THE HISTORY

OF

ISRAEL AND JUDAH.

HISTORY OF

ISRAEL AND JUDAH

FROM THE

BIRTH OF SOLOMON TO THE REIGN OF AHAB

BY THE

REV. ALFRED EDERSHEIM

M.A. (OXON.), D.D., PH.D.

AUTHOR OF "THE LIFE AND TIMES OF JESUS THE MESSIAH"

FLEMING H. REVELL COMPANY

NEW YORK   CHICAGO   TORONTO

Publishers of Evangelical Literature

PREFACE.

THE period of Israel's history treated in this Volume has a two-fold special interest : political and religious. Beginning with the later years of David's reign, when the consciousness and the consequences of the great sin of his life had, so to speak, paralysed the strong hand which held the reins of government, we are, first, led to see how, in the Providence of God, the possibility of a great military world-monarchy in Israel (comp. Ps. xviii. 43-45)—such as those of heathen antiquity—was for ever frustrated. Another era began with Solomon : that of peaceful development of the internal resources of the country ; of rapid increase of prosperity ; of spread of culture ; and, through friendly intercourse with other nations, of introduction of foreign ideas and foreign civilisation. When it is remembered that the building of the Temple preceded the legislation of Lycurgus in Sparta by about one hundred and twenty years ; that of Solon in Athens by more than four hundred years ; and the building of Rome by about two hundred and fifty years, it will be perceived that the kingdom of Solomon presented the dim possibility of the intellectual, if not the political Empire of the world. What Jerusalem was in the high-day of Solomon's glory is described in a chapter of this history. But, in the Providence of God, any such prospect passed away, when, after only eighty years' duration, the Davidic kingdom was rent into two rival and hostile states. Yet, although this catastrophe was intimated by prophecy, as Divine judgment upon Solomon's unfaithfulness, there was nothing either abrupt or out of the order of rational causation in its accomplishment. On the contrary, the causes of this separation lay far back in the tribal relations of Israel ; they manifested themselves once and again in the history of the Judges and of Saul; made themselves felt in the time of David; appeared in that of Solomon; and only reached their final issue, when the difficult task of meeting them devolved upon the youthful inexperience and misguided folly of a Rehoboam. All this is fully explained in the course of this history. After their separation, the two kingdoms passed, in their relations, through three stages : the first one of hostility ; the second one of alliance, which commenced with the reign of Jehoshaphat and of Ahab, and ended with the slaughter of the kings of Judah and Israel by Jehu ; and the third again one of estrangement and of hostility. Of these three periods the first is fully traced, and the beginning of the second marked in the present Volume.

From the political we turn to the religious aspect of this history. It was indeed true, that the empire of the world was to be connected with the Davidic kingdom (Ps. ii.)—but not in the sense of founding a great military monarchy, nor in that of attaining universal intellectual supremacy, least of all, by conformity to the ways and practices of heathen worship, magic, and theurgy. The exaltation of Zion above the hills, and the flowing of all nations unto it, was to be brought about by the going forth of the Law out of Zion, and of the Word of Jehovah from Jerusalem (Is. ii. 2, 3). This—to confine ourselves to the present period of our history—had been distinctly implied in the great promise to David (2 Sam. vii.) ; it was first typically realised in the choice of Jerusalem as the City of God (Ps. xlvi. ; xlviii. ; lxxxvii.); and further presented in its aspect of peace, prosperity, and happiness in the reign of Solomon (Ps. lxxii.) to which the prophets ever afterwards pointed as the emblem of the higher blessings in the Kingdom of God (Mic. iv. 4 ; Zech. iii. 10, comp. with 1 Kings iv. 25). But the great work of that reign, alike in its national and typical importance, was the building of the Temple at Jerusalem. This also has been fully described in the following pages.

But already other elements were at work. The introduction of heathen worship commenced with the decline of Solomon's spiritual

life. After his death, the apostasy from God attained fearful proportions, partially and temporarily in Judah, but permanently in
Israel. In the latter, from the commencement of its separate
national existence under Jeroboam, the God-chosen Sanctuary at
Jerusalem, and the God-appointed priesthood were discarded; the
worship of Jehovah transformed; and by its side spurious rites
and heathen idolatry introduced, till, under the reign of Ahab, the
religion of Baal became that of the State. This marks the high-
point of apostasy in Israel. The evolving of principles of con-
trariety to the Divine Covenant slowly but surely led up to the
final destruction of the Jewish Commonwealth. But, side by
side with it, God in great mercy placed an agency, the origin,
character, and object of which have already been indicated in
a previous Volume. The Prophetic Order may be regarded as
an extraordinary agency, by the side of the ordinary economy of
the Old Testament; and as intended, on the one hand, to com-
plement its provisions, and, on the other, to supplement them,
either in times of religious declension, or when, as in Israel, the
people were withdrawn from their influences. Hence the great extension of the Prophetic Order in such periods, and especially in
the kingdom of the ten tribes. But when, during the reign of Ahab,
the religion of Jehovah was, so to speak, repudiated, and the
worship of Baal and Astarte substituted in its place, something
more than even the ordinary exercise of the Prophetic Office was
required. For the prophet was no longer acknowledged, and the
authority of the God, Whose Messenger he was, disowned. Both
these had therefore to be vindicated, before the prophetic agency
could serve its purpose. This was achieved through what must be
regarded, not so much as a new phase, but as a further development
of the agency already at work. We mark this chiefly in the
ministry of Elijah and Elisha, which was contemporary with the
first open manifestation of Israel's national apostasy.

Even a superficial reader will observe in the ministry of these
two prophets, as features distinguishing it from that of all other
prophets—indeed, we might almost say, from the whole history

of the Old Testament—the *frequency* and the *peculiar character* of their miracles. Three points here stand out prominently: their *unwonted accumulation;* their seeming characteristic of *mere assertion of power;* and their apparent purpose of *vindicating the authority of the prophet.* The reason and object of these peculiarities have already been indicated in our foregoing remarks. But in reference to the characteristic of *power* as connected with these miracles, it may be remarked that its exhibition was not only necessary for the vindication of the authority of the prophet, or rather of Him in Whose Name he spake, but that they also do not present a mere display of power. For, it was always associated with an ultimate moral purpose: in regard to the Gentiles or to Israel—the believing or the unbelieving among them; and in all the leading instances (which must rule the rest) it was brought about not only in the Name of Jehovah, but by calling upon Him as the direct Agent in it (comp. for the present Volume 1 Kings xvii. 4, 9, 14, 20–22). Thus viewed, this extraordinary display of the miraculous appears, like that in the first proclamation of Christianity among the heathen, "for a sign, not to them that believe, but to them that believe not" (1 Cor. xiv. 22)—as Bengel explains, in order that, drawn and held thereby, they might be made to listen.

But even so, some further remarks may here be allowed; not, indeed, in the way of attempted disquisition on what must always be a prime postulate in our faith, but as helps in our thinking. It seems to me, that miracles require for their (objective) possibility—that is, subjectively viewed for their credibility[1]—only one postulate: that of the True and the Living God. It is often asserted, that miracles are not the traversing of the established, but the outcome of a higher order of things. This, no doubt, must be metaphysically true; but practically it is only a hypothetical statement, since, admittedly, and, as the very idea of miracles implies, we know nothing of this higher nature or order of things. But may we not

[1] I do not mean for the credibility of one or another special miracle, but for that of miracles in general.

assert that a miracle does not seem so much an interference with the laws of Nature—of which at most we have only partial and empirical knowledge—as with the laws and habits of our own thinking concerning Nature? And if so, does not this place the question on quite another footing?

Given, that there is a God (be the seeming hypothetication forgiven !), and in living connection with His rational creatures—and it seems to follow that He must teach and train them. It equally follows, that such teaching must be adapted to their stage and capacity (power of receptiveness). Now in this respect all times may be arranged into two periods: that of outward, and that of inward spiritual communication (of Law and Persuasion). During the former the miraculous could scarcely be called an extraordinary mode of Divine communication, since men generally, Jews and Gentiles alike, expected miracles. Outside this general circle (among deeper thinkers) there was only a "feeling after God," which in no case led up to firm conviction. But in the second stage personal determination is the great characteristic. Reason has taken the place of sense; the child has grown to the man. The ancient world as much expected an argument from the miraculous as we do from the purely rational or the logically evidential. That was their mode of apprehension, this is ours. To them, in one sense, the miraculous was really not the miraculous, but the expected; to us it is and would be interference with our laws and habits of thinking. It *was* adapted to the first period; it is *not* to the second.

It would lead beyond our present limits to inquire into the connection of this change with the appearance of the God-Man and the indwelling of the Holy Ghost in the Church. As we have shown in a previous Volume, under the Old Testament the Holy Spirit was chiefly known and felt as a *power*. The "still small voice" marks the period of transition. "Prophetism" was, so to speak, the introduction of the "still small voice" into the world—first in a preparatory manner; in the fulness of time, as in all fulness, in the Christ; and finally as indwelling in the Church of God.

These remarks will show what kind of questions are incidentally raised in the course of this history. Even in this respect the reader will have noticed progression in the successive Volumes of this Bible History. Otherwise also, it is hoped, he will mark it in these pages and in the Notes, in the fuller and more critical treatment of all questions. A new feature here is the introduction of a few Jewish and Rabbinical notices, which may prove interesting and useful. In general, while I have endeavoured to make my investigations thoroughly independent, and, so far as I could, original, it will, I trust, be also found that I have not neglected any sources of information within my reach. But above all, I would ever seek to keep steadily in view, as my main object, the practical and spiritual interest of this history. It all leads up to the Person of Christ, the Miracle of Miracles—the Miracle which gives meaning and unity to all others, and which is the truest evidence of them all. Thank God, we have sufficient and most firm historical ground for our faith in Him, as well as the inward teaching and the assurance of the Holy Ghost; sufficient, not indeed to supersede the necessity of faith, but to make that "blessed faith," so well grounded, so glorious, so joyous, and so transforming in its power, not only reasonable to us, but of obligatory duty to all men.

ALFRED EDERSHEIM.

LODERS VICARAGE, BRIDPORT:
Easter, 1880.

CONTENTS.

CHAPTER I.
Close of David's Reign.

CHAPTER II.

CHAPTER III.
Appendix to the History of David.

CHAPTER IV.
Reign of Solomon.

CHAPTER XI.

Jeroboam, first King of Israel.

CHAPTER XII.

Abijah and Asa, Kings of Judah.

CHAPTER XIII.

Asa, King of Judah.—Nadab, Baasha, Elah, Zimri, Tibni, and Omri, Kings of Israel.

HISTORY OF JUDAH AND ISRAEL

FROM THE BIRTH OF SOLOMON.

CHAPTER I.

Jewish View of the History of David—Amnon's Crime—Absalom's Vengeance—Flight of Absalom—The Wise Woman of Tekoah—Absalom returns to Jerusalem—His Conspiracy—David's Flight.

(2 SAM. XIII.—XVI.)

IN studying the history of the Old Testament, every thoughtful Christian must feel that a special interest attaches to the views and interpretations of the ancient Synagogue. Too often they are exaggerated, carnal, and even contrary to the real meaning of Holy Scripture. But, on the other hand, there are subjects on which we may profitably learn from Jewish teaching. Among them are some of the opinions expressed by the Rabbis on the history and character of David. A brief review of these may be helpful, and serve both as retrospect of the past, and as preparation for the study of the closing years of his reign.

Considering the important part which David sustains in the history of Israel, the views expressed by the ancient Synagogue are, on the whole, remarkably free from undue partiality. But beyond this there is a shrewd discernment of real under apparent motives, and a keen appreciation of the moral bearing of actions. The bright side of David's character is dwelt upon: his true humility,[1] the affectionateness of his

---

[1] Tradition instances this curious (if not historically accurate) evidence of it, that the coins which he had struck bore on one side the emblem of a shepherd's staff and scrip, and on the reverse a tower (*Ber. R.* 39).

disposition, the faithfulness of his friendship, and, above all, his earnest heart-piety, which distinguished him not only from the monarchs of heathen nations, but from all his contemporaries, and made him for all time one of the heroes of faith. On the other hand, his failings and sins are noted, and traced to self-indulgence, to rashness in arriving at conclusions, to suspiciousness in listening to every breath of slander, and even to a tendency to revengefulness,—all, we may observe, truly Oriental failings, the undisguised account of which is, of course, evidential of the truthfulness of the narrative. But what the Rabbis lay special stress upon is, that, while David kept indwelling sin in check, he failed in the full subdual, or rather in the moral renovation, of the heart. This led to his final and terrible sin. Of course, the Rabbis take a defective view of the case, since it would be more correct to reverse their statement. Nor should we omit to notice their conception of the higher aspects of his history. The typical bearing of his life is not lost sight of, and in every phase of it they point forward to " David's better Son." They also delight in marking throughout the overruling guidance of God : how the early training and history of David were intended to fit him for his calling; how, in Divine Providence, his failings and sins were, so to speak, ever reflected in their punishment,—as, for example, his rashness in dividing the inheritance of Mephibosheth with his unworthy servant in the similar loss sustained by Rehoboam, David's grandson ; how his life is full of deeper lessons ; and how in the fifteenth Psalm he embodies in brief summary the whole spiritual outcome of the Law (this is noticed in *Macc.* 24 *a*).

But of special interest in this history are the views taken of David's repentance, and of the consequences which followed from his great sin. David is here set before us as the model and ideal of, and the encouragement to, true repentance. In fact, tradition goes even further. It declares that the sin of Israel in making the golden calf and the fall of David were only recorded—it might almost seem, that they were only allowed—for the sake of their lessons about repentance. The former showed that, even if the whole congregation had erred and strayed, the door of mercy was still open to them; the latter, that not only for Israel as a whole, but for each individual sinner, however low his fall, there was assurance of forgiveness, if with true penitence he turned to God. The one case proved that nothing was too great for God to pardon; the other that there was not any one beneath His gracious notice. Be they many, or only one solitary individual, the ear of God was equally open to the cry of the repentant (comp. *Av. Sar.* 4. *b*, 5. *a*). The other point to which the Rabbis call attention is, that all the trials of David's later life, and all the judgments which overtook him and his house, might be traced up to his great sin, which, though personally pardoned, made itself felt in its consequences throughout the whole of his after-history (comp. especially *Sanh.* 107. *a* and *b*, where there are some interesting notices about David).

It cannot be doubted that there is deep truth in this view. For, although David was graciously forgiven, and again received into God's favour, neither he nor his government ever wholly recovered from the moral shock of his fall. It is not merely that his further history was attended by an almost continuous succession of troubles, but that these troubles, while allowed of God in judgment, were all connected with a felt and perceptible weakness on his part, which was the consequence of his sin. If the figure may be allowed: henceforth David's hand shook, and his voice trembled; and both what he did and what he said, alike in his own household and in the land, bore evidence of it.

As we reckon, it must have been about the twentieth year of his reign,[1] when the sin of his son Amnon proved the beginning of a long series of domestic and public troubles. In

---

[1] Both Absalom and Tamar were the children of Maacah, daughter of the king of Geshur, whom David married after his enthronement in Hebron (2 Sam. iii. 3). Amnon was the son of Ahinoam, the Jezreelitess (2 Sam. iii. 2).

this instance also it was carnal lust which kindled the devouring flame. The gloss of the LXX. is likely to be correct, that David left unpunished the incest of Amnon with Tamar, although committed under peculiarly aggravating circumstances, on account of his partiality for him as being his first-born son. This indulgence on the part of his father may also account for the daring recklessness which marked Amnon's crime. The sentence of the Divine law upon such sin was, indeed, unmistakeable (Lev. xx. 17). But a doting father, smitten with moral weakness, might find in the remembrance of his own past sin an excuse for delay, if not a barrier to action ; for it is difficult to wield a heavy sword with a maimed arm.

Two years had passed since this infamous deed. But there was one who had never forgiven it. Absalom had not forgotten the day when his brave and noble sister, after having vainly offered such resistance as she could, driven with her shame from the door of her heartless brother, had brought back the tale of her disgrace,—her maiden-princess's "sleeved upper garment"[1] rent, in token of mourning, her face defiled with ashes, her hand upon her head, as if staggering under its burden,[2] and bitterly lamenting her fate. So fair had she gone forth on what seemed her errand of mercy ; so foully had she been driven back ! These two years had the presence in his home of a loved sister, now "desolate" for ever, kept alive the remembrance of an irreparable wrong. The king had been "very wroth "—no more than that ; but Absalom would be avenged, and his revenge should not only be signal, but overtake Amnon when least suspecting it, and in the midst of his pleasures. Thus Amnon's sin and punishment would, so to speak, be in equipoise. Such a scheme could not, however, be immediately carried out. It required time, that so all suspicion might be allayed. But then, as Absalom's plan of revenge was

---

[1] This is the correct rendering, and not "garment of divers colours," as in our Authorised Version (2 Sam. xiii. 18, 19). The maiden princesses seem to have worn as mark of distinction a sleeved cloak-like upper garment. Comp. the Hebrew of ver. 18.

[2] In the East burdens are carried on the head.

peculiarly Oriental, these long delays to make sure of a victim are also characteristic of the lands of still, deep passion. At the same time, the readiness with which Jonadab, Amnon's cousin (xiii. 3) and clever adviser in wickedness, could suggest, before it was correctly known, what had taken place (vers. 32, 33), shows that, despite his silence, Absalom had not been able effectually to conceal his feelings. Perhaps the king himself was not quite without suspicion, however well Absalom had played his part. And now follows the terrible history. It is the time of sheep-shearing on Absalom's property, not very far from Jerusalem—a merry, festive season in the East. Absalom pressingly invites to it the king and his court, well knowing that such an invitation would be declined. But if the king himself will not come, at least let the heir-presumptive be there; and, if the king somewhat sharply takes up this suspicious singling out of Amnon, Absalom does not ask him only, but all the king's sons.

The consent has been given, and the rest of the story is easily guessed. Absalom's well-concerted plan; the feast; the merriment; the sudden murder; the hasty flight of the affrighted princes; the exaggerated evil tidings which precede them to Jerusalem; the shock to the king and his courtiers; then the partial relief on the safe arrival of the fugitives, followed by the horror produced as they tell the details of the crime—all this is sketched briefly, but so vividly that we can almost imagine ourselves witnesses of the scene. It was well for Absalom that he had fled to his maternal grandfather at Geshur. For all his life long the king could not forget the death of his firstborn, although here also time brought its healing to the wound. Absalom had been three years in Geshur—and "King David was restrained from going out after Absalom,[1] because he was comforted concerning Amnon."

Great as Absalom's crime had been, we can readily understand

---

[1] That is, in a hostile sense, as the same expression is used in Deut. xxviii. 7. The Hebrew text seems to admit no other translation than that which we have given. The Authorised Version, through following the Rabbis, is evidently incorrect.

that popular sympathy would in large measure be on the side of the princely offender. He had been provoked beyond endurance by a dastardly outrage, which the king would not punish because the criminal was his favourite. To the popular, especially the Eastern mind, the avenger of Tamar might appear in the light of a hero rather than of an offender. Besides, Absalom had everything about him to win the multitude. Without any bodily blemish from head to foot, he was by far the finest-looking man in Israel. Common report had it that, when obliged once a year, on account of its thickness, to have his long flowing hair cut, it was put, as a matter of curiosity, in the scales, and found amounting to the almost incredible weight of twenty shekels.[1] How well able he was to ingratiate himself by his manners, the after history sufficiently shows. Such was the man who had been left in banishment these three years, while Amnon had been allowed—so far as the king was concerned—to go unpunished !

Whether knowledge of this popular sympathy or other motives had induced Joab's interference, there seems no doubt that he had repeatedly interceded for Absalom;[2] till at last he felt fully assured that "the heart of the king was against[3] Absalom" (xiv. 1). In these circumstances Joab resorted to a not uncommon Eastern device. At Tekoah, about two hours south of Bethlehem, lived "a wise woman," specially capable of aiding Joab in a work which, as we judge, also commanded her sympathy. Arrayed in mourning, she appeared before the king to claim his interference and protection. Her two sons—so she said—had quarrelled; and as

[1] The Hebrew "200 shekels" must depend on a copyist's mistake, the lower stroke of כ, 20, having been obliterated, thereby making the numeral ר, 200.

[2] We infer this not only from 2 Sam. xiv. 22, but also from the ready guess of the king (ver. 19).

[3] This is certainly the correct translation. Comp. the similar use of the expression in Dan. xi. 28. If, as the Authorised Version puts it, the king's heart had been *toward* Absalom, there would have been no need to employ the woman of Tekoah, nor would the king have afterwards left Absalom for two full years without admitting him to his presence (xiv. 28).

no one was present to interpose, the one had killed the other. And now the whole family sought to slay the murderer !

True, he was guilty—but what mattered the "avenging of blood" to her, when thereby she would lose her only remaining son, and so her family become extinct? Would the death of the one bring back the life of the other—"gather up the water that was spilt"? Was it needful that she should be deprived of both her sons? Thus urged, the king promised his interference on her behalf. But this was only the introduction to what the woman really wished to say. First, she pleaded, that if it were wrong thus to arrest the avenging of blood, she would readily take the guilt upon herself (ver. 9). Following up this plea, she next sought and obtained the king's assurance upon oath, that there should be no further "destroying" merely for the sake of avenging blood (ver. 11). Evidently the king had now yielded in principle what Joab had so long sought. It only remained to make clever application of the king's concession. This the woman did; and, while still holding by the figment of her story (vers. 16, 17), she plied the king with such considerations, as that he was always acting in a public capacity; that lost life could not be restored; that pardon was God-like, since He "does not take away a soul, but deviseth thoughts not to drive away one driven away;"[1] and, lastly, that, to her and to all, the king was like the Angel of the Covenant, whose "word" was ever "for rest."

David could have no further difficulty in understanding the real meaning of the woman's mission. Accordingly, Joab obtained permission to bring back Absalom, but with this condition, that he was not to appear in the royal presence. We regard it as evidence of the prince's continued disfavour, that Joab afterwards twice refused to come to him, or to take a message to the king. It was a grave mistake to leave such a proud, violent spirit to brood for two years over supposed wrongs. Absalom now acted towards Joab like one wholly

---

[1] This is the correct rendering of the latter clauses of 2 Sam. xiv. 14.

reckless—and the message which Joab finally undertook to deliver was in the same spirit. At last a reconciliation took place between the king and his son—but only outwardly, not really, for already Absalom had other schemes in view.

Once more we notice here the consequences of David's fatal weakness, as manifest in his irresolution and half-measures. Morally paralysed, so to speak, in consequence of his own guilt, his position sensibly and increasingly weakened in popular estimation, that series of disasters, which had formed the burden of God's predicted judgments, now followed in the natural sequence of events. If even before his return from Geshur Absalom had been a kind of popular hero, his presence for two years in Jerusalem in semi-banishment must have increased the general sympathy. Whatever his enemies might say against him, he was a splendid man—every inch a prince : brave, warm-hearted, and true to those whom he loved —witness even the circumstance, told about Jerusalem, that he had called that beautiful child, his only daughter, after his poor dishonoured sister (2 Sam. xiv. 27), while, unlike an Oriental, he cared not to bring his sons prominently forward.[1] Daring he was—witness his setting Joab's barley on fire; but an Eastern populace would readily forgive, rather like in a prince, what might almost be called errors on the side of virtue. And now Absalom was coming forward like a real prince ! His state-carriage and fifty outrunners would always attract the admiration of the populace. Yet he was not proud—quite the contrary. In fact, never had a prince taken such cordial interest in the people, nor more ardently wished to see their wrongs redressed; nor yet was there one more condescending. Day by day he might be seen at the entering of the royal palace, where the crowd of suppliants for redress were gathered. Would that he had the power, as he had the will, to see them righted ! It might not be the king's blame; but there was a lack of proper officials to take cognisance of

[1] It is remarkable and exceptional that the name of his daughter is mentioned, and not those of his sons.

such appeal-cases—in short, the government was wrong, and
the people must suffer in consequence. As we realize the
circumstances, we can scarcely wonder that thus "Absalom
stole the hearts of the men of Israel."[1]

How long this intrigue was carried on we cannot accurately
determine,[2] and only once more wonder at the weakness
of the king who left it so entirely unnoticed. That the conspiracy which Absalom had so carefully prepared, though kept
very secret, was widely ramified, appears from the circumstance,
that, immediately on its outbreak, he could send "spies throughout all the tribes," to ascertain and influence the feelings of
the people generally, and to bid his adherents, on a precon-
certed signal, gather around him. More than that, it seems
likely that Ahithophel, one of David's privy councillors, and
deemed the ablest of his advisers, had, from the first, been in
the secret, and, if so, probably directed the conspiracy. This
would explain the strange coincidence of Ahithophel's absence
from Jerusalem at the time of the outbreak, and his presence
at his native Giloh, not far from Hebron (Josh. xv. 51). Nor
is it likely that a man like Ahithophel would so readily have
obeyed the summons of Absalom if he had been till then a
stranger to his plans, and had not had good reason to expect
success. And, indeed, if his advice had been followed, the
result would have answered his anticipations.

The place chosen for the rising was Hebron, both on account
of the facilities it offered for retreat in case of failure, and
as the city where formerly (in the case of David) a new royalty
had been instituted; perhaps also as the birthplace of Absalom,
and, as has been suggested, because the transference of the
royal residence to Jerusalem may have left dissatisfaction

[1] Keil notices that by similar means Agamemnon obtained the supreme
command of the Greek army (*Euripides*, Iphigenia, v. 337, seq.).

[2] The notice in the text: "after forty years" (2 Sam. xv. 7) is manifestly a clerical error. Most interpreters (with the Syrian, Arabic, and
Josephus) read "four years;" but it is impossible to offer more than a
hypothesis.

C

in Hebron. Absalom obtained the king's permission to go thither, on pretence of paying a vow made at Geshur. It was a clever device for entrapping two hundred influential persons from Jerusalem to invite them to accompany him, on pretext of taking part in the sacrificial feast. Arrived at Hebron, the mask was thrown off, and the conspiracy rapidly assumed most formidable proportions. Tidings of what had passed speedily reached Jerusalem. It was a wise measure on the part of the king to resolve on immediate flight from Jerusalem, not only to avoid being shut up in the city, and to prevent a massacre in its streets, but to give his adherents the opportunity of gathering around him. Indeed, in the hour of danger, the king seemed, for a brief space, his old self again. We can quite understand how, in David's peculiar state of mind, trials in which he recognised the dealings of God would rouse him to energy, while the even tenor of affairs left him listless. No weakness now—outward or inward ! Prudence, determination, and courage in action ; but, above all, a constant acknowledgment of God, self-humiliation, and a continuous reference of all to Him, marked his every step. In regard to this, we may here notice the progress of David's spiritual experience, marking how every act in this drama finds expression in the Book of Psalms. As Abraham perpetuated his progress through the land by rearing an altar unto Jehovah in every place where he sojourned, so David has chronicled every phase in his inner and outer life by a Psalm—a waymark and an altar for lone pilgrims in all ages. First, we turn to Psalms xli. and lv.—the former in which the designation Jehovah, the latter in which that of Elohim, prevails,[1]—which become more full of meaning if (with Professor Delitzsch) we infer from them, that during the four years Absalom's plot was ripening, the king was partially incapacitated by some illness. These two Psalms, then, mark the period *before* the conspiracy actually broke out, and find their typical counterpart in the treachery of Judas

---

[1] The circumstance that some are "Jehovah" and some "Elohim" Psalms often determines their position in the Psalter.

Iscariot.[1] Read in this light, these Psalms afford an insight into the whole history of this rising—political as well as religious. Other two Psalms, iii. and lxiii., refer to David's flight; while the later events in, and the overthrow of the conspiracy, form the historical background of Psalms lxi.. xxxix., and lxii.

When leaving Jerusalem in their flight, the king and his followers made a halt at "the far house."[2] Besides his family, servants and officials, his body-guard (the *Cherethi* and *Pelethi*), and the six hundred tried warriors, who had been with him in all his early wanderings, accompanied him.[3] In that hour of bitterness the king's heart was also cheered by the presence and stedfast adherence of a brave Philistine chieftain, *Ittai*, who had cast in his lot with David and with David's God. He had brought with him to Jerusalem his family (2 Sam. xv. 22) and a band of adherents (ver. 20); and his fidelity and courage soon raised him to the command of a division in David's army (xviii. 2).

It was winter, or early spring,[4] when the mournful procession passed through a crowd of weeping spectators over the Kidron, to take the way of the wilderness that led towards Jericho and the Jordan. At the foot of the Mount of Olives they again paused. Here the Levites, headed by Zadok the priest, put down the Ark, which had accompanied David, until the high-priest Abiathar, and the rest of the people who were to join the king, came up out of the city. They were wise as well as good words with which David directed the Ark of God to be

[1] Psa. lv. 22, in the version of the LXX., is quoted by St. Peter (1 Pet. v. 7).

[2] Probably the last house in the suburbs of Jerusalem. The rendering in our Authorised Version (2 Sam. xv. 17): "in a place that was far off," is not only incorrect, but absolutely meaningless.

[3] It is impossible to suppose that these six hundred were natives of Gath. Everything points to his old companions-in-arms, probably popularly called "Gathites," as we might speak of our Crimean or Abyssinian warriors.

[4] Kidron—"the dark flowing"—was only a brook during the winter and early spring rains.

taken back. At the same time he established communication with the city through the priests.[1] He would wait by "the fords" of the wilderness [2] till the sons of the two priests should bring him trustworthy tidings by which to guide his further movements.

It reads almost like prophecy, this description of the procession of weeping mourners, whom Jerusalem had cast out, going up "the ascent of the olive-trees," and once more halting at the top, "where it was wont to worship God !"[3] A little before, the alarming news had come that Ahithophel had joined the conspiracy. But now a welcome sight greeted them. Hushai, the Archite (comp. Josh. xvi. 2), David's friend and adviser, came to meet the king, and offered to accompany him. But the presence of unnecessary non-combatants would manifestly have entailed additional difficulties, especially if of the age of Hushai. Besides, a man like the Archite might render David most material service in Jerusalem, if, by feigning to join the conspirators, he could gain the confidence of Absalom, and so, perhaps, counteract the dreaded counsels of Ahithophel. Accordingly, Hushai was sent back to the city, there to act in concert with the priests.

Twice more David's progress was interrupted before he and his men reached *Ayephim*.[4] First it was Ziba, who, deeming this a good opportunity for securing to himself the coveted property of his master, came on pretext of bringing provisions for the fugitives, but really to falsely represent Mephibosheth

[1] The expression (2 Sam. xv. 27), rendered in the Authorised Version : "Art thou not a seer ?" is very difficult. Keil and others, by slightly altering the punctuation, translate : "Thou seer !"

[2] So the *Chethib*, or written text, has it ; the *Keri*, or emendated text, has "plains." The former seems the more correct. The "fords" were, of course, those where the Jordan was crossed.

[3] This is the correct rendering, and not as in the Authorised Version (2 Sam. xv. 32) : "where he worshipped God."

[4] The Authorised Version translates 2 Sam. xvi. 14 : "they came *weary* ;" but the word *Ayephim* is evidently intended as the name of a place, though it may mean "weary," somewhat in the sense of our "Traveller's Rest."

as engaged in schemes for recovering the throne of Israel amidst the general confusion. The story was so manifestly improbable, that we can only wonder at David's haste in giving it credence, and according to Ziba what he desired. Another and sadder interruption was the appearance of Shimei, a distant kinsman of Saul. As David, surrounded by his soldiers and the people, passed Bahurim, on the farther side of the Mount of Olives, Shimei followed on the opposite slope of the hill, casting earth and stones at the king, and cursing him with such words as these : " Get away ! get away ! thou man of blood ! thou wicked man !" thus charging him, by implication, with the death, if not of Saul and Jonathan, yet of Abner and Ishbosheth. Never more truly than on this occasion did David act and speak like his old self, and, therefore, also as a type of the Lord Jesus Christ in similar circumstances (comp. Luke ix. 52–56). At that moment, when he realised that all which had come upon him was from God, and when the only hope he wished to cherish was not in human deliverance, but in God's mercy, he would feel more than ever how little he had in common with the sons of Zeruiah, and how different were the motives and views which animated them (2 Sam. xvi. 10). Would that he had ever retained the same spirit as in this the hour of his deepest humiliation, and had not, after his success, relapsed into his former weakness ! But should not all this teach us, that, however necessary a deep and true sense of guilt and sin may be, yet if sin pardoned continueth sin brooded over, it becomes a source, not of sanctification, but of moral weakness and hindrance ? Let the dead bury their dead, but let *us* arise and follow Christ—and, " forgetting those things which are behind, and reaching forth unto those things which are before," let us " press toward the mark for the prize of the high calling of God in Christ Jesus " (Phil. iii. 13, 14).

CHAPTER II.

Ahithophel's twofold Advice—Hushai prevents imminent Danger—David is
informed, and crosses the Jordan—The Battle in the Forest—Death of
Absalom—Mourning of David—David's Measures—Return to Gilgal—
Barzillai and Joab as Representative Men of their Period — Federal
Republican Rising under Sheba—Murder of Amasa—Death of Sheba

(2 SAM. XVI.—XX.)

DAVID had not left the capital a moment too soon. He
had scarcely quitted the city when Absalom and his
forces appeared, and took possession of it. Hushai the
Archite was one of the first to welcome him with feigned
allegiance. There was a touch of boastful self-confidence about
the manner in which the new king received his father's old
counsellor, which the experienced man of the world well knew
how to utilise. By skilful flattery of his vanity, Absalom was
soon gained, and Hushai obtained access to his counsels.
Thus far everything had prospered with Absalom. Jerusalem
had been occupied without a struggle; and the new king now
found himself at the head of a very large force, though of
wholly undisciplined troops. But Ahithophel at least must have
known that, though David had fled, his cause was far from lost
On the contrary, he was at the head of veteran warriors, filled
with enthusiasm for their leader, and commanded by the ablest
generals in the land. Besides, account must also be taken of
the reaction which would undoubtedly set in. The flush of
confidence on the part of Absalom's raw levies, caused by
success where no resistance had been offered, would pass away
in measure as the real difficulties of their undertaking daily
more and more appeared; while, on the other hand, sympathy

with David, and adherents to his cause, would increase in the same proportion. In these circumstances even a much less sagacious adviser than Ahithophel, whose counsel was regarded in those days as if a man had inquired of the oracle of God, would have felt that Absalom's chief, if not his sole chance of success, lay in a quick and decisive stroke, such as should obviate the necessity of a protracted campaign. But first Ahithophel must secure himself, and, indeed, all the adherents of Absalom.

Considering the vanity and folly of Absalom, of which his easy reception of Hushai must have afforded fresh evidence to Ahithophel, and David's well-known weakness towards his children, it was quite possible that a reconciliation might yet take place between the usurper and his father. In that case Ahithophel would be the first, the other leaders in the rebellion the next, to suffer. The great aim of an unscrupulous politician would therefore be to make the breach between father and son publicly and absolutely permanent. This was the object of the infamous advice which Ahithophel gave Absalom (2 Sam. xvi. 21, 22), though, no doubt, he represented it as affording, in accordance with Oriental custom, public evidence that he had succeeded to the throne. While recoiling with horror from this unnatural crime, we cannot but call to mind the judgment predicted upon David (2 Sam. xii. 11, 12), and note how, as so often was the case, the event, supernaturally foretold, happened, not by some sudden interference, but through a succession of natural causes.

Having thus secured himself and his fellow-conspirators, Ahithophel proposed to select 12,000 men, make a rapid march, and that very night surprise David's followers—weary, dispirited, greatly outnumbered, and not yet properly organised. Had this advice been followed, the result would probably have been such as Ahithophel anticipated. A panic would have ensued, David fallen a victim, and with his death his cause been for ever at an end. But a higher power than the wisdom of the renowned Gilonite guided events. In the language of

Holy Scripture, "Jehovah had appointed to defeat the good counsel of Ahithophel" (2 Sam. xvii. 14). But, as first explained to Absalom and the council of Israelitish elders, Ahithophel's advice at once commended itself to their acceptance. Hushai seems not to have been present at that meeting. He was too prudent to intrude unbidden into the king's council-chamber. Besides, he had made arrangements for communicating with David before any measure of his enemies could have been executed. Just outside the city-wall, by the "*En-Rogel*," "the Fuller's Fountain"—for they dared not show themselves in the city—the two young priests, Jonathan and Ahimaaz the swift-footed (2 Sam. xviii. 23), waited in readiness to carry tidings to David.

Although Absalom had followed Ahithophel's vile advice, by which no immediate danger was incurred, it was another thing to take so decisive a step as to risk the flower of his army in a night attack upon David. If Ahithophel had retired from the royal presence in the expectation of seeing his counsel immediately carried out, he was soon to find himself disappointed. Hushai was next sent for, and consulted as to the measure proposed by Ahithophel. It was easy for the old statesman to conjure up difficulties and dangers to one so inexperienced and so irresolute as Absalom, and still more, by means of unlimited flattery, to turn one so vain into another course. Absalom had only to speak, and all Israel would gather to him from Dan even to Beer-sheba,—they would light upon David like the dew upon the grass; or if he fled into a city, why, cart-ropes would suffice to drag it, to the smallest stone, into the nearest river! On the other hand, this was the worst time for attacking David and his men when they were desperate. The idea of a night surprise was altogether inadmissible, bearing in mind David's great experience in such warfare; while any mishap, however small, would be fatal to Absalom's cause. We scarcely wonder, even taking the merely rational view of it, that in such a council-chamber the advice of Hushai should have prevailed, although we recognise none the less devoutly, the

Hand of God in ordering all. There was one, however, who did not deceive himself as to the consequences of this fatal mistake. Ahithophel knew, as if he had already witnessed it, that from this hour Absalom's cause was lost. His own course was soon and decisively chosen. He returned to his city, set his affairs in order, and, with the deliberate cynicism of a man who has lost all faith, committed that rare crime in Israel, suicide. Typical as the history of David is throughout, we cannot fail to see here also a terrible prefiguration of the end of him, who, having been the friend and companion of the Lord Jesus—perhaps regarded as the "wise adviser" among the simple disciples—betrayed his Master, and, like Ahithophel, ended by hanging himself (Matt. xxvii. 5).

Meanwhile, Hushai had communicated with the priests in Jerusalem. His counsel had, indeed, been adopted; but it was impossible to know what one so irresolute as Absalom might ultimately do. At any rate, it was necessary David should be informed, so as to secure himself against a surprise. A trusty maidservant of the priest carried the message to the young men by the "Fuller's Fountain." At the last moment their enterprise was almost defeated. A lad—probably one of those stationed to watch any suspicious movement—noticed their hurried departure in the direction of David's camp. Happily, the young men had observed the spy, and got the start of those sent after them. It was not the first nor yet the last time that an Israelitish woman wrought deliverance for her people, when at Bahurim the two young priests were successfully hidden in an empty well, and their pursuers led astray (2 Sam. xvii. 18–20). And here we gladly mark how different from the present inmates of Eastern harems were the mothers, wives, and daughters of Israel, — how free in their social intercourse, and how powerful in their influence : the religious and social institutions of the Old Testament forming in this respect also a preparation for the position which the New Testament would assign to woman. But to return. Coming out of their concealment, the two priests reached the encampment safely, and informed David of his danger. Ere the morning light he and all his followers had put the Jordan between them and their enemies; and anything like a surprise was henceforth impossible.

It all happened as Ahithophel had anticipated. The revolution now changed into a civil war, of which the issue could not be doubtful. David and his forces fell back upon Mahanaim, "a strong city in a well-provisioned country, with a mountainous district for retreat in case of need, and a warlike and friendly population."[1] Here adherents soon gathered around him, while wealthy and influential heads of clans not only openly declared in his favour, but supplied him with all necessaries. We are inclined to regard the three mentioned in the sacred narrative (2 Sam. xvii. 27) as representative men : *Shobi*, of the extreme border-inhabitants, or rather foreign tributaries (comp. 2 Sam. x. 2); *Machir*, of the former adherents of Saul; and *Barzillai*, of the wealthy land-owners generally.

With Absalom matters did not fare so well. Intrusting the command of his army to a relative, Amasa, the natural son of one Ithra, an Ishmaelite,[2] and of Abigail, David's step-sister,[3] he crossed the Jordan to offer battle to his father's forces. These must have considerably increased since his flight from Jerusalem (comp. 2 Sam. xviii. 1, 2), though, no doubt, they were still greatly inferior in number to the undisciplined multitude which followed Absalom. David divided his army into three corps, led by Joab, Abishai, and Ittai—the chief command being entrusted to Joab, since the people would not allow the king himself to go into battle. The field was most skilfully chosen for an engagement with undisciplined

[1] *Speaker's Commentary*, Vol. II. p. 429.

[2] This is the correct reading, as in 1 Chron. ii. 17. The word "Israelite" in 2 Sam. xvii. 25 is evidently a clerical error.

[3] From 2 Sam. xvii. 25, it appears that both Abigail and Zeruiah, though David's sisters, were not the daughters of Jesse, David's father, but of Nahash. It follows, that David's mother had been twice married : first to Nahash and then to Jesse, and that Abigail and Zeruiah were David's step-sisters.

superior numbers, being a thick forest near the Jordan,[1] which, with its pitfalls, morasses, and entanglements, destroyed more of Absalom's followers than fell in actual contest. From the first the battle was not doubtful; it soon became a carnage rather than a conflict.

One scene on that eventful day had deeply and, perhaps, painfully impressed itself on the minds of all David's soldiers. As they marched out of Mahanaim on the morning of the battle, the king had stood by the side of the gate, and they had defiled past him by hundreds and by thousands. One thing only had he been heard by all to say, and this he had repeated to each of the generals. It was simply: "Gently,[2] for my sake, with the lad, with Absalom!" If the admonition implied the existence of considerable animosity on the part of David's leaders against the author of this wicked rebellion, it showed, on the other hand, not only weakness, but selfishness, almost amounting to heartlessness, on the part of the king. It was, as Joab afterwards reproached him, as if he had declared that he regarded neither princes nor servants, and that it would have mattered little to him how many had died, so long as his own son was safe (2 Sam. xix. 6). If such was the impression produced, we need not wonder that it only increased the general feeling against Absalom. This was soon to be brought to the test. In his pursuit of the rebels, one of Joab's men came upon a strange sight. It seems that, while Absalom was riding rapidly through the dense wood in his flight, his head had somehow been jerked in between the branches of one of the large spreading terebinths—perhaps, as Josephus has it (*Ant.* vii. 10, 2), having been entangled by the flowing hair. In this position the mule which he rode—perhaps David's royal mule —had run away from under him; while Absalom, half suffocated and disabled, hung helpless, a prey to his pursuers.

[1] It is impossible to decide whether this "Wood of Ephraim" was west or east of the Jordan. From the context, the latter seems the more probable.

[2] So literally in the Hebrew text.

But the soldier who first saw him knew too well the probable consequences of killing him, to be tempted to such an act by any reward, however great. He only reported it to Joab, but would not become his tool in the matter. Indeed, Joab himself seems to have hesitated, though he was determined to put an end to Absalom's schemes, which he must have resented the more, since but for his intervention the prince would not have been allowed to return to Jerusalem. And so, instead of killing, he only wounded Absalom with pointed staves,[1] leaving it to his armour-bearers finally to despatch the unhappy youth. His hacked and mangled remains were cast into a great pit in the wood, and covered by a large heap of stones. A terrible contrast, this unknown and unhonoured criminal's grave, to the splendid monument which Absalom had reared for himself after the death of his sons! Their leader being dead, Joab, with characteristic love for his countrymen, sounded the *rappel*, and allowed the fugitive Israelites to escape.

But who was to carry to the king tidings of what had happened? Joab knew David too well to entrust them to any one whose life he specially valued. Accordingly, he sent a stranger, a Cushite; and only after repeated entreaty and warning of the danger, allowed Ahimaaz also to run with the news to Mahanaim. Between the outer and the inner gates of that city sat the king, anxiously awaiting the result of that decisive day. And now the watchman on the pinnacle above descried one running towards the city. Since he was alone, he could not be a fugitive, but must be a messenger. Soon the watchman saw and announced behind the first a second solitary runner. Presently the first one was so near that, by the swiftness of his running the watchman recognised Ahimaaz. If so, the tidings which he brought must be good, for on no other errand would Ahimaaz have come. And so it was! Without giving the king time for question, he rapidly announced

[1] The Hebrew word here used (*Shevet*) generally means sceptre, or else staff or rod, but not dart, as in the Authorised Version (2 Sam. xviii. 14).

the God-given victory. Whatever relief or comfort the news must have carried to the heart of David, he did not express it by a word. Only one question rose to his lips, only one idea of peace[1] did his mind seem capable of contemplating : " Peace to the lad, to Absalom ?" Ahimaaz could not, or rather would not, answer. Not so the Cushite messenger, who by this time had also arrived. From his language—though even he feared to say it in so many words—David speedily gathered the fate of his son. In speechless grief he turned from the two messengers, and from the crowd which, no doubt, was rapidly gathering in the gateway, and crept up the stairs leading to the chamber over the gate, while those below heard his piteous groans, and these words, oft repeated : " My son Absalom—my son ! My son Absalom ! Oh, would that I had died for thee ! Absalom, my son—my son!"

That was not a joyous evening at Mahanaim, despite the great victory. The townsmen went about as if there were public mourning, not gladness. The victorious soldiers stole back into the city as if ashamed to show themselves—as if after a defeat, not after a brilliant and decisive triumph. It was more than Joab could endure. Roughly forcing himself into the king's presence, he reproached him for his heartless selfishness, warning him that there were dangers, greater than any he had yet known, which his recklessness of all but his own feelings would certainly bring upon him. What he said was, indeed, true, but it was uttered most unfeelingly— especially remembering the part which he himself had taken in the death of Absalom—and in terms such as no subject, however influential, should have used to his sovereign. No doubt David felt and resented all this. But, for the present, it was evidently necessary to yield ; and the king received the people in the gate in the usual fashion.

---

[1] The first word of Ahimaaz as he came close to the king was : " Shalom," " Peace " (in our Authorised Version " All is well "). David's first word to Ahimaaz also was " Shalom." Only Ahimaaz referred to the public weal, David to his personal feelings.

The brief period of insurrectionary intoxication over, **the** reaction soon set in. David wisely awaited it in Mahanaim. The country recalled the national glory connected with his reign, and realised that, now Absalom had fallen, there was virtually an interregnum equally unsatisfactory to all parties. It certainly was neither politic nor right on the part of David under such circumstances to employ the priests in secret negotiations with the tribe of Judah for his restoration to the throne. Indeed, all David's acts now seem like the outcome of that fatal moral paralysis into which he had apparently once more lapsed. Such, notably, was the secret appointment of Amasa as commander-in-chief in the room of Joab, a measure warranted neither by moral nor by military considerations, and certainly, to say the least, a great political mistake, whatever provocation Joab might have given. We regard in the same light David's conduct in returning to Jerusalem on the invitation of the tribe of Judah only (2 Sam. xix. 14). Preparations for this were made in true Oriental fashion. The men of Judah went as far as Gilgal, where they had in readiness a ferry-boat, in which the king and his household might cross the river. Meantime, those who had cause to dread David's return had also taken their measures. Both Shimei, who had cursed David on his flight, and Ziba, who had so shamefully deceived him about Mephibosheth, went over Jordan "to meet the king."[1] As David was "crossing,"[2] or, rather, about to embark, Shimei, who had wisely brought with him a thousand men of his own tribe, Benjamin—the most hostile to David— entreated forgiveness, appealing, as evidence of his repentance, to his own appearance with a thousand of his clansmen, **as** the first in Israel to welcome their king. In these circumstances it would have been almost impossible not to pardon Shimei, though David's rebuff to Abishai, read in the light

[1] This **is** the correct rendering, and not, as in the Authorised Version, 2 Sam. xix. 17, last clause : "They went over Jordan before the king."

[2] This is the proper translation of the Hebrew word, and not, **as in our** Authorised Version (xix. 18) : "As he was come over Jordan."

of the king's dying injunctions to Solomon (1 Kings ii. 8, 9), sounds somewhat like a magniloquent public rebuke of the sons of Zeruiah, or an attempt to turn popular feeling against them. At the same time, it is evident that Shimei's plea would have lost its force, if David had not entered into separate secret negotiations with the tribe of Judah.

Ziba's motives in going to meet David need no comment. There can be little doubt that, well-informed as David must have been of all that had passed in Jerusalem, he could not but have known that the bearing and feelings of Mephibosheth had been the reverse of what his hypocritical servant had represented them (comp. 2 Sam. xix. 24). All the more unjustifiable was his conduct towards the son of Jonathan.[1] Both the language of irritation which he used towards him, and the compromise which he attempted (xix. 29), show that David felt, though he would not own, himself in the wrong. Indeed, throughout, David's main object now seemed to be to conciliate favour and to gain adherents—in short, to compass his own ends by his own means, which were those of the natural, not of the spiritual man ; of the Oriental, though under the influence of religion, rather than of the man after God's own heart. For, at the risk of uttering a truism, we must insist that there are only two courses possible—either to yield ourselves wholly to the guidance of the Holy Spirit, or else to follow our natural impulses. These impulses are not such as we may, perhaps, imagine, or suppose them to have become under the influence of religion. For the natural man always remains what he had been—what birth, nationality, education, and circumstances had made him. This consideration should keep us from harsh and, probably, erroneous judgments of others, and may likewise serve for our own warning and instruction.

Happily, this history also presents a brighter picture. It is

[1] The Talmud makes the following significant application : "In the hour when David said to Mephibosheth, Thou and Ziba shall divide the land, a *Bath Kol* (voice of God) came forth and said to him : Rehoboam and Jeroboam shall divide the kingdom" (*Shabb.* 56 b.).

that of the grand patriarchal chieftain, Barzillai, who had supported David in his adversity, and now came, despite the
weight of his years, to escort the king over the Jordan. No
reward or acknowledgment did he seek—in fact, the suggestion
seemed almost painful. A good and true man this, happy in
his independence, though not too proud to allow his son
Chimham to go to court—all the more that he had nothing
to gain by it. May we not legitimately infer, that his
conduct was influenced not merely by loyalty to his earthly
sovereign, but by the recognition of the higher spiritual truths,
and the hope for Israel and the world, symbolised by the reign
of David? For nearly eighty years Barzillai had watched in
distant Rogelim the varying fortunes of his loved people. He
remembered the time when Samuel was "judge;" he recalled
the hopes enkindled in the hearts of Israel when, after the
brilliant exploit in his own Jabesh-gilead, Saul was proclaimed
king. He had followed the waning glory of that same Saul—
for far and wide are tidings carried in the East, told by watch-
fires, and borne from home to home—until hope had almost
died out in his soul. Then came the story of David, and
increasingly, as he followed his career, or when some one
would repeat one of those new Psalms—so different from
the old war-songs in which Jewish deeds of valour had been
recorded—ascribing all to Jehovah, and making man of no
account, it all seemed to mark a new period in the history of
Israel, and Barzillai felt that David was indeed God's Anointed,
the symbol of Israel's real mission, and the type of its accomplishment. And at last, after the shameful defeat of Israel and
the sad death of Saul, he had hailed what had taken place in
Hebron. The capture of Jerusalem, the erection of a central
sanctuary there, and the subjection of Israel's enemies round
about, would seem to him bright links in the same chain.
And though David's sad fall must have grieved him to the
heart, it could never have influenced his views of Absalom's
conduct, nor yet shaken his own allegiance. And now that
David's reign, so far as its spiritual bearing was concerned, was

evidently coming to a close — its great results achieved, its spiritual meaning realised—he would feel that nothing could undo the past, which henceforth formed part of the spiritual inheritance of Israel, or rather of that of the world at large. And so, in the spirit of Simeon, when he had witnessed the incipient fulfilment of Israel's hopes, Barzillai was content to "turn back again" to his own city, to die there, and be laid in the grave of his father and mother, who had lived in times far more troubled than his own, and had seen but " far off" that of which he had witnessed the happy accomplishment.

On the other hand, we may, at this stage of our inquiries, be allowed to place by the side of Barzillai another representative man of that period. If Barzillai was a type of the spiritual, Joab was of the national aspect of Judaism. He was intensely Jewish, in the tribal meaning of the word, not in its higher, world-wide bearing : only Judæan in everything that outwardly marked Judaism, though not as regarded its inward and spiritual reality. Fearless, daring, ambitious, reckless, jealous, passionate, unscrupulous, but withal most loving of his country and people, faithful to, and, no doubt, zealous for his religion, so far as it was ancestral and national—Joab represented the one phase of Judaism, as Barzillai the other. Joab stands before us as a typical Eastern, or rather as the typical Eastern Judæan. Nor is it without deep symbolical meaning, as we trace the higher teaching of history, that Joab, the typical Eastern Judæan,—may we not say, the type of Israel after the flesh?—should, in carrying out his own purposes and views, have at last compassed his own destruction.

David's difficulties did not end with the crossing of Jordan. On the contrary, they seemed rather to commence anew. He had been received by the tribe of Judah; a thousand Benjamites had come for purposes of their own ; and probably a number of other tribesmen may have joined the king during his progress.[1] But the tribes, in their corporate capacity, had

---

[1] It is thus that we interpret the expression—" half the people of Israel "—in 2 Sam. xix. 40. Of course, it must not be taken literally, as appears from the whole context.

D

not been asked to take part in the matter, and both David and Judah had acted as if they were of no importance. Accordingly, when the representatives of Israel arrived in Gilgal, there was fierce contention between them and the men of Judah about this unjustifiable slight—the men of Judah being the more violent, as usual with those who do a wrong.

It needed only a spark to set the combustible material on fire. A worthless man, one Sheba, a Benjamite, who happened to be there, blew a trumpet, and gave it forth to the assembled representatives of the tribes that, since they had no part in David, they should leave him to reign over those who had selected him as their king. It was just such a cry as in the general state of excitement would appeal to popular feeling. David soon found himself deserted by his Israelitish subjects, obliged to return to Jerusalem with only his own tribesmen, and threatened by a formidable revolution in front. To suppress the movement before it had time to spread and disintegrate the country by everywhere exciting tribal jealousies —such was David's first care on his return to Jerusalem, after setting his household in order (2 Sam. xx. 3). But the fatal consequences of David's late conduct now appeared. True to his promise, he proposed to entrust to Amasa the command of the expedition against Sheba and what, to borrow a modern term, we may call the " Federal Republic." But, whether from personal incapacity, or, more probably, from the general want of confidence in, and dissatisfaction with, the new commander, Amasa did not even succeed in bringing together a force. As time was of the greatest importance,[1] David felt himself obliged again to have recourse to Abishai, or rather, through him, to Joab.[2] There was now no lack

[1] To use the pictorial Hebrew expression (2 Sam. xx. 6) : "lest he find him fenced cities, and tear out our eye." This seems to us a more suitable rendering than that either of our Authorised Version or of Ewald.

[2] The text mentions only dealings between David and Abishai, but the subsequent narrative shows that Joab was in command. From the relations between Joab and the king, it seems likely that David may have preferred to communicate with Joab through his brother.

of trusty warriors, and the expedition at once moved north-wards.

The forces, under the leadership of Abishai and Joab, had reached the great stone at Gibeon, when Amasa "came to meet them"[1] from the opposite direction, no doubt, on his way to Jerusalem. Joab was, as usual, "girt with his armour-coat as a garment, and upon it the girdle of the sword, bound upon his loins, in its scabbard; and it [the scabbard] came out, and it [the sword] fell out."[2] Amasa seems to have been so startled by this unexpected appearance of a host with another leader as to have lost all presence of mind. He saw not the sword which Joab picked up from the ground, and now held low down in his left hand, but allowed his treacherous relative to take him by the beard, as if to kiss him, so that the sword ran into the lower part of his body. Probably Joab, while determined to rid himself of his rival, had adopted this plan, in the hope of leaving it open to doubt whether Amasa's death had been the result of accident or of criminal intention. Then, as if there were not time for delay, Joab and Abishai left the body weltering where it had fallen, and hastened on their errand.

It was a dreadful sight; and not all the urgency of the soldier whom Joab had posted by the dead or dying man could prevent the people from lingering, horror-stricken, around him. At last the body had to be removed. It had been left on the ground, probably alike as a mark of contempt and a warning to others not to provoke the jealousy of Joab. And now David's army was in full chase after Sheba and his adherents. They followed him through the whole land up to the far north among the fortresses[3] by the Lake Merom,

---

[1] So 2 Sam. xx. 8, and not, as in the Authorised Version, "went before them."

[2] This is the correct rendering of the rest of ver. 8.

[3] These fortresses are grouped together in 1 Kings xv. 20; 2 Kings xv. 29; 2 Chron. xvi. 4. It has been ingeniously suggested that the expression: "all the Berites" (2 Sam. xx. 14), which gives no meaning, should be regarded as a masculine form of the word, and rendered: " all the fortresses."

where he was at last tracked to Abel, or rather, Abel-Beth-maachah. To this fortress Joab now laid siege. Its destruction, however, was averted by the wisdom of one of its women. Demanding speech of Joab from the city-wall, she reminded the general that the people of Abel had been famed, not for being rash in action, but rather wise and deliberate in counsel. Had Joab ever asked whether the town of Abel, which he was about to destroy, shared the views of Sheba, or took part in the rebellion? She, and, by implication, her fellow-citizens, were quite the contrary of turbulent conspirators. How, then, could Joab act so unpatriotically, so un-Jewishly, as to wish to destroy a city and a mother in Israel, and to swallow up the inheritance of Jehovah? And when Joab explained that it was not the destruction of a peaceable city, but the suppression of a rebellion which he sought, she proposed, as a speedy end to all trouble, that Sheba should be killed, and, in evidence of it, his head thrown over the wall. It was an easy mode of ridding themselves both of a troublesome visitor and of a terrible danger,—and the gory head cast at his feet convinced Joab that the rebellion was at an end, that he might retire from the city, dismiss his army, and return to Jerusalem. So ended the last rising against David—and, we may add, the political history of his reign.

CHAPTER III.

Appendix to the History of David.

The Famine—The Pestilence—The Temple Arrangements—David's Last Hymn and Prophetic Utterance.

(2 SAM. XXI.—XXIV.; 1 CHRON. XXI.—XXVII.)

WITH the suppression of the federal revolution under Sheba, the political history of David, as related in the Second Book of Samuel, closes. Accordingly, the account of this, the second part of his reign, concludes, like that of the first (2 Sam. viii. 16), with an enumeration of his principal officers (2 Sam. xx. 23 to the end). What follows in the Second Book of Samuel (xxi.–xxiv.), must be regarded as an Appendix, giving, first, an account of the famine which desolated the land (xxi. 1–14), probably in the *earlier* part, and of the pestilence which laid it waste, probably towards the *close* of David's reign (xxiv.); secondly, some brief notices of the Philistine wars (xxi. 15–22), and a detailed register of David's heroes (xxiii. 8–39), neither of which will require comment on our part; and, lastly, David's final Psalm of thanksgiving (xxii.), and his last prophetic utterances (xxiii. 1–7). All these are grouped together at the end of the Second Book of Samuel, probably because it was difficult to insert them in any other place consistently with the plan of the work, which, as we have repeatedly noted, was not intended to be a biography or a history of David, chronologically arranged. Perhaps we should add, that the account of the pestilence was placed last in the book (xxiv.), because it forms an introduction to the preparations made for the building of the Temple by Solomon. For, as we understand it, no sooner had the place been divinely pointed out where the Sanctuary should be reared, than David commenced such preparations for it as he could make. And here the First Book of Chronicles supplements most valuable notices, not recorded in any other part of Scripture. From these we learn what David did and ordered in his kingdom with a view to the building of the Temple and the arrangement of its future services (1 Chron. xxii.–xxix.). We have thus four particulars under which to group our summary of what we have designated as the Appendix to the History of David : the *famine ;* the *pestilence ;* the *Temple arrangements ;* and the *last Psalm and prophecy of the king.*

1. *The Famine* (2 Sam. xxi. 1–14).—There is not a more harrowing narrative in Holy Scripture than that connected with the famine which for three years desolated Palestine. Properly to understand it, we require to keep two facts in view. First, the Gibeonites, who, at the time of Joshua, had secured themselves from destruction by fraud and falsehood (Josh. ix. 3, etc.), were really heathens—Hivites, or, as they are called in the sacred text, Amorites, which was a general designation for all the Canaanites (Gen. x. 16; xv. 16; Josh. ix. 1; xi. 3; xii. 8, etc.). We know, only too well, the character of the Canaanite inhabitants of the land ; and although, after their incorporation with Israel, the Gibeonites must have been largely influenced for good, their habits of thinking and feeling would change comparatively little,[1]—the more so because, as there would be few, if any, intermarriages between them and native Israelites, they would be left, at least socially, isolated. This will account for their ferocious persistence in demanding the uttermost punishment prescribed by the law. The provisions of this law must be our second point of consideration. Here we have again to bear in mind the circumstances of the times, the existing moral, social, and national conditions, and the spiritual stage which Israel had then reached. The fundamental principle, laid down in Numb.

---

[1] In a previous volume of this *History* we have shown how much even a woman like Jael was influenced by tribal traditions—so to speak, the inherited taint of blood.

xxxv., was that of the holiness of the land in which Jehovah dwelt among His people. This holiness must be guarded (ver. 34). But one of the worst defilements of a land was that by innocent blood shed in it. According to the majestic view of the Old Testament, blood shed by a murderer's hand could not be covered up—it was, so to speak, a living thing which cried for vengeance, until the blood of him that had shed it silenced its voice (ver. 33), or, in other words, till the moral equipoise had been restored. While, therefore, the same section of the law provided safety in case of unintentional homicide (vers. 10–29), and regulated the old practice of "avenging blood," it also protected the land against crime, which it would not allow to be compensated for by money (ver. 31). Hence the Gibeonites were strictly within the letter of the law in demanding retaliation on the house of Saul, in accordance with the universally acknowledged Old Testament principle of the solidarity of a family; and David had no alternative but to concede their claim. This is one aspect of the question. The other must be even more reverently approached. We can only point out how they who lived in those times (especially such as the Gibeonites) would feel that they might cry to God for vengeance, and expect it from the Just and True One; and how the sternest lessons concerning public breach of faith and public crimes would be of the deepest national importance after such a reign as that of Saul.

The story itself may be told in few sentences. For some reason unrecorded—perhaps in the excess of his carnal zeal, but certainly without sufficient grounds—Saul had made havoc among the Gibeonites, in direct contravention of those solemn engagements into which Israel had entered, and which up to that time had been scrupulously observed. When, afterwards, a famine desolated the land for three years, and David sought the face of Jehovah, he was informed that it was due to the blood-guilt[1] which still rested on the house of Saul.

[1] It is thus we understand the expression (2 Sam. xxi. 1): "It is for Saul, and for his bloody house."

Upon this the king summoned the Gibeonites, and asked them what atonement they desired for the wrong done them, so that the curse which they had invoked might no longer rest on the inheritance of Jehovah. Their answer was characteristic. " It is not *a matter* to us of silver or of gold, in regard to Saul and his house, nor is it ours to put to death any one in Israel." "And he said : What say ye then? and I will do it for you."[1] Then came the demand, made with all the ferocity and irony of which they were capable, that the blood-vengeance which they, as Gibeonites, did not venture to take, should be executed for them, and that seven of Saul's descendants should be handed over to them that they might be nailed to the cross —of course *after* they were dead, for so the law directed [2]— as they termed it : "To Jehovah in Gibeah of Saul, the chosen of Jehovah."

Terrible as their demand was, it could not be refused, and the two sons of Rizpah, a foreign concubine of Saul, and five sons of Merab,[3] Saul's eldest daughter, were selected as the victims. Then this most harrowing spectacle was presented. From the commencement of the barley harvest in April till the early rains of autumn evidenced the removal of the curse from the land, hung those lifeless, putrescent bodies, which a fierce Syrian sun shrivelled and dried ; and beneath them, cease-less, restless, was the weird form of Saul's concubine. When she lay down at night it was on the coarse hair-cloth of mourners,

---

[1] We have translated literally 2 Sam. xxi. 4.

[2] The punishment of crucifixion, or impaling, is mentioned in Numb. xxv. 4. But that criminals were not crucified or impaled *alive*, but only *after* they were slain, appears from ver. 5. Similarly, in hanging, death always preceded the hanging (Deut xxi. 22, where our Authorised Version is not suf-ficiently distinct). The same remark applies to the punishment of *burning*, which was only executed on the dead body of the criminal (Lev. xx. 14), as appears from Josh. vii. 15 comp. with ver. 11. In these respects the Rabbi-nical Law was much more cruel, ordering literal strangulation, and burning by pouring down molten lead (comp. specially *Mishnah Sanh.* vii. 1–3).

[3] In 2 Sam. xxi. 8, by a clerical error, we have *Michal* instead of *Merab*. But it was the latter, not the former, who was married to Adriel the Meholathite (comp. 1 Sam. xviii. 19).

which she spread upon the rock ; but day and night was she on her wild, terrible watch to chase from the mangled bodies the birds of prey that, with hoarse croaking, swooped around them, and the jackals whose hungry howls woke the echoes of the night. Often has *Judæa capta* been portrayed as weeping over her slain children. But as we realise the innocent Jewish victims of Gentile persecution in the Middle Ages, and then remember the terrible cry under the Cross, this picture of Rizpah under the seven crosses, chasing from the slaughtered the vultures and the jackals, seems ever to come back to us as its terrible emblem and type.

"And it was told David what Rizpah, the daughter of Aiah, the concubine of Saul, had done. And David went [himself] and took the bones of Saul, and the bones of Jonathan his son, from the men of Jabesh-gilead, who had stolen them from the street of Bethshan, where the Philistines had hanged them, when the Philistines had slain Saul in Gilboa : and he brought up from thence the bones of Saul and the bones of Jonathan his son; and they gathered the bones of them that were crucified. And the bones of Saul and Jonathan his son buried they in the country of Benjamin in Zelah, in the sepulchre of Kish his father."

2. *The Pestilence.*—In regard to this event, it is of the greatest importance to bear in mind that it was sent in consequence of some sin of which Israel, as a people, were guilty. True, the direct cause and immediate occasion of it were the pride and carnal confidence of David, perhaps his purpose of converting Israel into a military monarchy. But this state of mind of their king was, as we are expressly told (2 Sam. xxiv. 1), itself a judgment upon Israel from the Lord, when Satan stood up to accuse Israel, and was allowed thus to influence David (1 Chron. xxi. 1). If, as we suppose, the popular rising under Absalom and Sheba was that for which Israel was thus punished, there is something specially corresponding to the sin alike in the desire of David to have the people numbered, and in the punishment which followed. Nor ought we to overlook

another Old Testament principle evidenced in this history: that of the solidarity of a people and their rulers.

It seems a confirmation of the view, that the sin of David, in wishing to ascertain the exact number of those capable of bearing arms, was due to carnal elation and pride, and that the measure was somehow connected with military ambition on his part, that both in 2 Sam. and in 1 Chron. this story follows an enumeration of the three classes of David's heroes, and of some of their most notable feats of arms.[1] The unwillingness of Joab and of the other captains, to whom the king entrusted the census, arose partly from the knowledge that such an attempt at converting all Israel into a large camp would be generally disliked and disapproved—a feeling with which he and his fellow-captains would, as Israelitish patriots, fully sympathise. But religious considerations also came in, since all would feel that a measure prompted by pride and ambition would certainly bring judgment upon the people (1 Chron. xxi. 3). Remonstrance having been vain, the military census was slowly and reluctantly taken, the Levites being, however, excluded from it (Numb. i. 47–54), and the royal order itself recalled before the territory of Benjamin was reached.[2] For already David's conscience was alive to the guilt which he had incurred. It was after a night of confession and prayer on the part of David, that Gad was sent to announce to him the punishment of his sin. For, the temporal punishment appropriately followed—not preceded—the confession of public sin. Left to choose between famine,[3] defeat, and pestilence, David

---

[1] The same inference may be drawn from 1 Chron. xxvii. 23, 24, where the enumeration is evidently connected with the military organisation of the nation.

[2] Comp. 1 Chron. xxi. 6 ; xxvii. 24. From this latter notice we also gather that the result of the census was *not* entered in the Chronicles of King David. We can therefore the less hesitate in supposing some want of accuracy in the numbers given. Of the two enumerations we prefer that in 2 Sam. xxiv. 9. However, 1,300,000, or even, according to 1 Chron. xxi. 5, 1,570,000 men capable of bearing arms, would only imply a total population of about five or six millions, which is not excessive.

[3] According to 1 Chron. xxi. 12, the famine was to be of *three* years' duration. The number "*seven*" in 2 Sam. xxiv. 13 must be a clerical error.

wisely and well cast himself upon the Lord, finding comfort only in the thought, which has so often brought relief to
those who realise it, that, even when suffering for sin, it is
well to fall into the hands of Jehovah. Nor was his unuttered
hope disappointed. The pestilence, terrible as it was in its
desolations, was shortened from three days to less than one
day : "from the morning to the time of the assembly," viz.,
for the evening sacrifice.[1]

Meanwhile "David and the elders, clothed in sackcloth"
(1 Chron. xxi. 16), were lying on their faces in humiliation
before the Lord. Significantly, it was as the Divine command
of mercy sped to arrest the arm of the Angel messenger of
the judgment, that he became visible to David and his
companions in prayer. Already he had neared Jerusalem, and
his sword was stretched towards it—just above Mount Moriah,
at that time still outside the city, where Aravnah[2] the Jebusite
had his threshing-floor. It was a fitting spot for mercy upon
Israel, this place where of old faithful Abraham had been
ready to offer his only son unto God ; fitting also as still
outside the city ; but chiefly in order that the pardoning and
sparing mercy now shown might indicate the site where, on
the great altar of burnt-offering, abundant mercy in pardon and
acceptance would in the future be dispensed to Israel. At
sight of the Angel with his sword pointed towards Jerusalem,
David lifted his voice in humblest confession, entreating that,
as the sin had been his, so the punishment might descend on
him and his household, rather than on his people. This
prayer marked the beginning of mercy. By Divine direction,
through Gad, David and they who were with him, went to
Aravnah to purchase the place thus rendered for ever memorable, in order to consecrate it to the Lord by an altar, on
which burnt and peace-offerings were brought. And this was
to be the site for the future "house of Jehovah God," and

---

[1] This is the proper rendering of 2 Sam. xxiv. 15.

[2] This seems to have been the original, while that of Ornan (1 Chron.
xxi. 15) and others are the Hebraised forms of the name.

for "the altar of the burnt-offering for Israel" (1 Chron. xxii. 1).

And God had both prepared and inclined the heart of the Jebusite for the willing surrender of the site for its sacred purposes. No doubt he was a proselyte, and probably (analogously to Rahab) had been an ally in the taking of Jerusalem under Joab. It seems that Aravnah and his four sons, while busy in that threshing-floor, had also seen the figure of the Angel high above them, and that it had struck terror into their hearts (1 Chron. xxi. 20). When, therefore, David and his followers came, they were prepared freely to give, not only the threshing-floor, but also all within it,[1] if only Jehovah were pleased to accept the prayer of the king (2 Sam. xxiv. 23). Thus most significantly, in its typical aspect, were Jew and Gentile here brought together to co-operate in the dedication of the Temple-site. It, no doubt, showed insight into Oriental character, though we feel sure it was neither from pride nor narrow national prejudice, that David refused to accept as a gift what had been humbly and, as we believe, heartily offered. But there was evident fitness in the acquisition of the place by money [2] on the part of David, as the representative of all Israel. And as if publicly and from heaven to ratify what had been done, fire, unkindled by man, fell upon the altar and consumed the sacrifices (1 Chron. xxi. 26). But from that moment the destroying sword of the Angel was sheathed at the command of God.

3. *David's Temple arrangements.*—Since the Lord had, in

[1] 2 Sam. xxiv. 23, reads in the Hebrew: "The whole, O king, does Aravnah give unto the king," and not as in the Authorised Version.

[2] Of the two statements of the price, we unhesitatingly take that in 1 Chron. xxi. 25 (the other in 2 Sam. depending on a clerical error, very common and easily accounted for in numerals). Bearing in mind that the common shekel was of half the value of the sacred, and that the proportion of gold to silver was about ten to one, the six hundred shekels of gold would amount to about £380. In *Siphré* 146 a., various attempts are made to conciliate the two diverging accounts—it need scarcely be said ineffectually. The learned reader will find a full discussion of the question in Ugolini's tractate *Altare Exterius* (Ugolini Thesaurus, Fol. Vol. x. pp. 504–506).

His Providence, pointed out the place where the Sanctuary was to be reared, David, with characteristic energy, began immediate preparations for a work, the greatness of which the king measured by his estimate of Him for Whose service it was designed (1 Chron. xxii. 5). It almost seems as if in these arrangements all David's former vigour had come back, showing where, despite his weaknesses and failings, the king's heart really was. Besides, the youth of his son and successor Solomon,[1] and the consideration that probably no other monarch would wield such influence in the land as he had possessed, determined David not to neglect nor defer anything that he might be able to do. First, he took a census of the "strangers,"[2] and set them to prepare the stone, iron, and timber work. His next care was to give solemn charge to Solomon concerning what was so much on his own heart. Recapitulating all that had passed, when he first proposed to "build an house unto the Name of Jehovah," he laid this work upon his son and God-appointed successor, as the main business of his reign. Yet not as a merely outward work to be done, but as the manifestation of spiritual religion, and as the outcome of allegiance to God and His law (1 Chron. xxii. 6–12). Only such principles would secure true prosperity to his reign (ver. 13). For himself, he had "by painful labour"[3] gathered great treasures,[4] which

[1] Solomon was probably at this time about twenty years of age.

[2] These were not only foreign settlers, but the descendants of the original inhabitants of the land whose lives had been spared. Such was their number that Solomon could employ no fewer than one hundred and fifty thousand of them to bear burdens, and to hew stones (1 Kings v. 15; 2 Chron. ii. 17).

[3] This, and not "in my trouble," is the correct rendering of 1 Chron. xxii. 14.

[4] Although, as we have often explained, clerical errors occur in the numerals in the historical books, it may be well to give the real equivalent of the silver and gold, mentioned in 1 Chron. xxii. 14. Bearing in mind the distinction between the sacred and the common shekel (2 Sam. xiv. 26; 1 Kings x. 17, compared with 2 Chron. ix. 16), it would amount to under £4,000,000. Immense as this sum is, Keil has shown that it is by no means out of proportion with the treasures taken as booty in antiquity (comp. *Bibl. Comment.* Vol. v. pp. 181–184).

were to be devoted to the building of the new Temple ; and he had made all possible preparations for it. Finally, summoning "the princes of Israel, with the priests and the Levites" (1 Chron. xxiii. 1, 2), and presenting to them his son Solomon as successor in the kingdom, he entreated their co-operation with him in what was to be the great work of the future—making it not a personal, but a national undertaking, expressive of this, that they had "set heart and soul to seek Jehovah" their God (1 Chron. xxii. 19).

It was in this solemn assembly of laity and priesthood that Solomon's succession was announced and accepted, and that the future organisation of the Temple Services was determined and fixed.[1] A census of the Levites gave their number, from thirty years and upwards, at 38,000 men. Of these 24,000 were appointed to attend to the general ministry of the sanctuary (xxiii. 28–32), 6,000 to act as "officers and judges," 4,000 for instrumental music, and 4,000 as choristers—the latter (and probably also the former class) being subdivided into adepts, of which there were 288 (xxv. 7), and learners (xxv. 8). As all the Levites, so these 288 adepts or trained choristers were arranged by lot into twenty-four courses, a certain number of "learners" being attached to each of them. Each course of Levites had to undertake in turn such services as fell to them. Those who had charge of the gates were arranged into classes, there being altogether twenty-four posts in the Sanctuary in which watch was to be kept (1 Chron. xxvi. 1–19). Similarly, the priests, the descendants of Aaron, were arranged by lot into twenty-four courses for their special ministry (1 Chron. xxiv. 1–19). Lastly, the sacred text gives a brief account of the work of those 6000 Levites whom David appointed as "scribes and judges" (1 Chron. xxvi. 29–32), and of the final arrangement of the army, and of all the other public offices (1 Chron. xxvii.).

---

[1] It is, of course, impossible here to enter into any critical examination of the chapters in 1 Chron., summarised in our text.

4. *David's last hymn and prophetic utterance* (2 Sam. xxii.– xxiii. 2–7).—The history of David appropriately closes with a grand hymn, which may be described as alike the programme and the summary of his life and reign in their spiritual aspect. Somewhat altered in language, so as to adapt it to liturgical purposes, it is inserted in our present Psalter as Ps. xviii., to which we accordingly refer. This grand hymn of thanksgiving is followed—to use the language of an eminent German critic [1]—by the prophetic testament of the king, in which he indicates the spiritual import and bearing of his kingdom. If Ps. xviii. was a grand Hallelujah, with which David quitted the scene of life, these his "last words" are the Divine attestation of all that he had sung and prophesied in the Psalms concerning the spiritual import of the kingdom which he was to found, in accordance with the Divine message that Nathan had been commissioned to bring to him. Hence these "last words" must be regarded as an inspired prophetic utterance by David, before his death, about *the King* and *the Kingdom* of God in their full and real meaning. The following is the literal rendering of this grand prophecy :

The Spirit of Jehovah speaks by me,[2]
And His Word *is* on my tongue![3]

Saith the God of Israel,
Speaks to me the Rock of Israel :
A Ruler over man,[4] righteous,
A Ruler in the fear of God—
And as the light of morning,[5] *when* riseth the sun[6]—

---

[1] Keil. We quote, of course, only the substance of his remarks.

[2] According to some "in me" or "into me," as Hos. i. 2. In that case, the first clause would indicate inspiration, and the second its human utterance.

[3] The Rabbis and others regard this as referring to all David's Psalms and prophecies.

[4] Not merely over Israel, but over mankind, indicating the future Kingdom of God, and the full application of the prophecy in its Messianic sense.

[5] Here the effects of that great salvation are described. The Rabbis, however, connect it with the previous verse, and regard it as a farther description of this ruler.

[6] The light of the morning of salvation—in opposition to the previous darkness of the night, the sun being the Sun of Righteousness.

Morning without clouds—
From the shining forth out of (after) rain (sprouts) the green out of the
     earth ! [1]
For is not thus my house with God? [2]
Since an everlasting covenant He hath made with me,
Provided (prepared) in all things, and preserved (kept, watched over)--
Then, all my salvation and all good pleasure,
Shall He not cause it to spring forth?

And (the sons of) Belial, as thorns cast away are they all [3]—
For they are not taken up in the hand [3]
And the man who toucheth them,
Provides himself (*lit.*, fills) with iron and shaft of spear, [4]
And in fire [5] are they utterly burned in their dwelling [6] (where
     they are).

---

[1] After a night of rain the sun shines forth and the earth sprouts. Comp.
Ps. lxxii. 6 ; Is. xlv. 8.

[2] Pointing to the promise in 2 Sam. vii.—as it were : Does not my house
stand in this relationship towards God, that alike the Just Ruler and the
blessings connected with His reign shall spring from it ?

[3] Here is an indication of the judgment to come upon the enemies of the
Messianic Kingdom.   Mark here the contrast between the consequences of
Belial and those of the morning light when green sprouts from the earth.
Mark also how, while the sprouting of the grass is a gradual and continuous
process, the burning of the castaway thorns is the final but immediate
judgment. Comp. Matt. xiii. 30.

[4] That is, they are not gathered together with the naked hand in order
to burn them, but people provide themselves with iron instruments held
by wooden handles.

[5] The fire a symbol of the Divine wrath.

[6] Other renderings have been proposed, but the one in the text conveys
the idea that the thorns are burned where they lie.

CHAPTER IV.

Adonijah's Attempt to Seize the Throne—Anointing of Solomon—Great Assembly of the Chiefs of the People—Dying Charge of David— Adonijah's Second Attempt and Punishment—Execution of Joab and of Shimei.

(1 KINGS I., II. ; 1 CHRON. XXIII. 1, XXVIII., XXIX.)

THE history of David, as told in the Book of Chronicles, closes with an account of what, in its bearing on the *theocracy*, was of greatest importance—the public charge to Solomon in regard to the building of the Temple and the preparations for the work. On the other hand, the Book of Kings[1] takes up the thread of *prophetic history* where the

---

[1] It should always be kept in view that (as stated in Vol. iv. p. 163) the history of Israel is presented in the Book of Kings from the *prophetic* point of view. In other words, it is a history written from the standpoint of 2 Sam. vii. 12-16. In the language of Winer (*Real-Wörterb.* vol. i. p. 412, note), " The history of the Old Testament was not regarded as an aggregate of facts, to be ascertained by diligent research and treated with literary ability, but as the manifestation of Jehovah in the events which occurred, for the understanding of which the influence of the Spirit of God was an essential condition." The Old Testament contains not merely secular history. Accordingly, its writers are designated in the Canon as "prophets." The "Book of Kings" was originally one work. Its division into two books was made by the LXX translators. Thence it passed into the *Vulgate*, and was introduced into our printed editions of the Hebrew Bible by Dan. Bomberg, at the beginning of the 16th century. In the LXX and *Vulgate* the books of Samuel and of Kings form one work, divided into four books. The Talmud (*Baba B.* 15 *a*) ascribes the authorship of the Book of Kings to Jeremiah, but the evidence seems insufficient. The author of the "Book of Kings" mentions three sources from which, at least partially, his information was derived : the Acts of Solomon (*once*, 1 Kings xi. 41), the Book of the Chronicles of the Kings of Judah (*sixteen* times), and the Book of the Chronicles of the Kings of Israel (*seventeen* times)—making in all thirty-four references. At the time of the composition of the Book of Chronicles the two last-mentioned works seem to have been either combined, or re-cast into one : the Book of the Kings of Judah and Israel (2 Chron.

previous writers had dropped it. The birth of Solomon had been the beginning of the fulfilment of that glorious promise (2 Sam. vii. 12–16), which gave its spiritual meaning and import to the institution of royalty in Israel. And the promises and the warnings embodied in that prediction form, so to speak, the background of the whole later history of the people of God.

Naturally, the first event recorded in this history is the formal installation of Solomon as the God-appointed successor of David (2 Sam. vii. 12 ; xii. 25 ; 1 Kings viii. 20 ; 1 Chron. xxviii. 5–7). It was somewhat hastened by an incident which, like so many others that caused trouble in Israel, must ultimately be traced to the weakness of David himself. It has already been noticed, in the history of Amnon and in that of Absalom, to what length David carried his indulgence towards his children, and what terrible consequences resulted from it. Both Amnon and Absalom had died violent deaths. A third son of David, Chileab, whose mother was Abigail,

---

xvi. 11 ; xxiv. 27, and other passages). Another important inference is to be derived from a comparison of the Books of Kings with those of Chronicles. Not unfrequently the two relate the same event in almost the same words. But while in the history of Solomon, as told in the Book of Kings, the reference is to the Acts of Solomon, in Chronicles (2 Chron. ix. 29) it is to the "Book of Nathan the prophet, the Prophecy of Ahijah the Shilonite, and the Visions of Iddo the Seer," showing that the work called the Acts of Solomon was based on these three prophetic compositions. Again, in the history of Rehoboam, we have in 2 Chron. xii. 15, a reference to the "Book of Shemaiah the Prophet," and to that of " Iddo the Seer, concerning genealogies ;" in the history of Abijah to the "Midrash of the prophet Iddo " (2 Chron. xiii. 22) ; in that of Uzziah to "the writing of Isaiah the prophet " (2 Chron. xxvi. 22) ; and in that of Manasseh to "the Book of Chosai" (2 Chron. xxxiii. 19). Without entering into further details, we only remark that passages from the prophecies of Isaiah (xxxvi.–xxxix.), and of Jeremiah (lii.) are inserted in 2 Kings, where, however, they are ascribed not to these prophetic books, but to the "Book of the Kings of Judah" (2 Kings xx. 20). These facts seem to show that the works from which the author of the Book of Kings quoted, were themselves based on earlier prophetic writings. It is only necessary to add in this note that the period embraced in the Books of Kings extends over 455 years.

seems also to have died. At least, so we infer from the silence of Scripture concerning him. These were the three eldest sons of David. The next in point of age was Adonijah the son of Haggith (2 Sam. iii. 2–4). Like his elder brother, Amnon, he had been born in Hebron ;[1] like Absalom, he was distinguished by personal attractions. But he also, as Amnon and Absalom, had all his life been fatally indulged by David. In the expressive language of Holy Scripture : "his father had not made him sorry all his days, saying, Why hast thou done so ?" (1 Kings i. 6.) The consequence may be easily guessed. By right of primogeniture the succession to the throne seemed his. Why, then, should he not attempt to seize upon a prize so coveted? His father had, indeed, sworn to Bathsheba that Solomon should be his successor (1 Kings i. 13, 30), and that on the ground of express Divine appointment ; and the prophet Nathan (ver. 11), as well as the leading men in Church and State, not only knew (as did most people in the land), but heartily concurred in it. But what mattered this to one who had never learned to subject his personal desires to a higher will? This supposed Divine appointment of his younger brother might, after all, have been only a matter of inference to David, and Nathan and Bath-sheba have turned it to account, the one because of the influence which he possessed over Solomon, the other from maternal fondness and ambition. At any rate, the prospect of gaining a crown was worth making an effort ; and the more quickly and boldly, the more likely of success.

It must be admitted that circumstances seemed specially to favour Adonijah's scheme. David was indeed only seventy years old ; but premature decay, the consequence of a life of exposure and fatigue, had confined him not only to his room (ver. 15), but to his bed (ver. 47). Such was his weakness, that the body had lost its natural heat, which could not be restored even by artificial means ; so that the physicians,

---

[1] Accordingly, Adonijah must have been between thirty-three and forty years of age at the time of his attempt to seize the throne.

according to the medical views of those times, had advised
bodily contact with a young, healthy subject.[1]　For this purpose
Abishag,[2] a fair maiden from Shunem, had been brought into
the king's harem.　In David's utter physical prostration,
Adonijah might reckon on being able to carry on his scheme
without interference from the king.　Indeed, unless David
had been specially informed, tidings of the attempt would
not even have reached his sick-chamber till it was too late.
The rebellion of Absalom had failed because David was in
full vigour at the time, and so ably supported by Abiathar
the priest and Joab the captain of the host.　But Adonijah
had attached these two to his interests.　It is not difficult
to understand the motives of Joab in trying to secure the
succession for one who would owe to him his elevation, not
to speak of the fact that the rival candidate for the throne
was Solomon, the "man of peace," the pupil of Nathan, and
the representative of the "religious party" in the land.　But it
is not so easy to account for the conduct of Abiathar, unless it
was prompted by jealousy of Zadok, who officiated at Gibeon
(1 Chron. xvi. 39).　As the latter was considered the principal Sanctuary (1 Kings iii. 4), the high-priest who officiated
there might have been regarded as entitled to the Pontificate,
when the temporary dual service of Gibeon and Jerusalem
should give place to the permanent arrangements of the
Temple.　If such was his motive, Abiathar may have also
wished to lay the new king under personal obligations.

From such a movement—which took advantage first of the

---

[1] Josephus (*Ant.* vii. 2) expressly states this to have been the advice
given by his *physicians.*　The practice was in accordance with the medical
views entertained not only in ancient, but even in comparatively modern
times.　Dr. Trusen devotes to the medical consideration of this subject a
special paragraph (§ 21, pp. 257–260) in his curious work, *Sitten, Gebr. u.
Krankh. d. alten Hebr.*

[2] The story of Abishag is only introduced in order to explain the occasion
of Adonijah's later execution.　Of course it must be viewed in the light
of the toleration of polygamy—nor could the object which the physicians
had in view have been otherwise secured.

indulgence, and then of the illness of David; which compassed aims that every one would know to be equally contrary to the Divine appointment and the express declarations of the aged king; and in which the chief agents were an ambitious priest and an unscrupulous military chieftain—those who were faithful to their God or to their monarch would, of course, keep aloof. Adonijah knew this, and accordingly excluded such from the invitation to the feast, at which it had been arranged his accession to the throne should be proclaimed. In other respects his measures closely resembled those taken by Absalom. For some time previous to his attempt he had sought to accustom the people to regard him as their future king by assuming royal state (1 Kings i. 5).[1] At length all seemed ready. It is characteristic that, in order to give the undertaking the appearance of religious sanction, the conspirators prepared a great sacrificial feast. We know the scene, and we can picture to ourselves that gathering in the shady retreat of the king's gardens, under an over-arching rock, close by the only perennial spring in Jerusalem—that of the Valley of Kidron—which now bears the name of the "fountain of the Virgin,"[2] at that time the *En-Rogel* ("Spring of the Spy," or else "of the Fuller"). But a higher power than man's overruled events. To outward appearance the danger was indeed most urgent, the more so that it was not known in the palace. But already help was at hand. Nathan hastened to Bathsheba, and urged on her the necessity of immediate and decisive action. If Adonijah were proclaimed king, Solomon, Bathsheba, and all their adherents would immediately be put out of the way. In such circumstances court-ceremonial must be set aside; and Bathsheba made her way into the king's sick-chamber. She spoke respectfully but earnestly; she told him fully what at that very moment was taking place in the king's gardens; she reminded him of his solemn oath about the succession, which had hitherto determined

[1] Comp. Josephus, *Ant.* vii. 14. 4.
[2] Comp. Bonar, *Land of Promise*, pp. 492-496.

her own conduct and that of Solomon's adherents; and, finally, she appealed to him as alone competent at this crisis to determine who was to be king. The interview had not terminated when, according to previous arrangement, Nathan was announced. He had come on the same errand as Bathsheba: to inform the king of what Adonijah and his adherents were doing, and that Solomon and the king's most trusted servants had been excluded from a feast, the object of which was not concealed. Had all this been done by direction of the king? If so, why had not he, so old and faithful a counsellor, been informed that Adonijah was to be proclaimed successor to the throne?

With whatever weakness David may have been chargeable, he always rose to the requirements of the situation in hours of decisive importance, when either the known will of God or else the interests of his kingdom were in question. In this instance his measures were immediate and decisive. Recalling Bathsheba, who had withdrawn during the king's interview with Nathan, he dismissed her with words of reassurance. Then he sent for Zadok, Nathan, and Benaiah, and gave them his royal command for the immediate anointing of Solomon as king over Judah and Israel. The scene is vividly portrayed in Scripture. The king's body-guard—the *Cherethi* and *Pelethi*—under the command of Benaiah, was drawn up in front of the royal palace. Soon a vast concourse of people gathered. And now the king's state-mule, richly caparisoned, was brought out. It was an unwonted sight, which betokened some great state event. Presently, the great news became known, and rapidly spread through the streets and up the bazaars: Solomon was about to be anointed king! The people crowded together, in hundreds and thousands, from all parts of the city. And now Solomon appeared, attended by Zadok the high priest, Nathan the prophet, and Benaiah the chief of the royal guard. The procession formed, and moved forward. To avoid collision with the party of Adonijah, it took an opposite or western direction to the valley of Gihon.[1] Here, by authority and express command of David, Solomon was anointed king with the sacred oil by the joint ministry of the high priest and the prophet. The ceremony ended, the blast of the trumpets proclaimed the accession of the new monarch, and the people burst into a ringing shout: "God save King Solomon!" The enthusiastic demonstrations of joy were truly Eastern. There were music of pipes and acclamations of the people, till the ground beneath seemed to rend with the noise. As the procession returned, the city rang with the jubilee, till it reached the royal palace, where King Solomon seated himself in solemn state on his father's throne, and received the homage of the court, while David gave public thanks that he had lived to see that day.

Meanwhile, out in the king's gardens, the strange shouts from the city had reached Adonijah and his guests. Joab had grown uneasy as he heard the well-known sound of the trumpet. The tidings travelled quickly, and already one was in waiting to explain its meaning. But it was not as Adonijah had hoped against hope. The son of Abiathar had come to inform the conspirators of what had just taken place in Gihon and in the royal palace. And now sudden terror seized those who had but lately been so confident in their feasting. Every one of the conspirators fled, foremost among them Adonijah; nor did he deem himself safe till he had reached the sacred precincts, and laid hold on the horns of the altar. This asylum he refused to quit, until Solomon had assured him by oath that his life would be spared—though on condition that his future conduct should give the king no cause for complaint.

The events just recorded, which are only briefly indicated in 1 Chron. xxiii. 1, were followed by a great assembly of the chief dignitaries in Church and State (1 Chron. xxviii., xxix.), when the accession of Solomon to the throne was formally confirmed, and he was anointed a second time (1 Chron. xxix. 22). We remember, that similarly both Saul and David were

[1] Such seems to me the right location of Gihon, and not that suggested in the *Speaker's Commentary*, vol. ii. p. 485.

anointed a second time, on publicly receiving the homage of
their subjects (1 Sam. xi. 15 ; 2 Sam. ii. 4 ; v. 3).   It was in this
great assembly that the aged king, speaking, as it were, from
his death-bed, laid before his people the deepest wishes of his
heart, and told his inmost thoughts concerning the character,
the stability, and the object of royalty in Israel.   Beginning
with an evident reference to the great promise given to him
and his house, David first solemnly owned, that the appointment to the royal office—more particularly his own election
and that of Solomon as his successor—was of God as Israel's
supreme King, and that the stability and welfare of the kingdom depended upon faithful allegiance to Jehovah, to which
he accordingly admonished Solomon and the people (1 Chron.
xxviii. 2–10).   Then, following further the line indicated in
the covenant-promise, David pointed out that the grand object
of his son's reign must be to build an house unto the LORD.
This would be the initial typical fulfilment of that to which
the prophetic promise pointed.   So deeply had the king this
work at heart, that he had already prepared all the plans for
the Temple ; and that he dedicated to this work the vast treasures which during his long reign he had accumulated, always
with this great purpose in view (1 Chron. xxviii. 11–xxix. 5).
But this was not a work which Solomon either could or should
undertake by himself.   He must be supported in it by a willing
people.   And when the representatives of Israel in that great
assembly readily and liberally promised of their substance,
David seemed to feel that the work of his life was indeed done,
and that God would now let "His servant depart in peace."
The solemn and joyous eulogy, and the earnest prayer for his
people, and for his son and successor on the throne, with which
David dismissed this assembly, form a most appropriate close
to his public career.

    Gladly would we here end our record of David's life.   But
Scripture, in its truthful narration, calls us to witness yet another
scene.   We stand by the death-bed of David, and hear his last
injunctions to his son and successor.   At this time Solomon

could not have been more than twenty years of age. Probably
he was even younger. However wise and well-disposed, the
temptations and difficulties of his position could not but
awaken fears in the heart of his father, and that in proportion
as he kept in view the terms of the Divine prediction concerning his house, with its warnings as well as its promises. In
regard to matters Divine and spiritual, only one plain advice need
he give to Solomon. Spiritual decidedness, faithfulness, and
obedience to God : such simply were the means by which
the promises given to David and his house would be inherited.
But all the greater were the political dangers which beset the
path of the youthful king : an unscrupulous military party,
headed by Joab ; a dissatisfied priestly faction, ready to plot
and join any rebellious movement ; and ill-suppressed tribal
jealousies, of whose existence Shimei had, at a critical period,
given such painful evidence. The leaders of two of these
parties had long forfeited their lives ; indeed, only the ne-
cessities of the time could have excused either the impunity
with which Joab's treachery and his murder of Abner and
Amasa had been passed over, or the indulgence extended to
such conduct as that of Shimei. On the other hand, gratitude
to such tried adherents in adversity as the family of Barzillai had
proved, was alike dictated by duty and by policy. It was not,
as some would have us believe, that on his death-bed David
gave utterance to those feelings of revenge which he was
unable to gratify in his lifetime, but that, in his most intimate
converse with his son and successor, he looked at the dangers
to a young and inexperienced monarch from such powerful
and unscrupulous partisans. In these circumstances it was only
natural that, before dying, he should have given to his son
and successor such advice for his future guidance as his long
experience would suggest ; and similarly that, in so doing, he
should have reviewed the chief dangers and difficulties which
had beset his own path, and have referred to the great public
crimes which, during his reign, had necessarily been left unpunished. The fact that, even before his death, an attempt had

been made to elevate Adonijah to the throne, contrary alike to the known will of God and the appointment of David, and that the chief actors in this had been Joab and Abiathar, must have recalled the past to his mind, and shown him that the fire had been smouldering these many years, and might at any time burst into flame. But, however natural, and even lawful, such feelings on the part of David, it is impossible to read his parting directions and suggestions to Solomon without disappointment and pain. Truly, even the most advanced of the "children were in bondage under the elements of the world" (Gal. iv. 3). How far did the type fall short of the reality, and how dim and ill-defined were the foreshadowings of Him, "Who when He was reviled, reviled not again; when He suffered, He threatened not; but committed Himself to Him that judgeth righteously!"

And yet events soon proved that David's apprehensions had been only too well grounded. The aged king died, and was buried in his own "City of David," amidst the laments of a grateful nation, which ever afterwards cherished his memory (Acts ii. 29). It seems that Adonijah, although obliged to submit to Solomon's rule, had not given up all hope of his own ultimate accession. The scheme which he conceived for this purpose lacked, indeed, the courage of open rebellion, but was characterised by the cunning and trickery of a genuine Oriental intrigue. To marry any of the late king's wives or concubines was considered in the East as publicly claiming his rights (2 Sam. xii. 8; xvi. 21, 22). If such were done by a rival, it would be regarded as implying an insult to which not even the weakest monarch could submit without hopelessly degrading his authority in public opinion (2 Sam. iii. 7). If Adonijah's primary object was to lower Solomon in public estimate, and that in a manner which he could neither resist nor resent, no better scheme could have been devised than that of his application for the hand of Abishag. By combined flattery and parade of his supposed wrongs and injuries he gained the queen-mother as unconscious accomplice and even instrument of his intrigue. Any scruples might be set aside by the plea, that there could be no wrong in his request, since, in the strict sense, Abishag had neither been the wife nor the concubine of David. To punish with death so cunning and mean an intrigue can scarcely be called excessive severity on the part of Solomon. It was rather a measure necessary, if tranquillity was to be preserved in the land, all the more that, by his own admission, Adonijah still entertained the opinion that rightfully the kingdom was his, and that "all Israel set their faces on him that *he* should reign" (1 Kings ii. 15).

Whether or not Abiathar and Joab were involved in this intrigue, is matter of uncertainty. At any rate an attempt so daring, and coming so soon after that in which these two had taken a leading part, called for measures which might prevent rebellion in the future, and serve as warning to the turbulent in Israel. That Joab felt conscious his conduct deserved the severest punishment, appears from the circumstance that he anticipated his sentence. On hearing of Adonijah's execution, he sought refuge within the sacred precincts of the Tabernacle. It would have been not only a dangerous precedent, but contrary to the express direction of the law (Ex. xxi. 12; Deut. xix. 11–13), to have allowed a criminal by such means to escape justice. However, it was not for his part in Adonijah's recent schemes that Joab now suffered the extreme penalty of the law, but for his former and still unpunished crimes, which his recent treasonable conduct seemed to bring afresh to view, just as some accidental ailment does a long latent fatal disease. As for Abiathar, in consideration of his office and former services to David, he was only removed from the Pontificate, and banished to his ancestral property at Anathoth, the city of the priests. But Holy Scripture calls us to mark, how by the deposition of Abiathar the Divine prediction against the house of Eli (1 Sam. ii. 31–36) was fulfilled, though in this instance also through a concurrence of intelligible causes.

There was now only one other left, who in heart and

mind, as well as in popular opinion, belonged to the party opposed to the reigning house. That old offender, Shimei, was still at large, and enjoying ill-deserved safety. Had he during those years learned to respect the dynasty which he had once so wantonly insulted, or did he still consider it too weak to resent insubordination on his part? The question was soon to be decided; for Solomon now ordered Shimei to remain permanently within the bounds of Jerusalem, at the same time warning him that any infringement of this command, from whatever cause, would be punished by death. Shimei, who had probably expected a far more severe sentence, received with gratitude this comparatively slight restriction upon his liberty. He must have known that most Eastern monarchs would have acted towards him in a very different spirit. Besides, the restriction was not more irksome than that which limited the safety of an ordinary manslayer by the condition of his remaining within the bounds of the city of refuge. Nor was the command in itself unreasonable, considering the necessity of watching Shimei's movements, and the importance of convincing the people that a strong hand now held the reins of government. But whatever outward acquiescence Shimei had shown, he had no idea of yielding such absolute obedience as in his circumstances seemed called for. On the first apparently trivial occasion,[1] Shimei left Jerusalem for the capital of Philistia without having sought the king's permission, and, upon his return, suffered the penalty which, as he well knew, had been threatened. By such measures of vigour and firmness "the kingdom was established in the hand of Solomon."

[1] It can scarcely be pretended that Shimei's personal presence at Gath was absolutely necessary for the recovery of his fugitive slaves. But even had it been so, if Shimei had been allowed to transgress the king's injunction, his obedience in this or any other matter could never afterwards have been enforced.

CHAPTER V.

Solomon marries the Daughter of Pharaoh—His Sacrifice at Gibeon—His Dream and Prayer—Solomon's Wisdom—Solomon's Officers and Court —Prosperity of the Country—Understanding and Knowledge of the King.

(1 KINGS III., IV., 2 CHRON. I.)

IT is remarkable, how often seemingly unimportant details in the sacred narrative gain a fresh meaning and new interest if viewed in their higher bearing and spiritual import. Nor is such application of them arbitrary. On the contrary, we conclude that Scripture was intended to be so read. This is evident from the circumstance that it is, avowedly, not a secular but a prophetic history,[1] and that, being such, it is not arranged according to the chronological succession of events, but grouped so as to bring into prominence that which concerns the kingdom of God. This plan of Scripture history is not only worthy of its object, but gives it its permanent interest and application.

What has just been stated is aptly illustrated by the opening account of King Solomon's reign. Of course, no chronological arrangement could have been here intended, since the list of Solomon's officers, given in 1 Kings iv., contains the names of at least two of the king's sons-in-law (vers. 11, 15), whose appointment must, therefore, date from a period considerably later than the commencement of his reign. What, then, we may ask, is the object of not only recording in a "prophetic history" such apparently unimportant details, but grouping them together irrespective of their dates? Without undervaluing them, considered as purely historical notices, we may venture to suggest a higher object in their record and arrange-

---

[1] As noticed in the previous part, and even indicated by the position in the Hebrew Canon of the historical books among "the Prophets."

ment. This detailed account of all the court and government appointments serves as evidence, how thoroughly and even elaborately the kingdom of Solomon was organised—and by obvious inference, how fully God had made good in this respect His gracious promises to King David. But may we not go even beyond this, and see in the literal fulfilment of these outward promises a pledge and assurance that the spiritual realities connected with them, and of which they were the symbol and type, would likewise become true in the Kingdom of Him Who was " David's better Son ? " Thus viewed, the Divine promise made to David (2 Sam. vii.) was once more like a light casting the lengthening shadows of present events towards the far-off future.

The first event of national interest that occurred was the marriage of Solomon with the daughter of Pharaoh. It was of almost equal political importance to Egypt and to Palestine. An alliance with the great neighbouring kingdom of Egypt might have seemed an eventuality almost unthought of among the possibilities of the new and somewhat doubtful monarchy in Israel. But, on the other hand, it may have been also of importance to the then reigning Egyptian dynasty (the 21st Tanite), which, as we know, was rapidly declining in authority.[1] To Israel and to the countries around, such a union would now afford evidence of the position and influence which the Jewish monarchy had attained in the opinion of foreign politicians. All the more are we involuntarily carried back in spirit to the period when Israel was oppressed and in servitude to Egypt. As we contrast the relations in the past and in the time of Solomon, we realise how marvellously God had fulfilled His promises of deliverance to His people. And here we again turn to the great promise in 2 Sam. vii., as alike instructive to Israel as regarded their present, and as full of blessed hope for their future. The time of the Judges had been one of struggle and disorganisation; that of David one of war and conflicts. But with Solomon the period of peace had begun, emblematic

[1] Comp. Stuart Poole, in Smith s *Bible Dict.*, vol. i. p. 511.

of the higher peace of the "Prince of Peace." Thus viewed, the account of the prosperity of the land and people, as further evidenced by the wealth displayed in the ordinary appointments of the Court ; by the arrangement of the country into provinces under officers for fiscal administration and civil government; and, above all, by the wisdom of Solomon, — who, while encouraging by example literature and study of every kind, chiefly aimed after that higher knowledge and understanding which is God-given, and leads to the fear and service of the Lord,—acquires a new and a spiritual meaning.

But to return to the sacred narrative. This marriage of Solomon with the daughter of Pharaoh—to which, from its frequent mention, so much political importance seems to have been attached—took place in the first years of his reign, although some time after the building of the Temple and of his own palace had commenced.[1] Such a union was not forbidden by the law,[2] nor was the daughter of Pharaoh apparently implicated in the charge brought against Solomon's other foreign wives of having led him into idolatry (1 Kings xi. 1–7). In fact, according to Jewish tradition, the daughter of Pharaoh actually became a Jewish proselyte. Still, Solomon seems to have felt the incongruity of bringing her into the palace of David, within the bounds of which "the Ark of the Lord" appears to have been located (2 Chron. viii. 11), and she occupied a temporary abode "in the City of David," till the new palace of Solomon was ready for her reception.

But the great prosperity which, as we shall presently see, the country enjoyed during the reign of Solomon, was due to higher than merely outward causes. It was the blessing of the Lord which in this instance also made rich—that blessing which

---

[1] From 1 Kings xi. 42, comp. with xiv. 21, we might infer that Solomon had married the Ammonitess Naamah before the death of his father. But as this seems incompatible with 2 Chron. xiii. 7, and for other reasons which will readily occur to the reader, the numeral indicating the age of Rehoboam (1 Kings xiv. 21) seems to be a copyist's mistake for 21.

[2] The law only forbade alliance with the Canaanites (Ex. xxxiv. 16; Deut. vii. 3).

it was Solomon's chief concern to obtain. From the necessity of the case, Israel, and even Solomon, still worshipped on the ancient "high places."[1] Of these the principal was naturally *Gibeon*—the twin height. For, right over against the city itself, on one of the two eminences ("mamelons") which gave it its name, the ancient Tabernacle which Moses had reared had been placed. Here Solomon, at the commencement of his reign, celebrated a great festival, probably to inaugurate and consecrate his accession by a public acknowledgment of Jehovah as the God of Israel. All the people took part in what was a service of hitherto unparalleled magnificence.[2] But something far better than the smoke of a thousand burnt-sacrifices offered in Israel's ancient Sanctuary, attested that the God, Who had brought Israel out of Egypt and led them through the Wilderness, still watched over His people. The services of those festive days were over, and king and people were about to return to their homes. As Solomon had surveyed the vast multitude which, from all parts of the country, had gathered to Gibeon, the difficulty must have painfully forced itself on him of wisely ruling an empire so vast as that belonging to him, stretching from Tiphsach (the Greek *Thapsacus*), "the fords," on the western bank of the Euphrates, in the north-east, to Gaza on the border of Egypt, in the south-west (1 Kings iv. 24). The conquests so lately made had not yet been consolidated; the means at the king's disposal were still comparatively scanty ; tribal jealousies were scarcely appeased ; and Solomon himself was young and wholly inexperienced. Any false step might prove fatal ; even want of some brilliant success might disintegrate what was but imperfectly welded together. On the other hand, had Israel's history not been a series of constant miracles, through the gracious Personal interposition of the Lord ? What, then, might Solomon not expect from His help?

Busy with such thoughts, the king had laid him down to rest

---

[1] Comp. the views expressed in the *Mishnah* on the lawfulness of such worship in vol. iii. of this "Bible History," p. 78.

[2] Similarly Xerxes offered a thousand oxen at Troy (Herod. vii. 43).

on the last night of his stay in Gibeon. Ordinarily dreams are without deeper significance. So Solomon himself afterwards taught (Eccles. v. 7); and so the spiritually enlightened among other nations, and the prophets in Israel equally declared (Job xx. 8; Is. xxix. 7). And yet, while most fully admitting this (as in Ecclus. xxxiv. 1–6), it must have been also felt, as indeed Holy Scripture teaches by many instances, that dreams might be employed by the Most High in the time of our visitation (Ecclus. xxxiv. 6). So was it with Solomon on that night. It has been well remarked, that Adonijah would not have thus dreamed after his feast at En-Rogel (1 Kings i. 9, 25), even had his attempt been crowned with the success for which he had hoped. The question which on that night the Lord put before Solomon, "Ask what I shall give thee?" was not only an answer to the unspoken entreaty for help expressed in the sacrifices that had been offered, but was also intended to search the deepest feelings of his heart. Like that of our Lord addressed to St. Peter, "Simon, son of Jonas, lovest thou Me?" it sounded the inmost depths of the soul. Such questions come, more or less distinctly, to us all, and that in every crisis of our lives. They may become fresh spiritual starting-points to us, seasons of greater nearness to God, and of spiritual advancement; or they may prove times of "temptation," if we allow ourselves to be "drawn away" and "enticed" of our own "lust."

The prayer of Solomon on this occasion once more combined the three elements of thanksgiving, confession, and petition. In his thanksgiving, acknowledgment of God mingled with humiliation; in his confession, a sense of inability with the expression of felt want; while his petition, evidently based on the Divine promise (Gen. xiii. 16; xxxii. 12), was characterised by singleness of spiritual desire. For, in order to know what he sought, when so earnestly craving for "understanding," we have only to turn to his own "Book of Proverbs." And, as in the case of all whose spiritual aim is single, God not only granted his request, but also added to what He gave "all things" other-

F

wise needful, thus proving that the "promise of the life that
now is" is ever connected with that of the life "which is to
come" (1 Tim. iv. 8), just as in our present condition the soul is
with the body.   Perhaps we may put it otherwise in this manner :
As so often, God extended the higher wisdom granted Solomon
even to the lower concerns of this life, while He added to it the
promise of longevity and prosperity—but only on condition
of continued observance of God's statutes and commandments
(1 Kings iii. 14). [1]   Such gracious condescension on the part
of the LORD called for the expression of fresh public thanksgiving, which Solomon rendered on his return to Jerusalem
(1 Kings iii. 15).

Evidence of the reality of God's promise soon appeared, and
that in a manner peculiarly calculated to impress the Eastern
mind.   According to the simple manners of the times, a cause
too difficult for ordinary judges was carried direct to the
king, who, as God's representative, was regarded as able to
give help to his people in all time of need.   In such paternal
dispensation of justice, there was no appeal to witnesses nor to
statute-books, which indeed would have been equally accessible
to inferior judges ; but the king was expected to strike out some
new light, in which the real bearings of a case would so appear
as to appeal to all men's convictions, and to command their
approval of his sentence.   There was here no need for anything
recondite—rather the opposite.   To point out to practical
common sense what *was* there, though unperceived till suddenly
brought to prominence, would more than anything else appeal
to the people, as a thing within the range of all, and yet showing
the wise guidance of the king.   Thus sympathy and universal
trust, as well as admiration, would be called forth, especially
among Orientals, whose wisdom is that of common life, and
whose philosophy that of proverbs.

The story of the contention of the two women for the one
living child, when from the absence of witnesses it seemed

[1] Accordingly, Solomon forfeited this promise on account of his later
idolatry.   He died at the age of about fifty-nine or sixty.

impossible to determine whose it really was, is sufficiently known. The ready wisdom with which Solomon devised means for ascertaining the truth would commend itself to the popular mind. It was just what they would appreciate in their king. Such a monarch would indeed be a terror to evil-doers, and a protection and praise to them that did well. It is probably in order to explain the rapid spread of Solomon's fame that this instance of his wisdom is related in Holy Scripture (1 Kings iii. 28).

The prosperity of such a reign was commensurate with the fact that it was based upon the Divine promises, and typical of far greater blessings to come. The notices in 1 Kings iv. and v. are strung together to indicate that prosperity by presenting to our view the condition of the Israelitish monarchy in the high-day of its glory. Wise and respected councillors surrounded the king.[1] The administration of the country was orderly, and the taxation not arbitrary but regulated. The land was divided, not according to the geographical boundaries of the "tribes," but according to population and resources, into twelve provinces, over each of which a governor was appointed. Among their number we find two sons-in-law of the king (iv. 11, 15), and other names well-known in the land (such as those of Baana, ver. 12, probably the brother of "the recorder," ver. 3, and Baanah, the son of Hushai, probably David's councillor, ver. 16). Had this policy of re-arranging the country into provinces been sufficiently consolidated, many of the tribal jealousies would have ceased. On the other hand, the financial administration, entrusted to these governors, was of the simplest kind. Apparently, no direct taxes were levied, but all that was requisite for the royal court and government had to be provided, each province supplying in turn what

[1] The word *Cohen* in 1 Kings iv. 2 ("Azariah, the son of Zadok the *priest*") should *not* be rendered "priest," but refers to a civil office—that of the king's representative to the people and his most intimate adviser. The same term is used of Zabud in ver. 5, where the Authorised Version translates "principal officer," and also of David's sons, 2 Sam. viii. 18. A grandson of Zadok could not have been old enough to be high-priest (comp. 1 Chron. vi. 10.)

was required for one month. Such a system could not indeed press heavily, so long as the country continued prosperous; but with a luxurious court, in hard times, or under harsh governors, it might easily become an instrument of oppression and a source of discontent. From 1 Kings xii. 4 we gather that such was ultimately the case. It need scarcely be added, that in each province the supreme civil government was in the hands of these royal officials; and such was the general quiet prevailing, that even in the extensive district east of the Jordan, which bordered on so many turbulent tributary nations, "one sole officer" (1 Kings iv. 19) was sufficient to preserve the peace of the country.

Quite in accordance with these notices are the references both to the prosperity of Israel, and to the extent of Solomon's dominions (1 Kings iv. 20, 21). They almost read like an initial fulfilment of that promise to Abraham: "Multiplying I will multiply thy seed as the stars of the heaven, and as the sand which is upon the sea shore; and thy seed shall possess the gate of his enemies" (Gen. xxii. 17). And if, compared with the simplicity of Saul's and even of David's court, that of Solomon seems luxurious in its appointments,[1] we must remember that it was intended to show the altered state of the Israelitish monarchy, and that even so the daily consumption was far smaller than at the court of the Persian monarchs in the high-day of their power and glory.[2]

---

[1] The provision made was not only for the court and its dependants, but also for the royal stables (1 Kings iv. 26–28). In verse 26 the number of his horses is by a clerical error given as 40,000 instead of 4000 (comp. 2 Chron. ix. 25). If, according to 1 Kings x. 26, 2 Chron. i. 14, Solomon had 1,400 chariots, each with two horses, and with, in most of them, a third horse as reserve, we have the number 4000.

[2] It is difficult to give the exact equivalent of the "thirty measures of fine flour and threescore of meal" (in all, ninety measures), 1 Kings iv. 22. According to the calculation of the Rabbis (*Bibl. Dict.* vol. iii. p. 1742) they would yield ninety-nine sacks of flour. Thenius (*Studien u. Krit.* for 1846, p. 73, etc.) calculates that they would yield two pounds of bread for 14,000 persons. But this computation is exaggerated. On competent authority I am informed that one bushel of flour makes up fourteen (four

But the fame which accrued to the kingdom of Solomon from its prosperity and wealth would have been little worthy of the Jewish monarchy, had it been uncombined with that which alone truly exalteth a nation or an individual. The views of Solomon himself on this subject are pithily summed up in one of his own "Proverbs" (iii. 13, 14): "Happy is the man that findeth wisdom, and the man that causeth understanding to go forth ; for merchandise (trading) with it, is better than merchandise with silver, and the gain from it than the most fine gold." [1] All this the "wise king" exemplified in his own person. God gave him "wisdom" not only far wider in its range, but far other in its character (Prov. i. 7 ; ix. 10) than that of the East, or of far-famed Egypt, or even of those deemed wisest in Israel, [2] "and understanding exceeding much, and largeness of heart, even as the sand that is on the sea-shore" [3] (1 Kings iv. 29). Not satisfied with the idle life of an Eastern monarch, he set

---

pound) loaves of bread ; consequently, one sack (= four bushels) fifty-six loaves, or 224 pounds of bread. This for ninety-nine sacks would give 22,176 pounds of bread, which at two pounds per person would supply 11,088—or, with waste, about 11,000 persons. Of this total amount of bread, the thirty-three sacks of "fine flour"—probably for court use—would yield 1,848 loaves, or 7,392 pounds of bread. The number of persons fed daily at the court of the kings of Persia is said to have been 15,000 (see *Speaker's Comm.*, p. 502). Thenius further calculates that, taken on an average, the thirty oxen and one hundred sheep would yield one and a half pounds of meat for each of the 14,000 persons. At the court of Cyrus, the daily provision seems to have been, 400 sheep, 300 lambs, 100 oxen, 30 horses, 30 deer, 400 fatted geese, 100 young geese, 300 pigeons, 600 small fowls, 3,750 gallons of wine, 75 gallons of new milk, and 75 of sour milk (comp. Bähr in Lange's *Bibel W.*, vol. vii. p. 29). But here also the computation of Thenius seems too large, bearing in mind that cattle and sheep in the East are much smaller than in the West.

[1] We translate literally.

[2] Comp. 1 Chron. ii. 6. Ethan, 1 Chron. vi. 44 ; xv. 17, 19 ; Ps. lxxxix. (inscr.) Heman, 1 Chron. vi. 33 ; xxv. 5 ; Ps. lxxxviii. (inscr.) Chalcol and Darda, sons of Mahol, perhaps—"*sacras choreas ducendi periti.*"

[3] A hyperbole not uncommon in antiquity. I feel tempted here to quote the similar expression of Horace (*Odes*, i. 28) :

"Te maris et terræ numeroque carentis arenæ
    Mensorem cohibent, Archyta."

the example of, and gave encouragement to study and literature—the range of his inquiries extending not only to philosophy and poetry,[1] but also to natural science in all its branches.[2] It must have been a mighty intellectual impulse which proceeded from such a king; it must have been a reign unparalleled in that age, as well as among that people, which Solomon inaugurated.

CHAPTER VI.

The Building of Solomon's Temple—Preparations for It—Plan and Structure of the Temple—Internal Fittings—History of the Temple—Jewish Traditions.

(1 KINGS V., VI., VII. 13–51, VIII. 6–9 ; 2 CHRON. II. III., IV., V. 7–10).

WHILE Solomon thus wisely and in the fear of God ordered his government, and the country enjoyed a measure of prosperity, wealth, and power never before or afterwards attained, the grand work of his reign yet remained to be done. This was the building of an " house unto the Name of Jehovah God." We have already seen how earnestly David had this at heart; how fully it corresponded with the Divine promise; and how fitly its execution was assigned to Solomon as the great task of his reign, viewing it as typical of that of " David's greater Son." As might be expected, all outward circumstances contributed to further the work. Israel, as a nation, was not intended to attain pre-eminence either in art or science. If

[1] Of these " Proverbs " only 915 verses have been preserved in the Book of that name ; of " the Songs," besides the Song of Songs, only Ps. lxxii. and cxxvii.

[2] The word rendered "hyssop" in the Authorised Version is either the mint, the marjoram, the *Orthotricum saxatile*, or, according to Tristram (*Nat. Hist. of the Bible*," p. 457), the caper (*Capparis spinosa*).

we may venture to pronounce on such a matter, this was the part assigned, in the Providence of God, to the Gentile world. To Israel was specially entrusted the guardianship of that spiritual truth, which in the course of ages would develop in all its proportions, till finally it became the common property of the whole world. On the other hand, it was the task assigned to that world, to develop knowledge and thought so as to prepare a fitting reception for the truth, that thus it might be presented in all its aspects, and carried from land to land in a form adapted to every nation, meeting every want and aspiration. This was symbolically indicated even in the building of Solomon's Temple. For, if that Temple had been exclusively the workmanship of Jewish hands, both the materials for it and their artistic preparation would have been sadly defective, as compared with what it actually became. But it was not so ; and, while in the co-operation of Gentiles with Israel in the rearing of the Temple we see a symbol of their higher union in the glorious architecture of that "spiritual house built up" of "lively stones," we also recognise the gracious Providence of God, which rendered it possible to employ in that work the best materials and the best artificers of the ancient world.

For it was in the good Providence of God that the throne of Tyre was at the time occupied by Hiram,[1] who had not only been a friend and ally of David, but to whom the latter had communicated his plans of the projected Temple-buildings. Indeed, Hiram had already furnished David with a certain proportion of the necessary materials for the work (1 Chron. xxii. 4). The extraordinary mechanical skill of the Phœnicians —especially of the Sidonians—was universally famed in the ancient world.[2] Similarly, the best materials were at their command. On the slopes of Lebanon, which belonged to their territory, grew those world-famed cedars with which the palaces

---

[1] Also written *Hirom* (1 Kings v. 10, 18—in the Hebrew, iv. 24, 32), and in 2 Chron. ii. *Huram.*

[2] Comp. the quotations in the *Speaker's Comment.* (II. p. 507a,) and Movers, *Phöniz.* II, i. pp. 86, etc.

of Assyria were adorned, and, close by, at Gebal (the ancient
Byblos, the modern *Jebeil*) were the most skilled workmen [1]
(Ezek. xxvii. 9). On the same slopes grew also the cypress, [2]
so suitable for flooring, its wood being almost indestructible,
and impervious to rot and worms; while the Phœnician
merchantmen brought to Tyre that "almug," "algum," or red
sandal-wood which was so valued in antiquity (comp. 1 Kings
x. 11). [3] The same skill as in the preparation of woodwork
distinguished the Phœnician carvers, stone-cutters, dyers,
modellers, and other craftsmen. To have at his disposal the
best artificers of Phœnicia, and these under a trained and celebrated "master" (2 Chron. ii. 13, 14), must have been of
immense advantage to Solomon. At the same time the
extensive preparations which David had made rendered the
work comparatively so easy, that the Temple-buildings, with
their elaborate internal fittings, were completed in the short
space of seven years (1 Kings vi. 37, 38), while the later rearing
of the king's palace occupied not less than thirteen years
(1 Kings vii. 1). But, although Solomon thus availed himself
of Phœnician skill in the execution of the work, the plan
and design were strictly Jewish, having, in fact, been drawn
long before, in the time of King David.

[1] Our Authorised Version translates wrongly, "stone-squarers" (1 Kings
v. 18), where the original has "Gebalites," *i.e.*, inhabitants of Gebal.

[2] There has been much controversy as to the meaning of the word
berosh, rendered in the Authorised Version (1 Kings v. 8, and many other
passages) by "fir." Differing from Canon Rawlinson, it seems to me,
for many reasons, most improbable that it was "the juniper," and on the
grounds explained in Gesenius' *Thesaurus* I. 246 *b*, 247 *a*, I regard it,
with almost all authorities, as the cypress. The Targumim and the Talmud
have the words *berotha* and *beratha*, with apparently the same signification.
Comp. Levy, *Chald. Wörterb. ü. d. Targ.* p. 118 *b*. Canon Tristram,
who is always trustworthy (*Nat. Hist. of the Bible*), speaks of it with caution.

[3] Most commentators are agreed that it was the "red sandal" wood.
It is curious to notice that this was apparently an article of ordinary
commerce. The "Ophir" (or Red Sea) fleet of King Solomon, on the
other hand, is only said to have brought "gold" (1 Kings ix. 28 ; 2 Chron.
viii. 17, 18). Remembering that this wood had to come from *Tyre*, there
is not the slightest inaccuracy in 2 Chron. ii. 8, as Zöckler and even Keil
seem to imagine.

The building of the Temple commenced in the second month (" *Siv*," "splendour"—the month of opening beauty of nature) of the fourth year of Solomon's reign, being the 480th from the Exodus[1] (1 Kings vi. 1). But there was this peculiarity about the work, that no sound of axe, hammer, or chisel was heard on Mount Moriah while the Holy House was rising, day by day, in beauty and glory. As Jewish tradition has it : " The iron is created to shorten the days of man, and the altar to lengthen them ; therefore it is not right that that which shortens should be lifted upon that which lengthens" (*Midd.* iii. 4). The massive timber used was not merely prepared but dressed before it was brought to the sea, to be conveyed in floats to Joppa, whence the distance to Jerusalem was only about forty miles (1 Kings v. 9). Similarly, those great, splendid (*not* "costly," as in the Authorised Version) hewed stones (1 Kings v. 17), bevelled at the edges, of which to this day some are seen in what remains of the ancient Temple-wall—the largest of them being more than thirty feet long by seven and a half high, and weighing above one hundred tons—were all chiselled and carefully marked before being sent to Jerusalem (1 Kings vi. 7). An undertaking of such magnitude would require, especially in the absence of modern mechanical appliances, a very large number of workmen. They amounted in all to 160,000 Palestinians, who were divided into two classes. The first comprised native Israelites, of whom 30,000 were raised by a "levy," which, taking the census of David as our basis, would be at the rate of considerably less than one in forty-four of the able-bodied male population. These 30,000 men worked by relays, 10,000 being employed during one month, after which they returned for two months to their homes. The second class of workmen, which consisted of strangers resident in Palestine (1 Kings v. 15 ; 2 Chron. ii. 17, 18), amounted to 150,000, of

[1] Doubt has been thrown on the accuracy of this date, which indeed is altered by the LXX ; but this, as it seems to us, on wholly insufficient grounds. Compare the Chronological Table at the beginning of Vol. III. of this " Bible History," and the detailed remarks of Bähr in Lange's *Bibel-Werk*, vol. vii. pp. 40*b*, 41*a*.

whom 70,000 were burden-bearers, and 80,000 "hewers in the mountains," or rather, as the expression always means, "stone-cutters." The two classes are carefully distinguished—the Israelites being free labourers, who worked under the direction of Hiram's skilled men ; while the others, who were the representatives of the ancient heathen inhabitants of Palestine, were really held to "bond-service" (1 Kings ix. 20, 21 ; 2 Chron. ii. 17, 18 ; viii. 7–9). The total number of men employed (160,000), though large, cannot be considered excessive, when compared, for example, with the 360,000 persons engaged for twenty years on the building of one pyramid (Pliny, *Hist. Nat.* xxxvi. 12. *apud* Bähr *u. s.*) Over these men 3,300 officers were appointed (1 Kings v. 16), with 550 "chiefs" (1 Kings ix. 23), of whom 250 were apparently native Israelites (2 Chron. viii. 10.)[1]

The number of skilled artificers furnished by Hiram is not mentioned, though probably the proportion was comparatively small. A very vivid impression is left on our minds of the transaction between the two kings. When Hiram sent a friendly embassy to congratulate Solomon on his accession, the latter replied by another, which was charged formally to ask help in the building about to be undertaken. The request was entertained by Hiram in the most cordial manner. At the same time, bearing in mind Eastern phraseology, and that a Phœnician ally of David would readily recognise the God of Israel as a "national Deity," there is no reason for inferring, from the terms of his reply, that Hiram was personally a worshipper of Jehovah (1 Kings v. 7; 2 Chron. ii. 12). The agreement seems to have been, that Solomon would undertake to provide for the support of Hiram's men, wheat, barley, and oil, to the amount specified in 2 Chron. ii. 10 ; while, so long as building materials were required, Hiram charged for them at an annual rate of 20,000 measures of wheat, and twenty

[1] There is no real discrepancy between the number of the "officers," as given respectively in Chronicles and in Kings. The sum total (3850) is in both cases the same—the arrangement in Chronicles being apparently according to nationality, and in the Book of Kings according to office (1 Kings, 3300 + 550 ; 2 Chron., 3600 + 250).

measures (about ten hogsheads) of "beaten oil,"—that is, the best in the market, which derived its name from its manufacture, the oil being extracted by beating the olives before they were quite ripe (1 Kings v. 11). In regard to these terms, it should be remembered that Phœnicia was chiefly dependent on Palestine for its supply of grain and oil (Ezek. xxvii. 17 ; Acts xii. 20). Lastly, the name of the "master-workman," whom Hiram sent, has also been preserved to us as Huram, or rather Churam,[1] a man of Jewish descent by the mother's side (2 Chron. ii. 13, 14; comp. 1 Kings vii. 14; 2 Chron. iv. 16).[2] Even the completeness and entirely satisfactory character of these arrangements proved, that in this respect also "Jehovah gave Solomon wisdom, as He had promised him" (1 Kings v. 12).

Without entering into details,[3] the general appearance and proportions of the Temple which Solomon built can be described without much difficulty. The Temple itself faced east—that is to say, the worshippers entered by the east, and, turning to the Most Holy Place, would look west ; while, if the veil had been drawn aside, the Ark in the innermost Sanctuary would have been seen to face eastwards. Entering then by the east, the worshipper would find himself in front of "a porch," which extended along the whole width of the Temple,—that is, twenty cubits, or about thirty feet—and went back a depth of ten cubits, or fifteen feet. The Sanctuary itself was sixty cubits (ninety feet) long, twenty cubits (thirty feet) wide, and thirty cubits (forty-five feet) high. The height of the porch is not mentioned in the Book of Kings, and the numeral given for it in 2 Chron. iii. 4, is evidently a copyist's error.[4] Probably it rose to a height

---

[1] The name is the same as that of the king himself.

[2] Our Authorised Version of 2 Chron. ii. 13 is entirely misleading. The sacred text mentions "Huram" as "Abi," "my father,"—not the father of King Hiram, but a title of distinction given to this able man (comp. the use of the word "*Ab*" in regard to Joseph, Gen. xlv. 8), and equivalent to "master."

[3] The literature of this subject is very large, and details are often most difficult.

[4] A height of 120 cubits would be out of all proportion, and, indeed, considering the width and length, almost impossible.

of about thirty cubits.[1] Of the total length of the Sanctuary, forty cubits were apportioned to the Holy Place, (which was thus sixty feet long, thirty wide, and forty-five high), and twenty cubits (thirty feet) to the Most Holy Place, which (1 Kings vi. 20) is described as measuring twenty cubits[2] (thirty feet) in length, width, and height. The ten cubits (fifteen feet) left above the Most Holy Place were apparently occupied by an empty room. Perhaps, as in the Temple of Herod, this space was used for letting down the workmen through an aperture, when repairs were required in the innermost Sanctuary. In that case the access to it would have been from the roof. The latter was, no doubt, flat.[3]

The measurements just given apply, of course, only to the *interior* of these buildings. As regards their *exterior* we have to add not only the thickness of the walls on either side, and the height of the roof, but also a row of side-buildings, which have, not inaptly, been designated as a "lean-to." These side-

[1] Of the textual alterations proposed, the first (מאה, 100, into אמות "cubits") seems the easiest, although it involves the elimination of the ו with which the next word in the Hebrew begins. On the other hand, "thirty cubits" seems a more suitable height, especially as the absence of its measurement in 1 Kings seems to convey that the "porch" had the same height as the main building. But this implies *two* alterations in the text, it being difficult to understand how, if the *numeral* 30 was originally written by a letter (ל, of which, it is supposed, the blotting out of the upper half made it appear like כ = 20), the copyist finding אמות written in full could have mistaken it for מאה, 100, which also ought to have been written with a letter (ק). It is, however, possible that instead of the full word, אמות, the MS. may have borne אמי, and the copyist have been thus misled.

[2] Thus the Most Holy Place would have had exactly double the proportions of that in the Tabernacle, while the height of the Holy Place was ten cubits (fifteen feet) higher.

[3] It is with great reluctance and becoming modesty—though without misgiving—that I differ from so justly famous an authority as Mr. Ferguson (Smith's *Bibl. Dict.* vol. III., Art. "Temple"). Mr. Ferguson, and after him most English writers, have maintained that the roof, both of the Tabernacle and of the Temple, was *sloping*, and not flat. This view is, to say the least, wholly unsupported by the text of Holy Scripture. Canon Rawlinson, indeed, speaks of Mr. Ferguson's view as "*demonstrated*," but, surely, without weighing the meaning of the word which he has italicised.

buildings consisted of three tiers of chambers, which surrounded
the Temple, south, west, and north—the east front being covered
by the "porch." On the side where these chambers abutted
on the Temple they seem to have had no separate wall. The
beams, which formed at the same time the ceiling of the first
and the floor of the second tier of chambers, and similarly those
which formed the ceiling of the second and the floor of the
third tier, as also those on which the roof over the third tier
rested, were *not* inserted within the Temple wall, but were laid
on graduated buttresses which formed part of the main wall of
the Temple. These buttresses receded successively one cubit
in each of the two higher tiers of chambers, and for the roofing
of the third, thus forming, as it were, narrowing steps, or receding
rests on which the beams of the chambers were laid. The
effect was that, while the walls of the Temple decreased one
cubit in thickness with each tier, the chambers increased one cubit
in width, as they ascended. Thus, if at the lowest tier the wall
including the buttress was, say, six cubits thick, at the next tier
of chambers it was, owing to the decrease in the buttress, only
five cubits thick, and at the third only four cubits, while above
the roof, where the buttress ceased, the walls would be only three
cubits thick. For the same reason each tier of chambers, built
on gradually narrowing or receding rebatements, would be one
cubit wider than that below, the chambers on the lowest tier
being five cubits wide, on the second six cubits, and on the third
seven cubits. If we suppose these tiers with their roof to have
been altogether sixteen to eighteen cubits high (1 Kings vi. 10),
and allow a height of two cubits for the roof of the Temple,
whose walls were thirty cubits high (the total height, including
roof, thirty-two cubits), this would leave an elevation of twelve
to fourteen cubits (eighteen to twenty-one feet) for the wall of
the Temple above the roof of "the chambers." Within this
space of twelve to fourteen cubits we suppose the "windows"
to have been inserted—south and north, the back of the Most
Holy Place (west) having no windows, and the front (east) being
covered by the "porch." The use of the "chambers" is not

mentioned in the sacred text, but it seems more probable that they served for the deposit of relics of the ancient Tabernacle, and for the storage of sacred vessels, than that they were the sleeping apartments of the ministering priesthood. Access to these "chambers" was gained by a door in the middle of the southern façade, whence also a winding stair led to the upper tiers (1 Kings vi. 8). The windows of the Temple itself, which we have supposed to have been above the roof of the "chambers," were with "fixed lattices"[1] (1 Kings vi. 4), which could not be opened, as in private dwellings, and were probably constructed, like the windows of old castles and churches, broad within, but mere slits externally. While these protracted works were progressing, the LORD in His mercy gave special encouragement alike to Solomon and to the people. The word of the LORD, which on this occasion came to the king (1 Kings vi. 11–13)—no doubt through a prophet—not only fully confirmed the promise made to David (2 Sam. vii. 12, etc.), but also connected the "house" that was being built to the LORD with the ancient promise (Ex. xxv. 8; xxix. 45) that God would dwell in Israel as among His people. Thus it pointed king and people beyond that outward building which, rising in such magnificence, might have excited only national pride, to its spiritual meaning, and to the conditions under which alone it would fulfil its great purpose.[2]

Thus far we have given a description of the exterior of the Temple.[3] It still remains to convey some idea of its internal arrangements. If we may judge by the description of Ezekiel's Temple (Ezek. xl. 49), and by what we know of the Temple of Herod, some steps would lead up to the porch,

[1] Not as in our Authorised Version : "windows of narrow lights."

[2] A fuller description of the Temple, and a detailed discussion of the various points in controversy among writers on the subject, would lead beyond the limit which we must here assign ourselves.

[3] Some have imagined that the Most Holy Place was, like the chancel in most churches, lower than the Holy Place (ten feet). Lundius has drawn the porch to the height of a gigantic steeple. Many (mostly fanciful) sketch-plans of the Temple have been drawn ; but it would be out of place here to enter into further details.

which, as we imagine, presented the appearance of an open colonnade of cedar, set in a pavement of hewn stones, and supporting a cedar-roof covered with marble. The most prominent objects here were the two great pillars, Jachin and Boaz, which Hiram cast by order of Solomon (1 Kings vii. 15–22). These pillars stood, as we are expressly told, *within* "the porch" (1 Kings vii. 21), and must have served alike architectural, artistic, and symbolical purposes. Added after the completion of the "House," perhaps for the better support of the roof of the "porch," their singular beauty must have attracted the eye, while their symbolical meaning appeared in their names. Jachin ("He supports"), Boaz ("in Him is strength"), pointed beyond the outward support and strength which these pillars gave, to Him on Whom not only the Sanctuary but every one who would truly enter it must rest for support and strength. Some difficulty has been experienced in computing the height of these pillars, including their "chapiters," or "capitals" (1 Kings vii. 15–22). It seems most likely that they consisted of single shafts, each eighteen cubits high and twelve in circumference,[1] surmounted by a twofold "chapiter" — the lower of five cubits, with fretted network depending, and ornamented with two rows of one hundred pomegranates; the higher chapiter four cubits high (1 Kings vii. 19), and in the form of an opening lily. The symbolical significance of the pomegranate and of the lily—the one *the* flower, the other *the* fruit of the Land of Promise, and both emblematic of the pure beauty and rich sweetness of holiness —need scarcely be pointed out. If we compute the height of these pillars with their chapiters at twenty-seven cubits,[2] we have three cubits left for the entablature and the roofing of the porch $(18+5+4+3=30)$.

"The porch," which (in its tablature) was overlaid with gold (2 Chron. iii. 4), opened into the Holy Place by folding doors,

---

[1] Canon Rawlinson has shown that the columns of the Egyptian temples were thicker than those of Solomon's.

[2] Other calculations have also been proposed, as by Bähr and Merz.

each of two leaves, folding back upon each other. **These** doors, which were the width of a fourth of the wall (1 Kings vi. 33), or five cubits, were made of cypress-wood, and hung by golden hinges on door-posts of olive-wood. They were decorated with carved figures of cherubim between palm-trees,[1] and above them opening flower-buds and garlands, the whole being covered with thin plates of gold, which showed the design beneath. Within the Sanctuary all the sacred furniture was of gold, while that outside of it was of brass. In truth, the Sanctuary was a golden house. The floor, which was of cypress-wood, was overlaid with gold; the walls, which were panelled with cedar, on which the same designs were carved as on the doors, were covered with gold, and so was the ceiling. It need scarcely be said, how it must have glittered and shone in the light of the sacred candlesticks, especially as the walls were encrusted with gems (2 Chron. iii. 6). There were ten candlesticks in the Holy Place, each seven-branched, and of pure gold. They were ranged right and left before the Most Holy Place[2] (1 Kings vii. 49). The entrance to the Most Holy Place was covered by a veil "of blue and purple, and crimson, and byssus," with "wrought cherubs thereon" (2 Chron. iii. 14). Between the candlesticks stood the "altar of incense," made of cedar-wood and overlaid with gold (1 Kings vi. 20, 22; vii. 48); while ten golden tables of shewbread (2 Chron. iv. 8) were ranged right and left. The implements necessary for the use of this sacred furniture were also of pure gold (1 Kings vii. 49, 50).

Two folding-doors, similar in all respects to those already described, except that they were of oleaster wood, and not a fourth, but a fifth of the wall (=4 cubits), opened from the

---

[1] Probably they were in panels, each having two cherubs and a palm tree.

[2] Keil supposes that only two of these candlesticks stood before the Most Holy Place, while the other eight were ranged, four and four, along the side walls, five tables of shewbread being placed in the interstices *behind* them, along each of the side walls. In that case, however, it would not have been easy to go round the tables.

Holy Place into the Most Holy. These doors we suppose to have always stood open, the entrance being concealed by the great veil, which the High-priest lifted, when on the Day of Atonement he went into the innermost Sanctuary.[1] Considerable difficulty attaches to a notice in 1 Kings vi. 21, which has been variously translated and understood. Two interpretations here specially deserve attention. The first regards the "chains of gold before the Oracle," as chain-work that fastened together the cedar-planks forming the partition between the Holy and the Most Holy Place—somewhat like the bars that held together the boards in the Tabernacle. The other, which to us seems the more likely,[2] represents the partition boards between the Holy and the Most Holy Place, as not reaching quite to the ceiling, and this "chain-work" as running along the top of the boarding. For some opening of this kind seems almost necessary for ventilation, for letting out the smoke of the incense on the Day of Atonement, and to admit at least a gleam of light, without which the ministrations of the High-priest on that day, limited though they were, would have been almost impossible. The only object within the Most Holy Place was the Ark overshadowed by the Cherubim. It was the same which had stood in the Tabernacle. But Solomon placed on either side of it (south and north) a gigantic figure of a Cherub, carved out of oleaster wood, and overlaid with gold. Each was ten cubits high; and the two, with their outspread wings, which touched over the Mercy - Seat, ten cubits wide. Thus, the two cherubim with their outspread wings reached (south and north) from one wall of the Sanctuary to the other (1 Kings vi. 23–28). But, whereas the Mosaic Cherubim looked inwards and downwards towards the Mercy-

[1] This we conclude from the circumstance, that otherwise there would have been no use of a veil, and that we do not read of the High-priest opening the doors on the Day of Atonement.

[2] Most writers suppose that these chains were drawn inside to further bar access to the Most Holy Place. But no mention is made of their existence or removal on the Day of Atonement. The view we have expressed is that of the Rabbis.

G

Seat, those made by Solomon looked outwards towards the Holy Place, with probably a slight inclination downwards (2 Chron. iii. 13). Another notice has raised differences of opinion. From 1 Kings viii. 8, we learn that the "staves" by which the Ark was carried were "drawn forward" ("lengthened," not "drawn out," as in the Authorised Version), so that their heads were visible from the Holy Place. As these "staves" were never to be drawn out (Ex. xxv. 15), and as all view of the interior of the Most Holy Place was precluded, this could only have been effected (as the Rabbis suggest) by drawing the staves forward, so that their heads would slightly bulge out on the veil. Of course this would imply that the staves faced east and west—not, as is generally supposed, south and north. Nor is there any valid objection to this supposition.

Descending from "the Porch," we stand in the "inner" (1 Kings vi. 36) or "Court of the Priests" (2 Chron. iv. 9). This was paved with great stones, as was also the outer or "Great Court" (2 Chron. iv. 9) of the people. Within the "inner" or Priests' Court, facing the entrance to the Sanctuary, was "the altar of burnt-offering" (1 Kings viii. 64), made of brass, and probably filled within with earth and unhewn stones. It was ten cubits high, and twenty cubits in length and breadth at the base—probably narrowing as it ascended, like receding buttresses [1] (2 Chron. iv. 1). Between the altar and the porch stood the colossal "sea of brass," five cubits high, and thirty cubits in circumference (1 Kings vii. 23–26; 2 Chron. iv. 2–5). Its upper rim was bent outwards, "like the work of the brim of a cup, in the shape of a lily-flower." Under the brim it was ornamented by two rows of opening flower-buds, ten to a cubit. This immense basin rested on a pedestal of twelve oxen, three looking to each point of the compass. Its object was to hold

---

[1] This was certainly the structure of the altar in the Temple of Herod (comp. *Midd.* iii. 1). In general, I must here refer the reader to the description of that Temple in *The Temple, its Ministry and Services at the Time of Jesus Christ,* and to my translation of the Mishnic Tractate *Middoth,* in the Appendix to *Sketches of Jewish Social Life in the Days of Christ.* Our present limits prevent more than the briefest outline.

the water in which the priests and Levites performed their ablutions. For the washing of the inwards and of the pieces of the sacrifices, ten smaller "lavers" of brass were provided, which stood on the right and left "side of the House" (1 Kings vii. 38; 2 Chron. iv. 6). They were placed on square "bases," or, rather, waggons of brass, four cubits long and broad, and three cubits high, which rested on "four feet" (not "corners," as in the Authorised Version, 1 Kings vii. 30) upon wheels, so as to bring them readily to the altar. Bearing in mind the height of the altar, this accounts for their being four cubits high (+4 cubits for the laver itself). The sides of these waggons were richly ornamented with figures of lions, oxen, and cherubs, and beneath them were "garlands, pensile work."[1] Although it is not easy to make out all the other details, it seems that the tops of these "bases" or waggons had covers, which bulged inwards to receive the lavers, the latter being further steadied by supports ("undersetters" in the Authorised Version, or rather "shoulder-pieces"). The covers of the waggons were also richly ornamented. Lastly, in the Priests' Court, and probably within full view of the principal gate, stood the brazen scaffold or stand (2 Chron. vi. 13) from which King Solomon offered his dedicatory prayer, and which seems to have always been the place occupied in the Temple by the kings (2 Kings xi. 14; xxiii. 3). To this a special "ascent" led from the palace (1 Kings x. 5), which was, perhaps afterwards, roofed over for protection from the weather.[2] The Priests' Court was enclosed by a wall consisting of three tiers of hewn stones and a row of cedar beams (1 Kings vi. 36).

From the court of the priests steps led down to the "outer court" of the people (comp. Jer. xxxvi. 10), which[3] was surrounded by a solid wall, from which four massive gates, covered

---

[1] See *Speaker's Comment.* ii., p. 521—not; as in our Authorised Version, "certain additions made of thin work" (1 Kings vii. 29).

[2] This was "the covert for the Sabbath" (2 Kings xvi. 18). The Rabbis hold it to have been the exclusive privilege of the kings to sit down within the Priests' Court.   [3] This appears from 1 Chron. xxvi. 13-16.

with brass, opened upon the Temple-mount (2 Chron. iv. 9). In this court were large colonnades and chambers, and rooms for the use of the priests and Levites, for the storage of what was required in the services, and for other purposes. The principal gate was, no doubt, the eastern (Ezek. xi. 1), corresponding to the "Beautiful Gate" of New Testament times. To judge by the analogy of the other measurements, as compared with those of the Tabernacle, the Court of the Priests would be 100 cubits broad, and 200 cubits long, and the Outer Court double these proportions (comp. also Ezek. xl. 27).[1]

Such, in its structure and fittings, was the Temple which Solomon built to the Name of Jehovah God. Its further history to its destruction, 416 years after its building, is traced in the following passages of Holy Scripture : 1 Kings xiv. 26 ; xv. 18, etc. ; 2 Chron. xx. 5 ; 2 Kings xii. 5, etc. ; xiv. 14 ; xv. 35 ; 2 Chron. xxvii. 3 ; 2 Kings xvi. 8 ; xviii. 15, etc. ; xxi. 4, 5, 7 ; xxiii. 4, 7, 11 ; xxiv. 13 ; xxv. 9, 13–17).[2]

[1] It is with exceeding reluctance that I forbear entering on the symbolical import of the Temple, of its materials, structure, and arrangements. But such discussions would evidently be outside the plan and limits of this Bible History.

[2] Comparing the Temple of Solomon with that of Herod, the latter was, of course, much superior, not only as regards size, but architectural beauty. To understand the difference, plans of the two should be placed side by side. We add a few remarks which may interest the reader. From being so largely constructed of cedar-wood, the Temple is also figuratively called "Lebanon" (Zech. xi. 1). Among the Jewish legends connected with the Temple, one of the strangest is that about a certain worm Shamir, which, according to *Aboth* v. 6, was among the ten things created on the eve of the world's first Sabbath, just before sunset (see also *Sifré on Deut.* p. 147, *a*). In *Gitt.* 86, *a* and *b*, we are informed by what artifices Solomon obtained possession of this worm from Ashmedai, the prince of the demons. This worm possessed the power, by his touch, to cut the thickest stones, and was therefore used by Solomon for this purpose (comp. also generally *Gitt.* 68 *a*, and *Sotah* 48 *b*). According to *Joma* 53*b*, 54*b*, the Ark was placed upon what is called the "foundation stone of the world." So early as in the *Targum Pseudo-Jonathan* on Exod. xxviii. 30, we read that the ineffable Name of God was engraved upon this stone, and that God at the first sealed up with it the mouth of the great deep. This may serve as a specimen of these legends. Perhaps we should add that, according to later Rabbis, the roof of the Temple was not quite flat, but slightly sloping, yet probably not higher in any part than the parapet around

CHAPTER VII.

Dedication of the Temple—When it took place—Connection with the Feast of Tabernacles—The Consecration Services—The King's part in them —Symbolical meaning of the great Institutions in Israel—The Prayer of Consecration—Analogy to the Lord's Prayer—The Consecration Thanksgiving and Offerings.

(1 KINGS VIII. ; 2 CHRON. V.—VII. 11.)

A T length the great and beautiful house, which Solomon had raised to the Name of Jehovah, and to which so many ardent thoughts and hopes attached, was finished. Its solemn dedication took place in the year following its completion, and, very significantly, immediately before, and in connection with, the Feast of Tabernacles. Two questions, of some difficulty and importance, here arise. The first concerns the circumstance that the sacred text (1 Kings vii. 1-12) records the building of Solomon's palace immediately after that of the Temple, and, indeed, almost intermingles the two accounts. This may partly have been due to a very natural desire on the part of the writer not to break the continuity of the account of Solomon's great buildings, the more so as they were all completed by the aid of Tyrian workmen, and under the supervision of Hiram. But another and more important consideration may also have influenced the arrangement of the narrative. For, as has been suggested, these two great undertakings of Solomon bore a close relation to each other. It was not an ordinary Sanctuary, nor was it an ordinary royal residence which Solomon reared. The building of the Temple marked that the preparatory period of Israel's unsettledness had passed, when God had walked with them "in tent and tabernacle"— or, in other words, that the Theocracy had attained not only fixedness, but its highest point, when God would set "His Name for ever" in its chosen centre. But this new stage of the Theocracy was connected with the establishment of a firm and settled kingdom in Israel, when He would "establish the throne of that kingdom for ever" (compare 2 Sam. vii. 5–16). Thus the dwelling of God in His Temple and that of Solomon in his house were events between which there was deep internal connection, even as between the final establishment of the Theocracy and that of David's royal line in Israel. Moreover, the king was not to be a monarch in the usual Oriental, or even in the ancient Western sense. He was to be regarded, not as the *Vicegerent* or *Representative* of God, but as *His Servant*, to do His behest and to guard His covenant. And this might well be marked, even by the conjunction of these two buildings in the Scripture narrative.

These considerations will also help us to understand why the Feast of the Dedication of the Temple was connected with that of Tabernacles (of course, in the year following). It was not only that, after "the eighth month," when the Temple was completed, it would have been almost impossible, considering the season of the year, to have gathered the people from all parts of the country, or to have celebrated for eight days a great popular festival ; nor yet that of all feasts, that of Tabernacles, when agricultural labour was at an end, probably witnessed the largest concourse in Jerusalem.[1] But the Feast of Tabernacles had a threefold meaning. It pointed back to the time when, "strangers and pilgrims" on their way to the Land of Promise, Israel, under its Divine leadership, had dwelt in tents. The full import of this memorial would be best realised at the dedication of the Temple, when, instead of tent and tabernacle, the glorious house of God was standing in all its beauty, while the stately palace of Israel's king was rising. Again, the Feast of Tabernacles was essentially one of thanksgiving, when at the

---

[1] The Temple was completed in the eighth month ; its dedication took place in the seventh of the next year. Ewald suggests that it was dedicated before it was quite finished. But this idea can scarcely be maintained.

completion, not only of the harvest, but of the ingathering of the fruits, a grateful people presented its homage to the God to Whom they owed all, and to Whom all really belonged. But what could raise this hymn of praise to its loudest strains, if not that they uplifted it within those sacred walls, symbolical of God's gracious Presence as King in His palace in the midst of His people, whose kingdom He had established? Lastly, the Feast of Tabernacles—the only still unfulfilled Old Testament type—pointed forward to the time of which the present state of Israel was an initial realisation, when the Name of the LORD should be known far and wide to earth's utmost bounds, and all nations seek after Him and offer worship in His Temple. Thus, however viewed, there was the deepest significance in the conjunction of the dedication of the Temple with the Feast of Tabernacles.

But, as previously stated, there is yet another question of somewhat greater difficulty which claims our attention. To judge by the arrangement of the narrative, the dedication of the Temple (1 Kings viii.) might seem to have taken place *after* the completion of Solomon's palace, the building of which, as we know, occupied further thirteen years (1 Kings vii. 1). Moreover, from the circumstance that the second vision of God was vouchsafed "when Solomon had finished the building of the house of the LORD, and the king's house, and all Solomon's desire which he was pleased to do" (1 Kings ix. 1), it has been argued, that the dedication of the Temple must have taken place immediately before this vision, especially as what was said to him seems to contain pointed reference to the consecration prayer of Solomon (1 Kings ix. 3, 7, 8). But, even if that vision took place at the time just indicated,[1] the supposed inference from it cannot be maintained.

---

[1] At the same time, I confess that I am by no means convinced that such was the case. The language of 1 Kings ix. 1 should not be too closely pressed, and may be intended as a sort of general transition from the subject previously treated to that in hand. The brief notices in 2 Chron. vii. seem rather to favour this idea.

For, although part of the sacred vessels may have been made during the time that Hiram was engaged upon Solomon's palace, it is not credible that the Temple should, after its completion, have stood deserted and unused for thirteen years. Nor are the arguments in favour of this most improbable assumption valid. The appeal to 1 Kings ix. 1 would oblige us to date the dedication of the Temple even later than the completion of Solomon's palace, viz., after he had finished all his other building operations. As for the words which the LORD spake to Solomon in vision (2 Kings ix. 3–9), although bearing reference to the Temple and the king's dedication prayer, they are evidently intended rather as a general warning, than as an answer to his petition, and are such as would befit the period of temptation, *before* Solomon, carried away by the splendour of his success, yielded himself to the luxury, weakness, and sin of his older age. From all these considerations we conclude that the Feast of the Dedication, which lasted seven days, took place in the seventh month, that of Ethanim, or of "flowing brooks"[1] (the later Tishri), of the year after the completion of the Temple (eleven months after it), and immediately before the Feast of Tabernacles, which, with the concluding solemnity, lasted eight days.

The account of the dedication of the Temple may be conveniently ranged under these three particulars: the *Consecration-Services*, the *Consecration-Prayer*, and the *Consecration-Thanksgiving* and *Festive Offerings*. But before describing them, it is necessary to call attention to the remarkable circumstance that the chief, if not almost the sole prominent agent in these services, was the *king*, the high-priest not being even mentioned. Not that Solomon in any way interfered with, or arrogated to himself the functions of the priesthood, but that, in the part which he took, he fully acted up to the spirit of the monarchical institution as founded in Israel. Solomon was not "king" according to the Saxon idea of *cyning*—cunning,

[1] This rendering of the term "Ethanim," seems preferable to that of "gifts," viz., fruits (Thenius), or of "stand still," viz., equinox (Böttche).

mighty, illustrious, the embodiment of strength. According to the terms of the Covenant, all Israel were God's *servants* (Lev. xxv. 42, 55; comp. Isa. xli. 8, 9; xliv. 1, 2, 21; xlv. 4; xlix. 3, 6; Jer. xxx. 10, and others). As such they were to be "a kingdom of priests" (Exod. xix. 6)—"the priest," in the stricter sense of the term, being only the representative of the people, with certain distinctive functions *ad hoc.* But what the nation was, as a whole, that Israel's theocratic king was *pre-eminently :* the servant of the LORD (1 Kings viii. 25, 28, 29, 52, 59). It was in this capacity that Solomon acted at the dedication of the Temple, as his own words frequently indicate (see the passages just quoted). In this manner the innermost and deepest idea of the character of Israel and of Israel's king as "the servant" of the LORD, became, so to speak, more and more individualized during the progress of the Old Testament dispensation, till it stood out in all its fulness in the Messiah—the climax of Israel and of Israelitish institutions—Who is *the* Servant of Jehovah. Thus we perceive that the common underlying idea of the three great institutions in Israel, which connected them all, was that of the *Servant* of Jehovah. The prophet who uttered the voice of heaven upon earth was the servant of Jehovah (comp., for example, Numb. xii. 7, 8; Josh. i. 2; Isa. xx. 3, etc.).[1] So was the priest, who spake the voice of earth to heaven; and the king, who made heaven's voice to be heard on earth. That which gave its real meaning equally to this threefold function—downwards, upwards, outwards—was the grand fact that in each of them it was the Servant of Jehovah who was acting, or, in other words, that *God was all in all.* With these general principles in view we shall be better able to understand what follows.

1. *The Consecration-Services* (1 Kings viii. 1–21).—These commenced with the transference of the Ark and of the other

[1] It is impossible here to do more than indicate this train of thought. The reader will be able to make out a perfect *catena* of confirmatory passages, extending over almost all the books of Holy Scripture, or from age to age.

holy vessels from Mount Zion, and of the ancient Mosaic Tabernacle from Gibeon. The latter and the various other relics of those earlier services were, as we have suggested, placed in the chambers built around the new Sanctuary. In accordance with the Divine direction, the whole of this part of the service was performed by the Priests and Levites, attended by the king, "the elders of Israel, the heads of the tribes, and the princes (of the houses) of the fathers of Israel," who, as representatives of the people, had been specially summoned for the purpose. As this solemn procession entered the sacred courts, amidst a vast concourse of people, numberless offerings were brought. Then the Ark was carried to its place in the innermost Sanctuary.[1] As the priests reverently retired from it, and were about to minister in the Holy Place [2]—perhaps to burn incense on the Golden Altar—"the cloud," as the visible symbol of God's Presence, came down, as formerly at the consecration of the Tabernacle (Ex. xl. 34, 35), and so filled the whole of the Temple itself, that the priests, unable to bear "the glory," had to retire from their ministry. But even here also we mark the characteristic difference between the Old and the New Dispensations, to which St. Paul calls attention in another connection (2 Cor. iii. 13–18). For whereas, under the preparatory dispensation God dwelt in a "cloud" and in "thick darkness," we all now behold "the glory of God" in the Face of His Anointed.[3]

[1] The expression, 1 Kings viii. 9, seems to be incompatible with the notice in Hebrews ix. 4. But not only according to the Talmud (*Joma* 52. *b*), but according to uniform Jewish tradition (see *apud* Delitzsch *Comm. z. Br. an die Hebr.* p. 361), what is mentioned in Heb. ix. 4 had been really placed in the Ark, although the emphatic notice in 1 Kings viii. 9 indicates that it was no longer there in the time of Solomon. It may have been removed previous to, or after the capture of the Ark by the Philistines.

[2] The Book of Chronicles (2 Chron. v. 12-14) characteristically notes that the Priests and Levites were raising holy chant and music.

[3] Bähr here quotes this ancient comment : *Nebulâ Deus se et representabat et velabat*, and Buxtorf (*Hist. Arcæ Foed.* ed. Bas. 1659, p. 115) adduces a very apt passage from Abarbanel.

This was the real consecration of the Temple. And now the king, turning towards the Most Holy Place, filled with the Sacred Presence, spake these words of dedication, brief as became the solemnity : " Jehovah hath said : to dwell in darkness—Building, I have built an house of habitation to Thee, and a settling-place for Thy dwelling ever !" In this reference to what Jehovah had said, it would not be any single utterance which presented itself to Solomon's mind. Rather would he think of them in their connection and totality—as it were, a golden chain of precious promises welded one to the other, of which the last link seemed riveted to the solemnity then enacting. Such sayings as Ex. xix. 9 ; xx. 21 ; Lev. xvi. 2 ; Deut. iv. 11 ; v. 22 would crowd upon his memory, and seem fully realised as he beheld the Cloudy Presence in the Holy House. Thus it is often not one particular promise or prophecy which is referred to when we read in Holy Scripture these words : " That it might be fulfilled," but rather a whole series which culminate in some one great fact (as, for example, in Matt. ii. 15, 23). Nor should we forget that, when the king spoke of the Temple as God's dwelling for *ever*, the symbolical character alike of the manifestation of His Presence and of its place could not have been absent from his mind. But the *symbolical* necessarily implies the *temporary*, being of the nature of an accommodation to circumstances, persons, and times. What was *for ever* was not the form, but the substance—not the manner nor the place, but the fact of God's Presence in the midst of His people. And what is real and eternal is the Kingdom of God in its widest sense, and God's Presence in grace among His worshipping people, as fully realised in Jesus Christ.

When the king had spoken these words, he turned from the Sanctuary to the people who reverently stood to hear his benedictory "address." [1] Briefly recounting the gracious promises and experiences of the past, he pointed to the present as their

---

[1] It is thus, and not as implying any actual benediction, either uttered or silent, that I understand the words 1 Kings viii. 14.

fulfilment, specially applying to it, in the manner already described, what God had said to David (2 Sam. vii. 7, 8).[1]

2. *The Prayer of Consecration.*—This brief address concluded, the king ascended the brazen pulpit-like platform "before the altar" (of burnt offering), and with his face, probably sideways towards the people, knelt down with hands outspread in prayer (comp. 2 Chron. vi. 12, 13).

It seems like presumption and impertinence to refer in laudatory terms to what for comprehensiveness, sublimeness, humility, faith, and earnestness has no parallel in the Old Testament, and can only be compared with the prayer which our Lord taught His disciples.[2] Like the latter, it consists of an introduction (1 Kings viii. 23–30), of seven petitions (the covenant-number, vers. 31–53), and of a eulogetic close (2 Chron. vi. 40–42). The Introduction sounds like an Old Testament version of the words "Our Father" (vers. 23–26), "which art in heaven" (vers. 27–30). It would be out of place here to enter into any detailed analysis. Suffice it to indicate the leading Scriptural references in it—as it were, the spiritual stepping-stones of the prayer—and one or another of its outstanding points. Marking how a review of the gracious dealings in the past should lead to *confidence* in present petitions (comp. Matt. xxi. 22; Mark xi. 24; James i. 6), reference should

---

[1] Compare the fuller account in 2 Chron. vi. 5, 6.

[2] It is one of its many extraordinary instances of "begging the question," that modern criticism boldly declares this whole prayer spurious, or rather relegates its composition to a much later date, even so far as the Babylonish exile! The only *objective* ground by which this *dictum* is supported, is the circumstance that the prayer is full of references to the Book of Deuteronomy—which modern criticism has *ruled* to be non-Mosaic, and of much later date—*ergo*, this prayer must share its fate! This kind of reasoning is, in fact, to derive from one unproved hypothesis another even more unlikely! For we have here, first, the accordant accounts (with but slight variations) in 1 Kings and 2 Chron.; while, secondly (as Bleek has remarked), the wording of the prayer implies a time and conditions when the Temple, Jerusalem, and the Davidic throne were still extant. To this we may add, that the whole tone and conception is not at all in accordance with, or what we would have expected at, the time of the exile.

be made in connection with verses 23–26 to the following passages : Ex. xv. 11 ; Deut. iv. 39 ; vii. 9 ; Josh. ii. 11 ; 2 Sam. vii. 12–22 ; xxii. 32 ; Ps. lxxxvi. 8.   In regard to the second part of the Introduction (vers. 27–30), we specially note the emphatic assertion, that He, Whose Presence they saw in the cloud, was really *in* "*heaven*," and yet "*our* Father," who art upon earth.   These two ideas seem carried out in it : (1) Not as heathenism does, do we locate God here ; nor yet will we, as carnal Israel did (Jer. vii. 4 ; Mic. iii. 11), imagine that *ex opere operato* (by any mere deed of ours) God will necessarily attend even to His own appointed services in His house.   Our faith rises higher—from the Seen to the Unseen—from the God of Israel to our Father ; it realises the spiritual relationship of *children*, which alone contains the pledge of His blessing ; and through which, though He be in heaven, yet faith knows and addresses Him as an ever-present help.   Thus Solomon's prayer avoided alike the two extremes of unspiritual realism and of unreal spiritualism.

The *first petition* (vers. 31, 32) in the stricter sense opens the prayer, which in ver. 28 had been outlined, according to its prevailing characteristics, as "petition," "prayer for mercy" (forgiveness and grace), and "thanksgiving" (praise).[1]   It is essentially an Old Testament "Hallowed be Thy Name," in its application to the sanctity of an oath as its highest expression, inasmuch as thereby the reality of God's holiness is challenged. The analogy between the *second petition* (vers. 33, 34) and that in the Lord's Prayer is not so evident at first sight.   But it is none the less real, since its ideal fulfilment would mark the coming of the kingdom of God, which neither sin from within nor enemy from without could endanger.   The references in this petition seem to be to Lev. xxvi. 3, 7, 14, 17 ; Deut. xxviii. 1–7, 15–25 ; and again to Lev. xxvi. 33, and 40–42, and Deut. iv. 26–28 ; xxviii. 64–68, and iv. 29–31 ; xxx. 1–5.   The organic

---

[1] In the Authorised Version, inaccurately, "prayer," "supplication," "cry ;" in the Hebrew, *Tephillah* (from the *Hithpael* of *Palal*), *Techinnah* (from the *Hithp.* of *Chanan*), and *Rinnah* (from *Ranan*).

connection, so to speak, between heaven and earth, which lies at the basis of the *third petition* in the Lord's Prayer, is also expressed in that of Solomon (vers. 35, 36). Only in the one case we have the New Testament realisation of that grand idea, or rather ideal, while in the other we have its Old Testament aspect. The references here are to Lev. xxvi. 19; Deut. xi. 17; xxviii. 23, 24. At the same time the rendering of our Authorised Version (1 Kings viii. 35): "When Thou afflictest them," should be altered to, "Because Thou humblest them," which indicates the moral effect of God's discipline, and the last link in the chain of true repentance.

The correspondence between the *fourth petition* in the Solomonic (vers. 37–40) and in our Lord's Prayer will be evident —always keeping in view the difference between the Old and the New Testament standpoint. But perhaps verses 38–40 may mark the transition from, and connection between the first and second parts of the prayer. The *fifth petition* (vers. 41–43), which concerns the acceptance of the prayers of strangers (not proselytes), is based on the idea of the great mutual forgiveness by those who are forgiven of God, fully realised in the abolition of the great *enmity* and separation, which was to give place to a common brotherhood of love and service —"that all the people of the earth may know Thy Name, to fear Thee, as Thy people Israel." Here also we note the difference between the Old and the New Testament form of the petition—a remark which must equally be kept in view in regard to the other two petitions. These, indeed, seem to bear only a very distant analogy to the concluding portion of the Lord's Prayer. Yet that there was real "temptation" to Israel, and real "deliverance from evil" sought in these petitions, appears from the language of confession put into the mouth of the captives (ver. 47), which, as we know, was literally adopted by those in Babylon[1] (Dan. ix. 5; Ps. cvi. 6). Here sin is

[1] It would seem almost too great a demand upon our credence, even by "advanced criticism," that, because these expressions were taken up by the exiles in Babylon, they originated at that time.

presented in its threefold aspect as *failure,* so far as regards the
goal, or *stumbling* and *falling* (in the Authorised Version "we
have sinned"); then as *perversion* (literally, making crooked);
and, lastly, as *tumultuous rebellion* (in the Authorised Version
"committed wickedness"). Lastly, the three concluding
verses (vers. 51–53) may be regarded either as the argument
for the last petitions, or else as an Old Testament version of
"Thine is the kingdom, and the power, and the glory." But
the whole prayer is the opening of the door into heaven—a door
moving, if the expression be lawful, on the two hinges of *sin*
and of *grace,* of *need* and of *provision.*

3. *The Consecration-Thanksgiving and Offerings.*—To the
prayer of Solomon, the descent of fire upon the great altar—
probably from out the Cloudy Presence [1]—which is recorded in
2 Chron. vii. 1, seems a most appropriate answer [2] (comp.
Lev. ix. 24). Little requires to be added to the simple account
of what followed. Rising from his knees, the king turned
once more to the people, and expressed the feelings of all
in terms of mingled praise and prayer, basing them on such
Scriptural passages as Deut. xii. 9, 10; Josh. xxi. 44, etc.;
xxiii. 14, and, in the second part of his address, on Lev. xxvi.
3–13; Deut. xxviii. 1–14. But it deserves special notice, that
throughout (as Thenius has well remarked) the tone is of the
loftiest spirituality. For, if the king asks for continued help and
blessing from the Lord, it is for the express purpose "that He
may incline our hearts to Him" (comp. Ps. cxix. 36; cxli. 4),
"to keep His commandments" (1 Kings viii. 58); and, if he looks
for answers to prayer (ver. 59), it is "that all the people of the
earth may know that Jehovah is God, and that there is none
else" (ver. 60).

[1] 2 Chron. vii. 1 does *not* necessarily imply that there was a second
manifestation of "the glory of Jehovah."

[2] It is certainly a fact, that this circumstance is not mentioned in the
narrative in the Book of Kings. But from this it is a very long and ven-
turesome step to the conclusion, that this is an addition or interpolation on
the part of the writer or editor of the Books of Chronicles, the more so as
"Kings" and "Chronicles" alternately record or omit other important
events.

Lastly, we have an account of the vast number [1] of festive offerings which Solomon and all Israel [2] brought, and of the Feast of Tabernacles [3] with which the solemn dedication-services concluded.

CHAPTER VIII.

The Surroundings of the Temple—Description of Jerusalem at the time of Solomon—The Palace of Solomon—Solomon's fortified Cities— External relations of the Kingdom—Internal State—Trade—Wealth —Luxury—The visit of the Queen of Sheba.

(1 KINGS IX., X.; 2 CHRON. VII. 11–IX. 28.)

WE have now reached the period of Solomon's greatest worldly splendour, which, as alas! so often, marks also that of spiritual decay. The building of the Temple was not the first, nor yet the last, of his architectural undertakings. Mount Moriah was too small to hold on its summit the Temple itself, even without its courts and other buildings. Accordingly,

[1] Canon Rawlinson (*Speaker's Commentary*, II. p. 533) has shown, by numerous quotations, that these sacrifices were not out of proportion to others recorded in antiquity. As to the time necessarily occupied in these sacrifices, we have the historical notice of Josephus (*Jewish War*, vi. 9, 3), that on one occasion not fewer than 256,000 Passover-lambs were offered, the time occupied being just *three hours* of an afternoon. It is also to be borne in mind that the killing and preparing of the sacrifices was *not* necessarily the duty of priests or even Levites, the strictly priestly function being *only that of sprinkling the blood*. Lastly, we are distinctly informed (1 Kings viii. 64) that supplementary altars—besides the great altar of burnt offering—were used on this occasion.

[2] We are expressly told in ver. 62, that these offerings were brought not only by the king but by all Israel.

[3] The Feast of Tabernacles lasted seven days and closed on the afternoon of the eighth with the *clausura* or solemn dismissal (comp. Lev. xxiii. 33–39).

as we learn from Josephus (*Ant.* xv. 11, 3), extensive substructures had to be reared. Thus, the level of the Temple-mount was enlarged both east and west, in order to obtain a sufficient area for the extensive buildings upon it. These rose terrace upon terrace—each court higher than the other, and the Sanctuary itself higher than its courts. We are probably correct in the supposition that the modern Mosque of Omar occupies the very site of the ancient Temple of Solomon, and that over the celebrated rock in it—according to Jewish tradition, the very spot where Abraham offered up Isaac—the great altar of burnt-offering had risen. Before the building of the Sanctuary itself could have been commenced, the massive substructures of the Temple must have been at least partially completed, although these and the outbuildings were probably continued during many years, perhaps many reigns, after the completion of the Temple.

The same remarks apply to another structure connected with the Temple, called " Parbar " (1 Chron. xxvi. 18). As already explained, the outer court of the Temple had *four* massive gates (1 Chron. xxvi. 13–16), of which the westernmost opened upon " Parbar " or " Parvarim " (perhaps " colonnade "). This seems to have been an annex to the western side of the Temple, fitted up as chambers, stables for sacrificial animals, etc. (2 Kings xxiii. 11, where our Authorised Version wrongly renders " Parvarim " by " suburbs "). From Parbar steps led down to the Tyropœon, or deep valley which intersected the city east and west.

Although anything like an attempt at detailed description would here be out of place, it seems desirable, in order to realise the whole circumstances, to give at least a brief sketch of Jerusalem, as Solomon found, and as he left it. Speaking generally, Jerusalem was built on the two opposite hills (east and west), between which the Tyropœon runs south-east and then south. The eastern hill is about 100 feet lower than the western. Its northern summit is Mount Moriah, which slopes down into Ophel (about 50 feet lower), afterwards the suburb of the priests. Some modern writers have regarded this as the ancient fort of the Jebusites, and as the site of the "City of David," the original Mount Zion. Although this is opposed to the common traditional view, which regards the *western* hill as Mount Zion, the arguments in favour of identifying it with the eastern hill seem very strong. These it would, of course, be impossible here to detail. But we may say that the history of David's purchase of the threshing-floor of Ornan the Jebusite (2 Sam. xxiv. 16–24; 1 Chron. xxi. 15–25) conveys these two facts: that the Jebusites *had* settlements on the western hill, and that David's palace (which, as we know, was in the City of David) was close by, only a little lower than Mount Moriah, since David so clearly saw from his palace the destroying Angel over the threshing-floor of Ornan. All this agrees with the idea, that the original stronghold of the Jebusites was on the slopes of Moriah and Ophel, and that David built his palace in that neighbourhood, below the summit of Moriah.[1] Lastly, if the term "Mount Zion" included Moriah, we can understand the peculiar sacredness which throughout Holy Scripture attaches to that name. Be this as it may, the regular quarter of the Jebusites was on the western hill, towards the slope of the Tyropœon, while the Jewish Benjamite quarter (the Upper City) was on the higher terrace above it (eastwards). Fort Millo was on the north-eastern angle of the Western City. Here King David had continued the wall, which had formerly enclosed the western hill northward and westward, drawing it eastward, so as to make (the western) Jeru-

---

[1] The above would give a new view of the taking of the fortress of Jebus by Joab. There undoubtedly existed a subterranean watercourse dug through the solid rock on which Jebus stood on Ophel, leading down to the "En-Rogel," or "Fountain of the Virgin." It is suggested, that with the connivance of Aravnah, Joab undertook the daring feat of climbing up into Jebus by this "gutter," and opening the gates to his comrades. This would also account for the presence of the Jebusite Aravnah on the neighbouring Moriah during the later years of David's reign, and explain the somewhat difficult passage, 2 Sam. **v. 8.** Comp. Warren's *Recovery of Jerusalem*, pp. 244-255.

salem a complete fortress (2 Sam. v. 9; 1 Chron. xi. 8). On the opposite (eastern) side of the Tyropœon was the equally fortified (later) Ophel. Solomon now connected these two fortresses by enlarging Millo and continuing the wall across the Tyropœon (1 Kings iii. 1; ix. 15; xi. 27).

Without referring to the various buildings which Solomon reared, it may be safely asserted that the city must have rapidly increased in population. Indeed, during the prosperous reign of Solomon it probably attained as large, if not larger, proportions than at any time before the Exile. The wealthier part of the population occupied the western terraces of the west hill—the Upper City—the streets running north and south. The eastern slopes of the west hill were covered by "the middle city" (2 Kings xx. 4, marginal rendering). It will have been noticed, that as yet only the *southern* parts of both the eastern and western hills of Jerusalem had been built over. King Solomon now reared the Temple on Mount Moriah, which formed the northern slope of the eastern hill, while the increase of the population soon led to building operations on the side of the western hill opposite to it. Here the city extended beyond the old wall, north of " the middle city," occupying the northern part of the Tyropœon. This was "the other" or "second part of the city" (2 Kings xxii. 14; 2 Chron. xxxiv. 22; Neh. xi. 9, the "maktesh" or "mortar" of Zeph. i. 11). Here was the real business quarter, with its markets, "fishgate," "sheepgate," and bazaars, such as the "Baker Street" (Jer. xxxvii. 21), the quarters of the goldsmiths and other merchants (Neh. iii. 8, 32), the "valley of the cheesemongers," etc. This suburb must have been soon inclosed by a wall. We do not know when or by whom the latter was commenced, but we have notices of its partial destruction (2 Kings xiv. 13; 2 Chron. xxv. 23), and of its repair (2 Chron. xxxii. 5).

We have purposely not taken account of the towers and gates of the city, since what has been described will sufficiently explain the location of the great palace which Solomon built during the thirteen years after the completion of the Temple

(1 Kings vii. 1–12; 2 Chron. viii. 1). Its site was the eastern terrace of the western hill, probably the same as that afterwards occupied by the palace of the Asmonæans (Maccabees) and of Agrippa II. The area covered by this magnificent building was four times that of the Holy House (not including its courts). It stood right over against the Temple. A descent led from the Palace into the Tyropœon, and thence a special magnificent "ascent" (2 Chron. ix. 4) to the royal entrance (2 Kings xvi. 18), probably at the south-western angle of the Temple. The site was happily chosen—protected by Fort Millo, and looking out upon the Temple-Mount, while south of it stretched the wealthy quarter of the city. Ascending from the Tyropœon, one would pass through a kind of ante-building into a porch, and thence into a splendid colonnade. This colonnade connected "the house of the forest of Lebanon," so called from the costly cedars used in its construction, with "the porch for the throne," where Solomon pronounced judgment (1 Kings vii. 6, 7). Finally, there was in the inner court, still further west, "the house where Solomon dwelt," and "the house for Pharaoh's daughter," with, of course, the necessary side and outbuildings (1 Kings vii. 8). Thus, the royal palace really consisted of three separate buildings. Externally it was simply of "costly stones" (ver. 9), the beauty of its design only appearing in its interior. Here the building extended along three sides. The ground-floor consisted of colonnades of costly cedar, the beams being fastened into the outer walls. These colonnades would be hung with tapestry, so as to be capable of being formed into apartments. Above these rose, on each side of the court, three tiers or chambers, fifteen on each tier, with large windows looking out upon each other. Here were the State apartments for court feasts, and in them were kept, among other precious things, the golden targets and shields (1 Kings x. 16, 17). Passing through another colonnade, one would next reach the grand Judgment- and Audience-halls, with the magnificent throne of ivory, described in 1 Kings x. 18–20; 2 Chron. ix. 17–19. And,

lastly, the innermost court contained the royal dwellings themselves.[1]

But this great Palace, the Temple, and the enlargement of Millo and of the city wall, were not the only architectural undertakings of King Solomon. Remembering that there were watchful foes on all sides, he either built or repaired a number of strong places. In the north, as defence against Syria, rose the ancient stronghold of Hazor (Josh. xi. 13; Judges iv. 2). The plain of Jezreel, the traditional battlefield of, as well as the highway into Palestine from the west and the north, was protected by Megiddo; while the southern approach from Egypt and the Philistine plain was guarded by Gezer, which Pharaoh had before this taken from the Canaanites and burnt, but afterwards given to his daughter as dowry on her marriage with Solomon. Not far from Gezer, and serving a similar defensive purpose, rose the fortress of Baalath, in the possession of Dan (comp. Josephus, *Ant.* viii., 6, 1). The eastern and north-eastern parts of Solomon's dominions were protected by Tamar or Tadmor, probably the Palmyra of the ancients,[2] and by Hamath-Zobah (2 Chron. viii. 4), while access to Jerusalem and irruptions from the north-western plain were barred by the fortification of Upper and Nether Bethhoron (1 Kings ix. 15–19; 2 Chron. viii. 3–6). Besides these fortresses, the king provided magazine-cities, and others where his chariots and cavalry were stationed—most of them, probably, towards the north. In all such undertakings Solomon employed the forced labour of the descendants of the ancient Canaanite inhabitants of Palestine, his Jewish subjects being chiefly engaged as overseers and officers in various departments (1 Kings ix. 20–23). But even thus, the diversion of so much labour and the taxation which his undertakings must have involved were felt as a

---

[1] In the description of Jerusalem and of Solomon's palace, I have largely availed myself of the Article in Riehm's *Hand-Wörterb. d. Bibl. Alterth.* Part viii. pp. 679–683, with which compare Unruh, *Das alte Jerusalem.*

[2] Comp. the admirable article of Mr. Twistleton, in Smith's *Bibl. Dict.* iii., pp. 1428–1430.

"grievous service" and "heavy yoke" (1 Kings xii. 4), all the more that Solomon's love of building and of Oriental splendour seems to have rapidly grown upon him. Thus, once more by a natural process of causation, the inner decay marked by luxury led to the weakening of the kingdom of Solomon, and scattered the seeds of that disaffection which, in the days of his degenerate son, ripened into open rebellion. So true is it, that in the history of Israel the inner and the outer always keep pace. But as yet Solomon's devotion to the services of Jehovah had not lessened. For we read that on the great festivals of the year (2 Chron. viii. 12, 13) he was wont to bring numerous special offerings.[1]

As regards the *foreign* relations of Solomon, reference has already been made (in ch. v.) to his marriage with the daughter of Pharaoh (1 Kings iii. 1), which took place in the first years of his reign. In all likelihood this Pharaoh was one of the last rulers of the (21st) Tanite dynasty. We know that their power had of late greatly declined, and Pharaoh may have been glad to ally himself with the now powerful ruler of the neighbouring country. On the new kingdom, however, such an alliance would shed great lustre, especially in the eyes of the Jews themselves. The frequent references to Pharaoh's daughter show what importance the nation attached to this union. It may be well here again to note, that the Egyptian princess, who brought to her husband the dowry of an important border-fortress (Gezer), was not in any way responsible for Solomon's later idolatry, no Egyptian deities being named among those towards whom he turned (1 Kings xi. 5–7).

Solomon's relations to Hiram, king of Tyre, at one time

---

[1] The expression "he burnt incense" (1 Kings ix. 25) has been regarded by Keil as a mistranslation—the text only implying the burning of the sacrifices. Bähr, more satisfactorily, refers it to the burning of incense on the great altar which accompanied all meat-offerings (Lev. ii. 1, 2). But on no consideration can it be supposed to imply, that Solomon arrogated to himself the priestly function of burning incense on the golden altar in the Holy Place (Thenius). How such an idea can be harmonised with the theory of the later origin of these books may be left to its advocates to explain.

threatened to become less friendly than they had been at first, and afterwards again became. It appears that, besides furnishing him with wood, Hiram had also advanced gold to Solomon (1 Kings ix. 11), amounting, if we may connect with this the notice in ver. 14, to 120 talents of gold, variously computed at £1,250,000 (Poole), £720,000 (S. Clarke), and £471,240 (Keil, whose estimate seems the most probable). We suppose it was in repayment of this sum that Solomon ceded to Hiram twenty cities in Northern Galilee, adjoining the possessions of Tyre. With these he might the more readily part, since the district was partially "Gentile" (Is. ix. 1). But Hiram, who probably coveted a strip of land along the coast, was dissatisfied with his new acquisition, and gave it the contemptuous designation of "the land of Cabul."[1] The district seems, however, to have been afterwards restored to Solomon[2] (2 Chron. viii. 2), no doubt on repayment of the loan and other compensation.

The later relations between Hiram and Solomon consisted chiefly in mercantile alliances. Although most writers regard the fleet which sailed to Ophir (1 Kings ix. 27, 28) as identical with "the navy of Tarshish" (1 Kings x. 22), yet the names, the imports, as well as the regularity in the passages of the latter ("every three years"), and the express statement that its destiny was Tarshish (2 Chron. ix. 21) seem opposed to this view. Opinions are also divergent as to the exact location of Ophir, and the share which Hiram had in the outfit of this expedition, whether he only furnished sailors (1 Kings ix. 27), or also the ships (2 Chron. viii. 18). In all probability the wood for these ships was cut in Lebanon by order of Hiram, and floated to Joppa, whence it would be transported by land (comp. 2 Chron. ii. 16) to Ezion-Geber and Elath, at the head of the Gulf of Akabah (the Red Sea), where the vessels would

[1] The derivation and meaning of the name are in dispute. Probably it is equivalent to "as nothing."

[2] This view is, however, opposed by some critics, though, as I think, on insufficient grounds.

be built under the direction of Phœnician shipwrights. **Upon**
the whole, it seems most likely that the Ophir whence they
fetched gold was Arabia. The sacred text does not inform us
whether these expeditions were periodical, the absence of such
notice rather leading to the supposition that this was not the
case, or at least that they were not continued. The total
result of these expeditions was an importation of gold to the
amount of 420 talents[1] (according to Keil about 1½ million
sterling). It was not only the prospect of such addition to the
wealth of the country, but that this was the first Jewish maritime expedition—in fact, the first great national trading undertaking, which gave it such importance in public estimation that
Solomon went in person to visit the two harbours where the
fleet was fitting out (2 Chron. viii. 17). According to 1 Kings
x. 11, the Phœnician fleet also brought from "Ophir" "precious
stones" and "almug-trees," or sandal-wood, which King Solomon used for "balustrades" in the Temple, for his own palace,
and for making musical instruments.

The success of this trading adventure may have led to another
similar undertaking, in company with the Phœnicians, to
Tartessus (Tarshish),[2] the well-known great mercantile emporium on the south coast of Spain. The duration of such an
expedition is stated in round numbers as *three years;* and the
trade became so regular that afterwards all the large merchantmen were popularly known as "Tarshish-ships" (comp. 1 Kings
xxii. 48; Ps. xlviii. 7; Is. ii. 16).[3] The imports from Tarshish
consisted of gold, silver, ivory,[4] apes, and peacocks (1 Kings x. 22).

---

[1] According to 2 Chron. viii. 18, by a clerical error (ב for כ), 450 talents.

[2] Critics are generally agreed that Tarshish is the Tartessus of Spain.
This was the great place for the export of silver, and a central depot whence
the imports from Africa, such as sandal-wood, ivory, ebony, apes, and
peacocks, would be shipped to all parts of the world. Compare here the
very conclusive reasoning of Canon Rawlinson, *u. s.* pp. 545, 546.

[3] From this passage Bähr and others have concluded that the Tarshish
fleet of King Solomon went to Ophir; but the inference is incorrect.

[4] The Hebrew terms are not easy to render. Most critics have, by a
slight alteration, translated them "ivory, ebony." But Keil and Bähr have
shown that this rendering is not sufficiently supported.

The two last-mentioned articles of import indicate the commencement of a very dangerous decline towards Oriental luxury. It has been well observed (by Ewald), that there was a moment in Israel's history when it seemed possible that David might have laid the foundation of an empire like that of Rome, and another when Solomon might have led the way to a philosophy as sovereign as that of Greece.[1] But it was an equally, if not more dangerous path on which to enter, and one even more opposed to the Divine purpose concerning Israel, when foreign trade, and with it foreign luxury, became the object of king and people. The danger was only too real, and the public display appeared in what the Queen of Sheba saw of Solomon's court (1 Kings x. 5), in the magnificence of his throne (vers. 19, 20), and in the sumptuousness of all his appointments (ver. 21). Two hundred large targets and three hundred smaller shields, all covered with beaten gold,[2] hung around the house of the forest of Lebanon; all the king's drinking vessels, and all the other appurtenances for State receptions were of pure gold; the merchants brought the spices of the East into the country (ver. 15); while traders, importers, and vassal chiefs swelled the immense revenue, which in one year[3] rose to the almost incredible sum of 666 talents of gold, which at the lowest computation amounts to upwards of $2\frac{1}{2}$ millions of our money, or only one million less than that of the Persian kings (Herod. iii. 95). Add to this the number of Solomon's chariots and horsemen, the general wealth of the country, and the importation of horses[4] from Egypt, which

[1] See Sir Edward Strachey's very thoughtful book on *Hebrew Politics in the Times of Sargon and Sennacherib*, p. 200.

[2] These shields were made of wood or of twisted material, and covered with gold, the amount of the latter being calculated for the targets at 9lbs., and for the smaller shields at $4\frac{1}{2}$lbs (Keil).

[3] 1 Kings x. 14 does not necessarily imply that this was the *annual* revenue, only that it came to him in one year. The 666 talents may perhaps be a round sum.

[4] Our Authorised Version renders 1 Kings x. 28 "linen yarn," but this is a mistranslation for: "And the bringing out of horses which was for Solomon from Egypt—and the troop of the merchants of the king brought a

made Palestine almost an emporium for chariots and horses;[1] and it will not be difficult to perceive on what a giddy height king and people stood during the later years of Solomon's reign.

It was this scene of wealth and magnificence, unexampled even in the East, as well as the undisputed political influence and supremacy of the king, combined with the highest intellectual activity and civilization in the country, which so much astounded the Queen of Sheba on her visit to Solomon's dominions. Many, indeed, were the strangers who had been attracted to Jerusalem by the fame of its king (1 Kings x. 24). But none of them had been so distinguished as she, whose appearance was deeply symbolical of the glorious spiritual destiny of Israel (Ps. lxxii. 10, 11; Is. lx. 6), and indicative of the future judgment on the unbelief of those who were even more highly favoured (Matt. xii. 42; Luke xi. 31). Sheba, which is to be distinguished from Seba, or Meroë in Ethiopia, was a kingdom in Southern Arabia,[2] on the shores of the Red Sea, and seems to have been chiefly governed by Queens. Owing to its trade, the population was regarded as the wealthiest in Arabia. It may have been that Solomon's fame had first reached the ears of the Queen through the fleet of Ophir. In consequence, she resolved to visit Jerusalem, to see, to test, and to learn for herself whether the extraordinary reports

---

troop (of horses) for a (definite) price." This would imply that there was a regular trading company which purchased the horses by contract. But the text seems to be here corrupt, and the LXX render, "From Egypt and from Koa" (doubtfully Thekoa), and that "the royal merchants fetched them from Koa for a definite price." In this case there would seem to have been annual horse fairs at Koa, at which the royal merchants bought at a contract price.

[1] The price mentioned in 1 Kings x. 29 amounts (according to Keil) for a chariot—of course, complete, with two or rather three horses, to £78, and for a (cavalry) horse, to £19 10s.

[2] Accordingly the story of the descent of the Ethiopian royal line from Solomon and the Queen of Sheba must be dismissed as unhistorical, although Judaism may have spread into Ethiopia from the opposite shores of Arabia.

which had reached her were true. But, whatever may have *specially* influenced her to undertake so novel a pilgrimage, three things in regard to it are beyond question. She was attracted by the fame of Solomon's *wisdom ;* she viewed that wisdom in connection with "the Name of Jehovah" (1 Kings x. 1 [1]); and she came to *learn.* What the higher import of this "wisdom" was, is explained by Solomon himself in Prov. iii. 14–18, while its source is indicated in Prov. ii. 4–6. Thus viewing it, no event could have been more important, alike typically and in its present bearing on the ancient world. The Queen had come, scarcely daring to hope that Eastern exaggeration had not led her to expect more than she would find. It proved the contrary. Whatever difficulty, doubt, or question she propounded, in the favourite Oriental form of "riddles,"[2] "whatever was with her heart,"[3] "Solomon showed (disclosed to) her all her words"[4] (the spoken and unspoken). And here she would learn chiefly this : that all the prosperity she witnessed, all the intellectual culture and civilisation with which she was brought into contact, had their spring above, with "the Father of lights." She had come at the head of a large retinue, bearing richest presents, which she left in remembrance and also in perpetuation of her visit—at least, if we may trust the account of Josephus, that the cultivation of balsam in the gardens of Jericho owed its origin to plants which the Queen had brought (Jos., *Ant.* viii. 6, 6). The notice is at least deeply symbolical. The spices of Sheba, so sweet and strong

---

[1] Without here entering on a detailed criticism of the precise meaning of the Hebrew expression *leShem Jehovah* ("to the name of Jehovah"), our inference from it can scarcely be called in question.

[2] Our Authorised Version renders "hard questions"— accurately as regards the import, but not the literal meaning of the word. Josephus relates, on the authority of Dius and Menander, some curious legends about "problems" propounded by Solomon to Hiram, which the latter could not solve, and had to pay heavy fines in consequence,—a like fate, however, overtaking Solomon in regard to the problems propounded to him by Abdemon (*Ag. Ap.* i. 17, 18). The love of the Easterns—especially the Arabs—for "riddles" is well known.

[3] So literally.   [4] So literally.

that, according to ancient accounts, their perfume was carried out far to sea, were to be brought to Jerusalem, and their plants to strike root in sacred soil (Ps. lxxii. 10, 11 ; Is. lx. 6). But now the balsam-gardens of Jericho, into which they were transplanted, are lying bare and desolate—for "the Queen of the South" hath risen up in judgment with that "generation ;" and what further "sign" can or need be given to the generation that turned from Him Who was "greater than Solomon?"

CHAPTER IX.

Solomon's Court—His Polygamy—Spread of Foreign Ideas in the Country —Imitation of Foreign Manners—Growing Luxury—Solomon's spiritual Decline—Judgment predicted—Solomon's Enemies: Hadad, Rezon, Jeroboam—Causes of popular discontent—Ahijah's prediction of the separation of the two Kingdoms—Jeroboam's Rebellion and Flight into Egypt—Death of Solomon.

(1 KINGS xi.)

A GREATER contrast could scarcely be imagined than that between the state of Solomon's court and of the country generally, and the directions and restrictions laid down in Deut. xvii. 16, 17 for the regulation of the Jewish monarchy. The first and most prominent circumstance which here presents itself to the mind, is the direct contravention of the Divine command as regarded the number of "princesses" and concubines which formed the harem of Solomon.[1] Granting that the notice in Cant. vi. 8 affords reason for believing that the numerals in 1 Kings xi. 3 may have been due to a mistake on the part of a copyist, still the sacred narrative expressly

---

[1] Bähr gives a number of instances, both from ancient and modern history, of far larger harems than that ascribed to Solomon.

states, that the polygamy of Solomon, and especially his alliances with nations excluded from intermarriage with Israel,[1] was the occasion, if not the cause, of his later sin and punishment. While on this subject we may go back a step further, and mark (with Ewald) what sad consequences the infringement of the primitive Divine order in regard to marriage wrought throughout the history of Israel. It is undoubtedly to polygamy that we have to trace the troubles in the family of David; and to the same cause were due many of those which came on David's successors. If Moses was obliged to tolerate the infringement of the original institution of God, "the hardness of heart" which had necessitated it brought its own punishment, especially when the offender was an Eastern king. Thus the sin of the people, embodied, as it were, in the person of their representative, carried national judgment as its consequence.

But the elements which caused the fall of Solomon lay deeper than polygamy. Indeed, the latter was among the effects, as well as one of the further causes of his spiritual decline. First among these elements of evil at work, we reckon the growing luxury of the court. The whole atmosphere around, so to speak, was different from what it had been in the primitive times which preceded the reign of Solomon, and still more from the ideal of monarchy as sketched in the Book of Deuteronomy. Everything had become un-Jewish, foreign, purely Asiatic. Closely connected with this was the evident desire to emulate, and even outdo neighbouring nations. Such wisdom, such splendour, such riches, and finally, such luxury, and such a court were not to be found elsewhere, as in the kingdom of which Jerusalem was the capital. An ominous beginning this of that long course of Jewish pride and self-exaltation which led to

---

[1] Properly speaking, only Canaanite women were excluded by the Law (Ex. xxxiv. 11-16; Deut. vii. 1-3). But alliance with those of other nations was contrary to the spirit of the law, at any rate so long as they continued idolaters. Comp. Ezra ix. 1; Neh. xiii. 23. There is a legend that Solomon married a daughter of Hiram, king of Tyre.

such fearful consequences. It is to this desire of surpassing other Eastern courts that the size of Solomon's harem must be attributed. Had it been coarse sensuality which influenced him, the earlier, not the later years of his reign, would have witnessed the introduction of so many strange wives. Moreover, it deserves special notice that the 700 wives of Solomon are designated as "princesses" (1 Kings xi. 3). Without pressing this word in its most literal meaning, we may at least infer that Solomon courted influential connections with the reigning and other leading families of the clans around, and that the chief object of his great harem was, in a worldly sense, to strengthen his position, to give evidence of his wealth and power as an Eastern monarch, and to form promising alliances, no matter what spiritual elements were thus introduced into the country. Closely connected with all this was the rapidly growing intercourse between Israel and foreign nations. For one reason or another, strangers, whom Israel hitherto had only considered as heathens, crowded to Jerusalem. By their presence king and people would not only become familiar with foreign ideas, but so-called toleration would extend to these strangers the right of public worship, or rather, of public idolatry. And so strong was this feeling, that, although Asa, Jehoshaphat, Joash, and Hezekiah put an end to all idolatry, yet the high places which Solomon had built on the southern acclivity of the Mount of Olives remained in use till the time of Josiah (2 Kings xxiii. 13), avowedly for the worship of those foreigners who came to, or were resident in, Jerusalem. Viewed in connection with what has just been stated, even the intellectual culture in the time of Solomon may have proved a source of serious danger.

All this may help us to form a more correct conception of the causes which led to the terrible decline in the spiritual history of Solomon, and this without either extenuating his guilt or, as is more commonly the case, exaggerating his sin. As Holy Scripture puts it, when Solomon was old, and less able to resist influences around, he so far yielded to his foreign wives as to build altars for their worship. This in the Scriptural and real sense was already to "go after Ashtoreth and Milcom" (1 Kings xi. 5). But the sacred text does not state that Solomon personally "served them;"[1] nor is there any reason for supposing that he either relinquished the service of Jehovah, or personally took part in heathen rites. To have built altars to "the abominations of the Gentiles,"[2] and to have tolerated, if not encouraged, the idolatrous rites openly enacted there by his wives, implied great public guilt. In the language of Scripture: "Solomon's heart was not perfect with Jehovah his God;" he "did evil in the sight of Jehovah, and went not fully after Jehovah." His sin was the more inexcusable, that he had in this respect the irreproachable example of David. Besides, even closer allegiance to the LORD might have been expected from Solomon than from David, since he had been privileged to build the Temple, and had on two occasions received personal communication from the Lord, whereas God had never *appeared* to David, but only employed prophets as intermediaries to make known His good pleasure.

It need scarcely be said, that public sin such as that of Solomon would soon bring down judgment. As preparatory to it we regard that solemn warning, when the LORD a second time appeared in vision to Solomon (1 Kings ix. 4-9). This being misunderstood or neglected, the actual announcement of judgment followed, probably through Ahijah. The terms of the sentence were terribly explicit. Solomon's kingdom would be rent from him, and given to his servant.

---

[1] Whenever the Jewish kings were personally guilty of idolatry, the Hebrew word *avad*, "served," is used. Comp. 1 Kings xvi. 31; xxii. 53; 2 Kings xvi. 3; xxi. 2-6, 20-22. Jewish tradition also emphatically asserts (*Shab.* 56 b.) that Solomon was not *personally* guilty of idolatry. The account of Josephus (*Ant.* viii. 7, 5) is worthless.

[2] Ashtoreth, the goddess of the Phœnicians, was worshipped with impure rites. Milcom, Malcom, or Molech, was the principal deity of the Ammonites, but must be distinguished from Moloch, whose terrible rites were only introduced at a later period (2 Kings xvi. 3). Chemosh was the sun-god and war-god of the Moabites; his name frequently occurs on the celebrated Moabite Stone.

Yet even so Divine mercy would accord a twofold limitation: the event foretold should not happen in the days of Solomon himself, and when it took place the kingdom should not be wholly taken away, but partially remain in his line. And this for the sake of David—that is, not from partiality for him, nor on account of any supposed superabundant merit, but because of God's promise to David (2 Sam. vii. 14–16), and for God's own glory, since He had made choice of Jerusalem as the place where He would for ever reveal His Name (1 Kings ix. 3).

But although execution of the judgment was stayed, indications of its reality and nearness soon appeared. Once more we mark a succession of natural and intelligible causes, of which the final outcome was the fulfilment of the Divine prediction. It will be remembered that, of the two great wars in which David was involved after his accession, the most formidable was that against the hostile combination of tribes along the eastern boundary of his kingdom.[1] The distance, the character of the country, the habits of the enemy—the alliance of so many nationalities, their determination, and the stubborn resistance which they offered, made this a really great war. We know that the armies of David, under the leadership of Joab and Abishai, were victorious at all points (2 Sam. viii.; x.; 1 Chron. xix.). But, although the enemy may have been subdued and even crushed for a time, it was, in the nature of things, impossible wholly to remove the elements of resistance. In the far south-east, terrible, almost savage, vengeance had been taken on Edom (1 Chron. xviii. 12). From the slaughter of the people a trusty band of Edomites had rescued one of the youthful royal princes, Hadad[2] (or Adad), and brought him

---

[1] Comp. the account of this war in vol. iv. of this Bible History, chapter xviii.

[2] Hadad, "the Sun," or "Sun-god"—an ancient name, perhaps a royal title among the Edomite princes (comp. Gen. xxxvi. 35). But it seems an ungrounded inference (by Ewald, Thenius, and even Canon Rawlinson) to connect him (as grandson) with the last king of the Edomites, who in 1 Chron. i. 50 is by a clerical error called Hadad instead of Hadar (comp. Gen. xxxvi. 39.)

ultimately to Egypt, where he met a hospitable reception from the then reigning Pharaoh—probably the predecessor of Solomon's father-in-law. If Pharaoh had at first been influenced by political motives in keeping near him one who might become a source of trouble to the growing Israelitish power, the young prince of Edom soon enlisted the sympathy and affection of his host (1 Kings xi. 14–19). He married the sister of Tahpenes,[1] the Gevirah, or queen dominant (principal) of Pharaoh's harem ; and their child was acknowledged and brought up among the royal princes of Egypt. When tidings of the death of David and afterwards of Joab reached Hadad, he insisted on returning to Edom, even against the friendly remonstrances of Pharaoh, who by this time would rather have seen him enjoying his peaceful retreat in Egypt than entering upon difficult and dangerous enterprises. But, although Hadad returned to his own country in the beginning of Solomon's reign, it was only towards its close—when growing luxury had enervated king and people—that his presence there became a source of trouble and anxiety.[2] This we infer, not only from 1 Kings iv. 24, but from such a notice as that in 1 Kings ix. 26.

But in the extreme north-east, as well as in the far south east, a dark cloud gathered on the horizon. At the defeat of Hadadezer by the troops of David (2 Sam. viii. 3 ; x. 18) one of the Syrian captains, Rezon by name, had "fled from his lord." In the then disorganized state of the country he gradually gathered around him a band of followers, and ultimately fell back upon Damascus, of which he became king. The sacred text leads us to infer that, although he probably did not venture on open warfare with Solomon, he cast off the

[1] The name occurs also on Egyptian monuments. Tahpenes, or rather Thacpenes, was also the name of an Egyptian goddess (Gesenius, *Thesaurus*, vol. iii., p. 1500 a.).

[2] The LXX have here an addition, upon which Josephus bases a notice (*Ant.* viii. 7, 6), to the effect that Hadad (Ader) raised the standard of revolt in Edom, but, being unsuccessful, combined with Rezon, and became king of part of Syria. The notice cannot be regarded as of historical authority.

Jewish suzerainty, and generally "was an adversary"—or, to use the pictorial language of the Bible, "abhorred Israel." [1]

Ill-suppressed enmity in Edom (far south-east), and more active opposition and intrigue at Damascus (in the north-east)— in short, the danger of a combination like that which had so severely taxed the resources of David : such, then, so far as concerned external politics, were the darkening prospects of Solomon's later years.   But the terms in which Holy Scripture speaks of these events deserve special notice.   We are told, that "Jehovah stirred up" or, rather, "raised up" these adversaries unto Solomon (1 Kings xi. 14, 23).   The expression clearly points to Divine Causality in the matter (comp. Deut. xviii. 15, 18; Judges ii. 18; 1 Sam. ii. 35; Jer. xxix. 15; Ez. xxxiv. 23).   Not, indeed, that the ambitious or evil passions of men's hearts are incited of God, but that while each, in the exercise of his free will, chooses his own course, the LORD overrules all, so as to serve for the chastisement of sin and the carrying out of His own purposes (comp. Psa. ii. 1, 2; Is. x. 1–3).

But yet another and far more serious danger threatened Solomon's throne.   Besides "adversaries" without, elements of dissatisfaction were at work within Palestine, which only needed favouring circumstances to lead to open revolt.   First, there was the old tribal jealousy between Ephraim and Judah.   The high destiny foretold to Ephraim (Gen. xlviii. 17–22; xlix. 22–26) must have excited hopes which the leadership of Joshua, himself an Ephraimite (Numb. xiii. 8), seemed for a time to warrant.   Commanding, perhaps, the most important territorial position in the land, Ephraim claimed a dominating power over the tribes in the days of Gideon and of Jephthah (Judg. viii. 1 ; xii. 1).   In fact, one of the successors of these Judges, Abdon, was an Ephraimite (Judg. xii. 13).   But, besides, Ephraim

[1] Canon Rawlinson (in the *Speaker's Commentary*, vol. ii., p. 550) arranges the succession of the Damascus kings as follows : Hadad-Ezer (Hadad I.), contemporary of David ; Rezon (usurper), contemporary of Solomon ; Hezion (Hadad II.), contemporary of Rehoboam ; Tabrimon (Hadad III.), contemporary of Abijam ; Ben-hadad (Hadad IV.), contemporary of Asa.

could boast not only of secular, but of ecclesiastical supremacy, since Shiloh and Kirjath-jearim were within its tribal possession. And had not Samuel, the greatest of the Judges, the one outstanding personality in the history of a decrepit priesthood, been, though a Levite, yet " from Mount Ephraim" (1 Sam. i. 1)? Even the authority of Samuel could not secure the undisputed acknowledgment of Saul, who was only too painfully conscious of the objections which tribal jealousy would raise to his elevation (1 Sam. ix. 21). It needed that glorious God-given victory at Jabesh-Gilead to hush, under strong religious convictions, those discordant voices, and to unite all Israel in acclamation of their new king. And yet the tribe of Benjamin, to which Saul belonged, was closely allied to that of Ephraim (Judg. xxi. 19–23). Again, it was the tribe of Ephraim which mainly upheld the cause of Ishbosheth (2 Sam. ii. 9); and though the strong hand of David afterwards kept down all active opposition, no sooner did his power seem on the wane than " a man of Mount Ephraim " (2 Sam. xx. 21) roused the tribal jealousies, and raised the standard of rebellion against him. And now, with the reign of King Solomon, all hope of tribal pre-eminence seemed to have passed from Ephraim. There was a new capital for the whole country, and that in the possession of Judah. The glory of the ancient Sanctuary had also been taken away. Jerusalem was the ecclesiastical as well as the political capital, and Ephraim had to contribute its wealth and even its forced labour to promote the schemes, to support the luxury, and to advance the glory of a new monarchy, taken from, and resident in, Judah!

But, secondly, the burden which the new monarchy imposed on the people must, in the course of time, have weighed very heavily on them (1 Kings xii. 4). The building of a great national Sanctuary was, indeed, an exceptional work which might enlist the highest and best sympathies, and make the people willing to submit to any sacrifices. But this was followed by the construction of a magnificent palace, and then by a succession of architectural undertakings (1 Kings ix. 15, 17–

19) on an unprecedented scale. However useful some of these might be, they not only marked an innovation, but involved a continuance of forced labour (1 Kings iv. 6; v. 13, 14; xi. 28), wholly foreign to the spirit of a free people, and which diverted from their proper channels the industrial forces of the country. Nor was this all. The support of such a king and court must have proved a heavy demand on the resources of the nation (1 Kings iv. 21–27). To have to pay enormous taxes, and for many long years to be deprived during so many months of the heads and the bread-winners of the family, that they might do what seemed slaves' labour for the glorification of a king, whose rule was every year becoming weaker, would have excited dissatisfaction even among a more enduring people than those tribes who had so long enjoyed the freedom and the privileges of a federated Republic.

It only needed a leader—and once more Ephraim furnished him. Jeroboam, the son of Nebat and of a widow named Zeruah, was a native of Zereda or Zererath [1] (Judg. vii. 22), within the territory of Ephraim. The sacred text describes him as a "mighty man of valour." His energy, talent, and aptitude pointed him out as a fit permanent overseer of the forced labour of his tribe. It was a dangerous post to assign to a man of such power and ambition. His tribesmen, as a matter of course, came to know him as their chief and leader, while in daily close intercourse he would learn their grievances and sentiments. In such circumstances the result which followed was natural. The bold, strong, and ambitious Ephraimite, "ruler over all the burden of the house of Joseph," became the leader of the popular movement against Solomon.

It was, no doubt, in order to foment the elements of discontent already existing, as well as because his position in the

---

[1] Most critics erroneously identify it with Zarthan (1 Kings vii. 46), or Zeredathah (2 Chron. iv. 17), which, however, lay outside the possession of Ephraim.

city must have become untenable, that "Jeroboam went out of Jerusalem" (1 Kings xi. 29). When "the prophet Ahijah the Shilonite found him in the way," Jeroboam had already planned, or rather commenced, his revolt against Solomon. Himself an Ephraimite (from Shiloh), the prophet would not only be acquainted with Jeroboam, but also know the sentiments of his tribesmen and the views of their new leader. It was not, therefore, Ahijah who incited Jeroboam to rebellion [1] by the symbolical act of rending his new garment in twelve pieces, giving him ten of the pieces,[2] while those retained were emblematic of what would be left to the house of David. Rather did he act simply as the Divine messenger to Jeroboam, *after* the latter had resolved on his own course. The event was, indeed, ordered of God in punishment of the sin of Solomon (vers. 11–13); and the intimation of this fact, with its lessons of warning, was the principal object of Ahijah's mission and message. But the chief actor had long before chosen his own part, being prompted, as Holy Scripture puts it, by a settled ambition to usurp the throne (1 Kings xi. 37); while the movement of which he took advantage was not only the result of causes long at work, but might almost have been forecast by any observer acquainted with the state of matters. Thus we learn once more how, in the Providence of God, a result which, when predicted, seems miraculous, and is really such, so far as the Divine operation is concerned, is brought about, not only through the free agency of man, but by a series of natural causes, while at the same time all is guided and overruled of God for His own wise and holy purposes.

Indeed, closely considered, the words of the prophet, so far from inciting Jeroboam to rebellion against Solomon, should

---

[1] This is the view of some German critics.

[2] Much needless ingenuity has been employed to show in what sense Jeroboam had ten "pieces" or tribes, and Rehoboam "one"—or rather two—assigned to him. The language must not be too closely pressed. The "one" tribe left to the house of David was no doubt Judah, including "little Benjamin" as the second of the twelve "pieces" or tribes.

rather have deterred him from it. The scene is sketched in vivid outline: Jeroboam, in whose soul tribal pride, disgust at his work, contempt for the king, irrepressible energy, and high-reaching ambition, combined with a knowledge of the feelings of his tribesmen, have ripened into stern resolve, has left Jerusalem. The time for secret intrigue and dissimulation is past; that for action has arrived. As he leaves the hated city-walls—memorials of Ephraim's servitude—and ascends towards the heights of Benjamin and Ephraim, a strange figure meets him. It is his countryman from Shiloh, the prophet Ahijah. No salutation passes between them, but Ahijah takes hold of the new square cloth or upper mantle in which he has been wrapped, and rends it in twelve pieces. It is not, as usually, in token of mourning (Gen. xxxvii. 29; xliv. 13; 2 Sam. xiii. 19), though sadness must have been in the prophet's heart, but as symbol of what is to happen—as it were, God's answer to Jeroboam's thoughts. Yet the judgment predicted is *not* to take effect in Solomon's lifetime (1 Kings xi. 34, 35);[1] and any attempt at revolt, such as Jeroboam seems to have made (vers. 26, 40),[2] was in direct contravention of God's declared will.

There were other parts of the prophet's message which Jeroboam would have done well to have borne in mind. David was always to "have a light before God" in Jerusalem, the city "which He had chosen to put His Name there" (1 Kings xi. 36). In other words, David was always to have a descendant on the throne,[3] and Jerusalem with its Temple was always to be God's chosen place; that is, Israel's worship was to continue in the great central Sanctuary, and the descendants of David were to be the rightful occupants of the throne till He came Who was

[1] I cannot adopt Canon Rawlinson's proposed rendering of ver. 34: "I will not take aught of the kingdom out of his hand."

[2] The expression "to lift up the hand," means actual revolt. Comp. 2 Sam. xviii. 28; xx. 21.

[3] That this is the meaning of the figurative expression "light," may be gathered from 1 Kings xv. 4; 2 Kings viii. 19; 2 Chron. xxi. 7; Psa. xviii. 28; lxxii. 17.

David's greater Son. God had linked the Son of David with His City and the Temple, so that the final destruction of the latter marked the fulfilment of the prophecies concerning the house of David. Thus gloriously did the promise stretch beyond the immediate future, with its troubles and afflictions. Lastly, so far as regarded Jeroboam, the promise of succession to the kingdom of Israel in his family was made conditional on his observance of the statutes and commandments of God, as David had kept them (ver. 38). But Jeroboam was of far other spirit than David. His main motive had been personal ambition. Unlike David, who, though anointed king, would make no attempt upon the crown during Saul's lifetime, Jeroboam, despite the express warning of God, "lifted up his hand against the king." The result was failure[1] and flight into Egypt. Nor did Jeroboam keep the statutes and commandments of the LORD; and after a brief reign his son fell by the hand of the assassin (1 Kings xv. 28). Lastly, and most important of all—the Messianic bearing of the promise to David, and the Divine choice of Jerusalem and its Temple, were fatally put aside or forgotten by Jeroboam and his successors on the throne of Israel. The schism in the kingdom became one from the Theocracy; and the rejection of the central Sanctuary resulted, as might have been expected, in the establishment of idolatry in Israel.

Nor did King Solomon either live or die as his father David. A feeble attempt—perhaps justifiable—to rid himself of Jeroboam, and no more is told of him than that, at the close of a reign of forty years,[2] he "slept with his fathers, and was buried in the city of David his father." So far as we know, in that death-chamber no words of earnest, loving entreaty to serve Jehovah were spoken to his successor, such as David

---

[1] Of course this is only an inference from the narrative.

[2] Josephus (*Ant.* viii. 7, 8) assigns him a reign of eighty years. But this must either be a clerical error, or depend on one in Josephus' copy of the LXX. Solomon probably died at the age of about sixty. The question of his final repentance, so largely discussed at one time by theologians, may be safely left—where the Bible has left it.

had uttered; no joyous testimony here as regarded the past, nor yet strong faith and hope as concerned the future, such as had brightened the last hours of David. It is to us a silent death-chamber in which King Solomon lay. No bright sunset here, to be followed by a yet more glorious morning. He had done more than any king to denationalise Israel. And on the morrow of his death: rebellion within the land; outside its borders—Edom and Syria ready to spring to arms, Egypt under Shishak gathering up its might; and only a Rehoboam to hold the rudder of the State in the rising storm.

CHAPTER X.

REHOBOAM, FIRST KING OF JUDAH.

Family of Solomon—Age of Rehoboam—His Character—Religious History of Israel and Judah—The Assembly at Shechem—Jeroboam's return from Egypt—Rehoboam's Answer to the Deputies in Shechem—Revolt of the Ten Tribes—The Reigns of Rehoboam and of Jeroboam—Invasion of Judah by Shishak—Church and State in Israel—Rehoboam's attempt to recover rule over the Ten Tribes—His Family History—Religious Decline in Israel, and its consequences.

(I KINGS XII.; XIV. 21-31; 2 CHRON. X.-XII.)

STRANGE as it may seem, despite the multifarious marriages of the king, his alliances with neighbouring nations, and his immense wealth, "the house of Solomon" was far from strong at the time of his decease. It may have been that Solomon left other sons besides Rehoboam, though it is strange that we find no notice of them, nor, indeed, of any child, except a casual remark about two of Solomon's daughters (1 Kings iv. 11, 15). If other children survived him, their position must have been far less influential than that of the sons of David, nor does Rehoboam's succession appear to have been ever contested by any member of the family.

Rehoboam, or rather *Rechavam* ("he who enlargeth the people"), must have been very young at his accession. This we gather from the expression by which they "who had grown up with him" are described, and from the manner in which his son and successor, Abijah, characterised the commencement of his reign (2 Chron. xiii. 7). There seems, therefore, considerable probability attaching to the suggestion, that the notice of his age at his accession—forty-one (1 Kings xiv. 21; 2 Chron. xii. 13)—is the mistake of a copyist, who in transcribing the figures misread the two letters כא—twenty-one—for מא—forty-one. This supposition is strengthened by the fact that Rehoboam was not the son of the Egyptian princess, who seems to have been Solomon's first wife, but of Naamah, an Ammonitess; [1] and we know that it was only after his religious decline (1 Kings xi. 1) that Solomon entered upon alliances with "strange women," among whom Ammonitesses are specially mentioned. [2]

Of the character of Rehoboam we know sufficient to form an accurate estimate. David had taken care to commit the upbringing of his son and successor to the prophet Nathan; and, so far as we can judge, the early surroundings of Solomon were such as not only to keep him from intimacy with light o: evil associates, but to train him in earnest piety. But when Rehoboam was born, King Solomon had already entered upon the fatal path which led to the ruin of his race; and the prince

[1] The LXX notice that she was the granddaughter of Nahash, king of Ammon.

[2] It is hardly credible that Solomon should have contracted such an alliance before his accession to the throne, which, of course, would be implied if Rehoboam was forty-one years old at the time of his father's death. The Rabbis find a parallel to the marriage of Solomon with Naamah in that of Ruth with Boaz (Jalkut, vol. ii., p. 32 *a*).

was brougnt up, like any other Eastern in similar circumstances, with the young nobles of a court which had learned foreign modes of thinking and foreign manners. The relation between the aristocracy and the people, between the king and his subjects, had changed from the primitive and God-sanctioned to that of ordinary Eastern despotism; and the notions which Rehoboam and his young friends entertained, appeared only too clearly in the first act of the king's reign. In general, we gather that Rehoboam was vain, weak, and impulsive; ready to give up under the influence of fear what he had desired and attempted when he deemed himself secure. Firm religious principles he had not, and his inclinations led him not only towards idolatry, but to a form of it peculiarly dissolute in its character (1 Kings xiv. 23, 24; 2 Chron. xi. 13–17; xii. 1). During the first three years of his reign he remained, indeed, faithful to the religion of his fathers, either through the influence of the Levites who had gathered around him from all Israel—though even in this case his motives might be rather political than conscientious—or else under the impression of the outward consequences of his first great mistake. But this mood soon passed away, and when the state-reasons for his early adherence to the worship of Jehovah had ceased to be cogent, or he felt himself secure on his throne, he yielded, as we have seen, to his real inclinations in the matter.

Here, at the outset of the separate history of the kingdoms of Judah and Israel, it may be well to take a general view of the relation of these two divisions of the Jewish people to Jehovah, their King. That the sin of Israel was much deeper, and their apostasy from God much sooner and more fully developed than in the case of Judah, appears from the circumstance, that the Divine judgment in the banishment of the people from their land overtook Israel 123 years earlier than Judah.[1] Yet at first sight it seems almost strange that such should have been the case. Altogether, the period of the

---

[1] See the Chronological Table at the end of this volume, and the remarks on the chronology of that period there appended.

separate existence of the two kingdoms (to the deportation of the ten tribes under Shalmaneser, about 722 B.C.) extended over 253 years. During that time, thirteen monarchs reigned over Judah, and twenty over Israel—besides two periods of probable interregnum, or rather of anarchy in Israel. The religious history of the ten tribes during these two and a half centuries may be written in very brief compass. Of all the kings of Israel it is uniformly said, that they "walked in the ways of Jeroboam, the son of Nebat," except of Ahab and his two sons (Ahaziah and Joram), under whose reigns the worship of Baal became the established religion of the country. It follows, that there was not a single king in Israel who really served the LORD or worshipped in His Temple. On the other hand, there were at least *five* kings in Judah distinguished for their piety (Asa, Jehoshaphat, Uzziah, Jotham, and Hezekiah), while of the other eight, *two* (Joash and Amaziah) continued for a considerable, and a *third* (Rehoboam) for a short period their profession of the religion of their fathers. Four of the other *five* kings acquired, indeed, a terrible notoriety for daring blasphemy. Abijam, the son and successor of Rehoboam, adopted all the practices of his father during the last fourteen years of that monarch's reign. During the reign of Joram the worship of Baal was introduced into Judah; and we know with what terrible consistency it was continued under Ahaziah and Athaliah, the measure of iniquity being filled by Ahaz, who ascended the throne twenty years before the deportation of the ten tribes, when the doors of the Sanctuary were actually closed, and an idol-altar set up in the Temple court. But, despite all this, idolatry never struck its roots deeply among the people, and this for three reasons. There was, *first*, the continued influence for good of the Temple at Jerusalem; and in this we see at least one providential reason for the existence of a central Sanctuary, and for the stringency of the Law which confined all worship to its courts. *Secondly*, the idolatrous kings of Judah were always succeeded by monarchs distinguished for piety, who swept away the rites of their pre

decessors; while, *lastly* and most remarkably, the reign of
the idolatrous kings was uniformly brief as compared with
that of the God-fearing rulers. Thus, on a review of the
whole period, we find that, of the 253 years between the accession of Rehoboam and the deportation of the ten tribes,
200 passed under the rule of monarchs who maintained the
religion of Jehovah, while only during 53 years His worship
was more or less discarded by the kings of Judah.[1]

We repeat, it were a mistake to ascribe the separation of the
ten tribes entirely to the harsh and foolish refusal of Rehoboam
to redress the grievances of the people. This only set the
spark to the inflammable material which had long been ac-
cumulating. We have seen how dissatisfaction had spread,
especially in the northern parts of the kingdom, during the
later part of Solomon's reign; how, indeed, a rising seems to
have been actually attempted by Jeroboam, though for the
time it failed. We have also called attention to the deep-seated
tribal jealousy between Ephraim and Judah, which ever and
again broke into open hostility (Judg. viii. 1–3; xii. 1–6;
2 Sam. ii. 9; xix. 42, 43). This, indeed, may be described
as the ultimate (secondary) cause of the separation of the two
kingdoms. And, if proof were required that the rebellion
against Rehoboam was only the outcome of previously existing
tendencies, we would find it even in the circumstance that
the language used by the representatives of Israel, when re-
nouncing the rule of Rehoboam, was exactly the same as that
of Sheba when he raised against David the standard of
what would be represented as the ancient federal Republic
of Israel (2 Sam. xx. 1 comp. with 1 Kings xii. 16). Still
more wrongful would it be to account for the conduct either
of Israel or of Jeroboam, or even to attempt vindicating it,

---

[1] We arrive at this result by the following computation:—Years of
public idolatry: under Rehoboam, 14; under Abijah, 3; under Joram, 6;
under Ahaziah, 1; under Athaliah, 6; under Ahaz, 16; or in all 46 years,
to which we add 7, for the later idolatrous reigns of Joash and Amaziah.
See Keil, *Bibl. Commentar*, vol. iii., pp. 137, 138.

on the ground of the prophecy of Ahijah (1 Kings xi. 29-39). The latter foretold an event in history, and explained the reason of what, in view of the promises to David, would otherwise have been unaccountable. But such prediction and announcement of judgment—even if known to the tribes—warranted neither their rebellion nor the usurpation of Jeroboam. It is, indeed, true that, as the Old Testament considers all events as directly connected with God, its fundamental principle being : Jehovah reigneth—and that not merely in a pseudo-spiritual, but in the fullest sense—this, as all other things that come to man, is ultimately traced up to the living God. So was the resistance of Pharaoh, and so are the sword, the pestilence, and the famine. For, all things are of Him, Who sendeth blessings upon His people, and taketh vengeance of their inventions ; Who equally ruleth in the armies of heaven, and among the inhabitants of the earth ; Who maketh the wrath of man as well as the worship of His people to praise Him ; Who always doeth marvellously, whether He accomplish His purposes by direct interposition from heaven, or, as much more frequently, through a chain of natural causation, of which He holds the first, and man the last, link. This grand truth, as fully expressed and applied in the sublime language of Ps. cxlvii., is the sheet-anchor of faith by which it rides out the storms of this world. Ever to look up straight to God, to turn from events and secondary causations to Jehovah as the living God and the reigning King, is that denial of things seen and affirmation of things unseen, which constitute the victory of faith over the world.

On the death of his father, Rehoboam seems to have at once, and without opposition, assumed the reins of government. His enthronement at Jerusalem implied the homage of Judah and its neighbour-tribe Benjamin. According to ancient custom, the representatives of the more distant tribes should have assembled at the residence of the king, when in a great popular assembly the royal dignity would be solemnly conferred, and public homage rendered to the new monarch

(comp. 1 Sam. xi. 15 ; 2 Sam. ii. 4 ; v. 3 ; 1 Chron. xxix. 22).
But, instead of repairing to Jerusalem, the representatives
of the ten tribes gathered at Shechem, the ancient capital
of Ephraim, where important popular assemblies had previously been held (Josh. viii. 30–35 ; xxiv. 1–28), and the
first claimant of royalty in Israel, Abimelech, had set up his
throne (Judg. ix. 1–23). Only one meaning could attach
to their choice of this place.[1]   They had indeed come to
make Rehoboam king, but only with full concessions to their
tribal claims.   All that they now required was an energetic
leader.   Such an one was to hand in the person of Jeroboam,
who in the reign of King Solomon had headed the popular
movement.   After the failure of his attempt, he had fled into
Egypt, and been welcomed by Shishak.   The weak (21st
Tanite) dynasty, with which King Solomon had formed a
matrimonial alliance, had been replaced by the vigorous and
martial rule of Shishak (probably about fifteen years before
the death of Solomon).   The rising kingdom of Palestine
—allied as it was with the preceding dynasty—was too
close, and probably too threatening a neighbour not to be
attentively watched by Shishak.   It was obviously his policy
to encourage Jeroboam, and to support any movement which
might divide the southern from the northern tribes, and
thus give Egypt the supremacy over both.   In point of fact,
five years later Shishak led an expedition against Rehoboam,
probably not so much for the purpose of humbling Judah as
of strengthening the new kingdom of Israel.

The sacred text leaves it doubtful whether, after hearing of
the accession of Rehoboam, Jeroboam continued in Egypt till
sent for by the representatives of the ten tribes, or returned
to Ephraim of his own accord.[2]   In any case, he was not in

---

[1] Jewish commentators expressly account for the gathering of the ten
tribes at Shechem on the ground of their intention to make Jeroboam their
king.

[2] The LXX version has here several additions about the mother of Jeroboam, his stay in Egypt, his conduct after his return, etc.   This is not the
place to discuss them in detail, but they may safely be rejected as *legendary*,
and, indeed, quite in the spirit of later Jewish tradition.

Shechem when the assembly of the Israelitish deputies met there, but was expressly sent for to conduct negotiations on their behalf.[1] It was a mark of weakness on the part of Rehoboam to have gone to Shechem at all; and it must have encouraged the deputies in their demands. Moderate as these sound, they seem to imply not only a lightening of the "heavy" burden of forced labour and taxation, but of the "grievous yoke" of what they regarded as a despotism, which prevented their free movements. It is on this supposition alone that we can fully account for the reply which Rehoboam ultimately gave them. The king took three days to consider the demand. First, he consulted Solomon's old advisers, who strongly urged a policy of at least temporary compliance. The advice was evidently ungrateful, and the king—as Absalom of old, and most weak men in analogous circumstances—next turned to another set of counsellors. They were his young companions—as the text throughout contemptuously designates them: "the children (the boys) who had grown up with him." With their notions of the royal supremacy, they seem to have imagined that such daring attempts at independence arose from doubt of the king's power and courage, and would be best repressed if sternly met by an overawing assertion of authority. Rehoboam was not to discuss their demands, but to tell them that they would find they had to deal with a monarch far more powerful and far more strict than his father had been. To put it in the vain-glorious language of the Eastern "boy-counsellors," he was to say to them: " My little finger is bigger than my father's hips. And now my father did lade upon you a heavy yoke, and I will add to your yoke; my father chastised you with whips [those of ordinary slaves], but I will chastise you with [so-called] 'scorpions'"[2]—or wnips

---

[1] Probably Jeroboam returned of his own account, but did not go to Shechem till he was sent for by the deputies of Israel. This accords with the two versions. There is no need further to discuss here the reading, or rather the proper punctuation of 1 Kings xii. 2, 3.

[2] So literally

armed with hooks, such as were probably used upon criminals
or recalcitrants.

Grossly foolish as this advice was, Rehoboam followed it
—the sacred writer remarking, in order to account for such
an occurrence: "for the turn (of events) was from Jehovah,
that He might perform His word which Jehovah spake
by the hand of Ahijah the Shilonite to Jeroboam the son
of Nebat."[1] The effect was, indeed, immediate. To the
shout of Sheba's ancient war-cry of rebellion the assembly
renounced their allegiance to the house of David, and the
deputies returned to their homes. Rehoboam perceived his
fatal error, when it was too late to retrieve its consequences.
Even his attempt in that direction was a mistake. The king
sent Adoram,[2] the superintendent of the tribute and of forced
labour[3]—the two forming apparently one department of the
king's dues—to arrange, if possible, matters with the rebellious tribes. But this seemed only like trifling with their
grievances, and a fresh insult. The presence of the hated
official called forth such feelings, that he was stoned, and
Rehoboam himself narrowly escaped[4] the same fate by flight
to Jerusalem.

The rebellion of the ten tribes was soon followed by
their formation into an independent kingdom. When, on
their return from Shechem, the deputies made known the
presence of Jeroboam, the tribes sent for him, and in a
popular assembly appointed him king over all Israel. Still,
it must not be thought that the whole land was absolutely
subject to him. When thinking of monarchy in Palestine, it
is always necessary to bear in mind the long-established and
great municipal rights and liberties which made every city

[1] So literally.

[2] As three persons of that name are mentioned (2 Sam. xx. 24; 1 Kings
v. 6; xii. 18) who must have lived at different times, may not "Adoram"
be the appellation of the office?

[3] The one Hebrew word means both—and probably the two belonged
to the same department of royal dues.

[4] This is implied in ver. 18; see the marginal rendering.

with its district, under its Elders, almost an independent state within the state.   Accordingly, we find it chronicled as a noteworthy fact (1 Kings xii. 17), that King Rehoboam reigned over those Israelites who were settled in Judæan towns—either wholly inhabiting, or forming the majority in them; while it is marked as a wise measure on the part of Rehoboam, that he distributed "his children throughout all the countries (districts) of Judah and Benjamin unto every fenced city"—no doubt, with the view of making sure of their allegiance.   It seems to have been otherwise within the domains of Jeroboam.   From 2 Chron. xi. 13–16 we learn that, on the substitution by Jeroboam and his successors of the worship of the golden calves for the service of Jehovah, the old religion was disestablished, and the Levites deprived of their ecclesiastical revenues, the new priesthood which took their place being probably supported by the dues of their office, and, if we may judge from the history of Ahab (1 Kings xviii. 19), by direct assistance from the royal treasury.   In consequence of these changes, many of the Levites seem to have settled in Judæa, followed perhaps by more or less extensive migrations of the pious laity, varying according to the difficulties put in the way of resorting to the great festivals in Jerusalem.   It would, however, be a mistake to infer the entire exodus of the pious laity or of the Levites.[1]   But even if such had been the case, the feeling in the ancient Levitical cities would for some time have continued sufficiently strong to refuse allegiance to Jeroboam.

And here a remarkable document throws unexpected light upon our history.   On the wall of the great Egyptian Temple of Karnak, Shishak has left a record of his victorious expedition against Judah.   Among the conquests there named 133 have been deciphered—although only partially identified—while 14 are now illegible.   The names ascertained have

---

[1] In point of fact, 2 Chron. xi. 16 does *not* necessarily imply any settlement of the pious laity in Judah; and even the evidence for that of the priests and Levites is not *quite* convincing (see the next chapter).

been arranged into three groups [1]—those of Judæan cities (the smallness of their number being accounted for by the erasures just mentioned); those of Arab tribes, south of Palestine; and those of Levitical and Canaanite cities within the territory of the new kingdom of Israel. It is the latter which here alone claim our attention. Any conquest of cities within the territory of Jeroboam might surprise us, since the expedition of Shishak was against Judah, and *not* against Israel—indeed, rather in alliance with Jeroboam and in support of his new kingdom. Another remarkable circumstance is, that these Israelitish conquests of Shishak are *all* of Levitical or else of ancient Canaanite cities, and that they are of towns in all parts of the territory of the ten tribes, and at considerable distances from one another, there being, however, no mention of the taking of the intervening cities. All these facts point to the conclusion, to which we have already been directed on quite independent grounds, that the Levitical and ancient Canaanite cities within the territory of Jeroboam did not acknowledge his rule. This is why they were attacked and conquered by Shishak on his expedition against Judah, as virtually subject to the house of David, and hence constituting an element not only of rebellion but of danger within the new kingdom of Israel. Before quitting this subject, these two remarks may be allowed: how wonderfully, and we may add, unexpectedly, documents of secular history—apparently accidentally discovered—confirm and illustrate the narratives of the Bible; and how wise, politically and religiously, how suited to the national life, were the institutions of the Old Testament, even when to our notions they seem most strange, as in the case of Levitical cities throughout the land. For, these cities, besides serving other most important purposes, formed also the strongest bond of political union, and at the same time the most powerful means of preserving throughout the country the unity of the faith in the unity of the central worship of

[1] Compare **Mr. Poole's** admirable article on "Shishak," in Smith's *Dictionary of the Bible*, vol. iii., pp. 1287-1295.

Jehovah at Jerusalem. Thus national union and religious purity were bound up together, and helped to preserve each other.

But to return. On the elevation of Jeroboam to the new throne of Israel, Rehoboam made one more attempt to recover the lost parts of David's kingdom. He assembled an army of 180,000 men [1] from Judah and Benjamin—the latter tribe having apparently become almost unified with Judah since the establishment of the political and religious capital in Jerusalem, through which ran the boundary-line between Judah and Benjamin. But the expedition was at its outset arrested by Divine direction through the prophet Shemaiah.[2] This abandonment of an expedition and dispersion of a host simply upon the word of a prophet, are quite as remarkable as the courage of that prophet in facing an army in such circumstances, and his boldness in so fully declaring as a message from Jehovah what must have been a most unwelcome announcement alike to king and people. Both these considerations are very important in forming an estimate, not only of the religious and political state of the time, and their mutual inter-relations, but of the character of "Prophetism" in Israel.

The expedition once abandoned was not again renewed, although throughout the reign of Rehoboam there were constant incursions and border-raids—probably chiefly of a predatory character—on the part of Judah and of Israel (1 Kings xiv. 30). The remaining notices of Rehoboam's reign concern the *internal* and *external* relations of Judah, as well as the *sad religious change* which passed over the country after the first three years of his rule. They are recorded, either solely or with much fuller details, in the Book of Chronicles (2 Chron. xi. 4 to xii. 16). The first measure referred to is the building of fifteen fortresses, of which thirteen were in the land of

---

[1] The LXX has 120,000, but the number in the Hebrew text is moderate (comp. 2 Sam. xxiv. 9).

[2] From 2 Chron. xii. 15 we learn that Shemaiah wrote a history of the reign of Rehoboam.

Judah—Hebron forming, as it were, the centre of them—and
only two (Zorah and Aijalon) within the later possession of
Benjamin.[1]   They served as a continuous chain of forts south
of Jerusalem, and to defend the western approaches into the
country.   The northern boundary was left wholly unprotected.
From this it would appear that Rehoboam chiefly dreaded
an incursion from Egypt, though it does not by any means
follow that these fortresses were only built after the campaign
of Shishak, which took place five years after the accession of
Solomon's son.

The next notice concerns the family relations of Rehoboam.
It appears that he had eighteen wives and sixty concubines
(thirty, according to Josephus, *Ant.* viii. 10, 1), following
in this respect the evil example of Solomon.   Of his wives
only *two*[2] are named : his cousin Mahalath, the daughter of
Jerimoth, a son of David (either the same as Ithream, 1
Chron. iii. 3, or the son of one of David's concubines,
1 Chron. iii. 9), and of Abihail, the daughter of Eliab, David's
eldest brother; and Maachah, the daughter, or rather, evidently,
the granddaughter of Absalom,[3] through his only child, Tamar
(2 Sam. xiv. 27; xviii. 18; comp. Jos. *Ant.* viii. 10, 1), who
had married Uriel of Gibeah (2 Chron. xiii. 2).   Maachah,
named after her paternal great-grandmother (the mother of
Absalom, 1 Chron. iii. 2), was the favourite of the king, and her
eldest son, Abijah, made "chief among his brethren," with
succession to the throne.   As already noticed, Rehoboam
took care to locate his other sons in the different districts of

---

[1] Originally they belonged to Dan (Josh. xix. 41, 42), but see 1 Chron.
vi. 66-69.

[2] Some commentators have regarded Abihail (2 Chron. xi. 18) as the
name of a *third* wife, and accordingly represented her, not as a daughter
but as a granddaughter of Eliab.   But even if this were not contrary to the
plain meaning of vers. 18, 19, a granddaughter of Eliab would have been
too old for the wife of Rehoboam.

[3] This appears clearly from 2 Chron. xiii. 2.   At the death of Solomon
the daughter of Absalom would be about fifty years of age.   In 2 Chron.
xiii. 2 the name is misspelt *Michaiah*.

his territory, giving them ample means for sustaining their rank, and forming numerous and influential alliances for them.[1] Altogether Rehoboam had twenty-eight sons and sixty daughters.

From these general notices, which must be regarded as referring not to any single period, but to the whole reign of Rehoboam, we pass to what, as regards the Scripture narrative, is the most important event in this history. The fact itself is told in fullest detail in the Book of Kings (1 Kings xiv. 22–24); its punishment at the hand of God in the Book of Chronicles (2 Chron. xii. 2, 12).

After the first three years of Rehoboam's reign a great change seems to have come over the religious aspect of the country. Rehoboam and Judah did not, indeed, openly renounce the worship of Jehovah. On the contrary, we find that the king continued to attend the house of the LORD in royal state, and that after the incursion of Shishak there was even a partial religious revival[2] (2 Chron. xii. 11, 12). Still the general character of this period was, that "Rehoboam forsook the law of Jehovah, and all Israel with him," that "he did evil in that he did not set his heart on seeking Jehovah" (2 Chron. xii. 1, 14, *lit.*), and, lastly, that "Judah did the evil in the sight of Jehovah, and provoked Him to jealousy (viewing the relation between the LORD and Israel as one of marriage, Numb. v. 14)—more than anything which their fathers had done by their sins which they sinned" (1 Kings xiv. 22). These sins consisted in building *Bamoth*, or "high places," *i.e.*, altars on every high hill, and setting up

---

[1] Our Authorised Version renders 2 Chron. xi. 23: "he desired many wives," which seems to imply that Rehoboam sought them for himself. But this is not the case. The original has it, that he "demanded (or sought)" these alliances for his sons, evidently to strengthen his connection with the noble families of the land.

[2] It must not be thought that there was a formal renunciation in Judah of the worship of Jehovah; but, side by side with it, other services were carried on, which Holy Scripture rightly describes as so inconsistent with it as to amount to idolatry.

in every grove *Mazzeboth*, or memorial-stones and pillars dedicated to Baal, and *Asherim*, or trunks of trees dedicated to Astarte (with all the vileness which their service implied).[1] This idolatry was, indeed, not new in Israel—though it had probably not been practised to the same extent. But in addition to this we now read of persons "consecrated" to the Syrian goddess, with the nameless abominations connected therewith. This form of heathen pollution was of purely Canaanite origin. As indicating the influence of the Canaanites upon Judah, it may perhaps be regarded as another evidence of the connection subsisting between Rehoboam and the ancient Canaanite cities within the territory of Israel.

The Divine punishment was not long withheld. Once more it came in the course of natural causation, through the political motives which influenced Shishak, and led him to support Jeroboam. In the fifth year of Rehoboam's reign Shishak marched a large army of Egyptians, Lybians, Sukkiim, ("tent-dwellers"? Arabs?), and Ethiopians, with 1200 chariots[2] and 60,000 horsemen, into Judæa, and, after taking the fenced cities along his route, advanced upon Jerusalem, where Rehoboam and his army were gathered. Once more the prophet Shemaiah averted a contest, which could only have ended in disaster. On showing them that the national danger, though apparently arising from political causes, was really due to their sin against Jehovah (2 Chron. xii. 2); and that it was needless to fight, since, as they had been God-forsaking, they were now God-forsaken (ver. 5)—the king and his princes humbled themselves. Thereupon the LORD intimated through His prophet, that He would "grant them deliverance for a little while," on condition of their submitting to Shishak. The reason for this : "that they may know My service, and the service of the kingdoms of the countries," as well as the

---

[1] The *Bamoth* would be on the heights, the Baal- and Astarte-worship in the groves.

[2] This number is thoroughly consistent with such notices as Exod. xiv. 7; 1 Kings x. 26, and other well-ascertained historical instances.

terms by which the promised deliverance was qualified, contained the most solemn warning of the ultimate consequences of apostasy. Yet the Divine forbearance continued other 370 years before the threatened judgment burst upon the nation. But at this time Jerusalem was spared. Voluntary submission having been made, Shishak entered the city, and contented himself with carrying away the treasures of the Temple and of the Palace, including among the latter the famous golden shields used by Solomon's body-guard on state occasions,[1] for which Rehoboam now substituted shields of brass.[2]

[1] These were kept in the guard-house, or "house of the runners," who kept watch at the entrance of the king's house—and not, as before, in the house of the forest of Lebanon (1 Kings x. 17).

[2] And yet the Rabbis speak of the reign of Rehoboam as one of the five brilliant periods (those of David, Solomon, Rehoboam, Asa, and Abijah, *Shem. R.* 15). The Rabbinical notices are collated in the *Nachalath Shim.*, p. 61, cols. *c* and *d*. There is a curious legend (*Pes.* 119, *a*), that Joseph gathered in Egypt all the gold and silver of the world, and that the children of Israel brought it up with them from Egypt. On the capture of Jerusalem, Shishak is said to have taken it, and the possession of this treasure is then traced through various wars to Rome, where it is said now to be.

CHAPTER XI.

JEROBOAM, FIRST KING OF ISRAEL.

Political Measures of Jeroboam—The Golden Calves—The New Priesthood and the New Festival—The Man of Elohim from Judah—His Message and Sign—Jeroboam Struck by Jehovah and miraculously Restored —Invitation to the Man of Elohim—Heathen view of Miracles—The Old Prophet—Return of the Man of Elohim to Bethel—Judgment on his Disobedience—Character of the Old Prophet and of the Man of Elohim—Sickness of the Pious Child of Jeroboam—Mission of his Mother to Ahijah — Predicted Judgment — Death of the Child — Remaining Notices of Jeroboam.

(1 KINGS XII. 25–XIV. 20.)

FROM the history of Judah under Rehoboam, we turn to that of the newly-established kingdom of Israel, the record of which is only found in the Book of Kings (1 Kings xii. 25—xiv. 20). The first object of Jeroboam ("He shall increase the people") was to strengthen the defences of his throne. For this purpose he fortified Shechem, the modern Nablûs—which he made his residence till he exchanged it for Tirzah (1 Kings xiv. 17)—and also the ancient Penuel (Gen. xxxii. 30, 31; Judges viii. 8), on the other side Jordan. As the latter place commanded the great caravan-route to Damascus and Palmyra, its fortification would serve the double purpose of establishing the rule of Jeroboam in the territory east of the Jordan, and of protecting the country against incursions from the east and north-east. His next measure, though, as he deemed it, also of a protective character, not only involved the most daring religious innovation ever attempted in Israel, but was fraught with the most fatal consequences to

Jeroboam and to Israel. How deeply Israel had sunk appears alike from the fact that the king acted with the approbation of his advisers [1]— no doubt the representatives of the ten tribes— and that the people, with the exception of the Levites and a minority among the laity, readily acquiesced in the measure. It implied no less than a complete transformation of the religion of Jehovah, and that for a purely political object.

The danger that, if the people regularly resorted to the great festivals at Jerusalem, their allegiance might be won back to their rightful king, who held rule in the God-chosen capital, was too obvious not to have occurred to a mind even less suspicious than that of an Oriental despot, who had gained his throne by rebellion. To cut off this source of dynastic and even personal peril, Jeroboam, with the advice of his council, introduced a complete change in the worship of Israel. In so doing, his contention would probably be, that he had not abolished the ancient religion of the people, only given it a form better suited to present circumstances—one, moreover, derived from primitive national use, and sanctioned by no less an authority than that of Aaron, the first High-priest.[2] It was burdensome and almost impossible to go up to the central Sanctuary at Jerusalem. But there was the ancient symbol of the "golden calf," [3] made by Aaron himself, under which the people had worshipped Jehovah in the wilderness. Appealing, perhaps at the formal consecration of these symbols, to the very words which Aaron had used (Ex. xxxii. 4), Jero-

[1] It has been suggested that the expression (1 Kings xii. 28): "the king took counsel," only refers to deliberation in his own mind. But the view given in the text seems the more rational, consistent, and accordant with the language of the original.

[2] The idea, that these golden calves of Jeroboam were intended as imitations of the cherubim over the ark (*Speaker's Comment.*), is manifestly untenable.

[3] It has been objected, that Jeroboam could not have wished to have recalled to Israel the service of the golden calf in the wilderness, in view of the punishment which followed that sin. But the words and the fact clearly point to it ; and many ways might be found of either ignoring or explaining away the consequences of Israel's conduct at that time.

boam made two golden calves, and located them at the southern
and the northern extremities of the territory of the ten tribes.
This was the more easy, since there were both in the south
and north "sacred" localities, associated in popular opinion
with previous worship. Such in the extreme south was Beth-el
—"the house of God and the gate of heaven"—consecrated
by the twofold appearance of God to Jacob; set apart by
the patriarch himself (Gen. xxviii. 11–19; xxxv. 1, 7, 9–15);
and where of old Samuel had held solemn assemblies (1 Sam.
vii. 16). Similarly, in the extreme north Dan was a "consecrated" place, where "strange worship" may have lingered
from the days of Micah (Judges xviii. 30, 31).

The setting up of the golden calves as the symbol of
Jehovah brought with it other changes. An "house of Bamoth,"
or Temple for the high-place altars, probably with priests'
dwellings attached, was reared. The Levitical priesthood was
extruded, either as inseparably connected with the old worship,
or because it would not conform to the new order of things,
and a new priesthood appointed, not confined to any tribe
or family, but indiscriminately taken from all classes of the
people,[1] the king himself apparently acting, in true heathen
fashion, as Chief Pontiff (1 Kings xii. 32, 33).[2] Lastly, the
great Feast of Tabernacles was transferred from the 7th to the
8th month, probably as a more suitable and convenient time for
a harvest-festival in the northern parts of Palestine, the date
(the 15th) being, however, retained, as that of the full moon.
That this was virtually, and would in practice almost immediately become idolatry, is evident. Indeed, it is expressly
attested in 2 Chron. xi. 15, where the service of the "Calves"
is not only associated with that of the *Bamoth,* or high-place
altars, but even with that of "goats"[3]—the ancient Egyptian

---

[1] Our Authorised Version renders "the lowest of the people." But this
is not implied in the original, which uses an expression conveying the idea
of all ranks and classes, in opposition to the Levites.

[2] This is implied in his offering the incense, which was the highest act
in worship.

[3] So literally, and not "devils," as in our Authorised Version and
according to the Rabbis.

worship of Pan under the form of a goat (Lev. xvii. 7). It
is true, the text does not imply, as our Authorised Version
suggests, that the new priests were taken "from the lowest
of the people." But the emphatic and more detailed repetition
of the mode of their appointment (1 Kings xii. 31, comp. xiii.
33), of which apparently the only condition was to bring an
offering of one young bullock and seven rams (2 Chron. xiii. 9),
enables us to judge on what class of people the conduct of
the religious services must soon have devolved.

A more daring attempt against that God-ordained symbolical
religion, the maintenance of which was the ultimate reason
for Israel's call and existence—so to speak, Israel's very *raison
d'être*—could not be conceived. It was not only an act of gross
disobedience, but, as the sacred text repeatedly notes, a system
devised out of Jeroboam's own heart, when every religious institution in Israel had been God-appointed, symbolical, and forming a unity of which no part could be touched without impairing
the whole. It was a movement which, if we may venture so
to say, called for immediate and unmistakable interposition
from on high. Here, then, if anywhere, we may look for the
miraculous, and that in its most startling manifestation. Nor
was it long deferred.

It was, as we take it, the first occasion on which this new
Feast of Tabernacles was celebrated—perhaps at the same
time also the dedication of the new Temple and the inaugura-
tion of its services. Bethel was in festive array, and thronged
by pilgrims—for no less a personage than the king himself was
to officiate as Chief Pontiff on that occasion. Connecting, as
we undoubtedly should do, the last verse of 1 Kings xii. with
the first of chapter xiii., and rendering it literally, we read that
on this feast which he "made" (*i.e.* of his own devising) "to the
children of Israel," the king "went up on the altar," that is,
up the sloping ascent which led to the circuit around the altar
on which the officiating priest stood. The sacrifices had
already been offered, and their smouldering embers and fat

had mingled with the ashes (1 Kings xiii. 3).[1]   And now the most solemn and central part of the service was reached.   The king went up the inclined plane to the middle of the altar [2] to burn the incense, when he was suddenly arrested, and the worshippers startled by a voice from among the crowd (comp. here the similar event in John vii. 37).   It was a stranger who spoke, and, as we know him, a Judæan, "a man of *Elohim*."   He had come "in [3] the word of Jehovah" (1 Kings xiii. 1)—not merely in charge of it, nor only in its constraining power, but as if the Word of Jehovah itself had come, and this "man of God" been carried in it to deliver the message which he "cried to the altar in the word of Jehovah" (ver. 2).   It was to the spurious and rival altar that he spake, and not to the king—for it was a controversy with spurious worship, and King Jeroboam was as nothing before Jehovah.   That altar, and the policy which had reared it, would be shivered — the altar desecrated,[4] and that by a son of David [5]—whereof he gave

---

[1] 1 Kings xiii. 3, not "ashes," as in the Authorised Version, but "fat" —or rather ashes laden with fat.

[2] Ver. 1 in the original : "Jeroboam stood upon the altar"—this because "going up" the inclined plane to the middle of the altar, he would stand on the circuit of the altar, when laying on it either sacrifices or incense.

[3] So literally.

[4] The most effectual mode of desecration would be by the bones of dead men (comp. Numb. xix. 16).   For the fulfilment of this prediction, see 2 Kings xxiii. 16.

[5] We would put the words in 1 Kings xiii. 2, "Josiah by name," within hyphens, thus : "—Josiah by name—," as not those of the original prophecy, but of the writer of the Book of Kings, being added for the purpose of pointing to the fulfilment of that prediction.   Our reasons for this view are : 1. That there is a similar, and in that case, unquestionable, explanatory addition by the writer in ver. 32, where the "cities of Samaria" are mentioned (see our note below) ; 2. That prophecy never deals in details ; 3. That the present would be the only exception to this rule. For, the mention of Cyrus by name in Isa. xliv. 28 ; xlv. 1, affords no parallel instance, since Cyrus, or Coresh, means "Sun," and may be regarded as the designation (appellation) of the Persian kings, which Cyrus afterwards made his own name (like Augustus Cæsar).   Keil, indeed, argues that Josiah was also an appellative title, meaning "Jehovah supports him"—but this explanation seems, to say the least, strained.   There is no

them immediate symbolic evidence that Jehovah had spoken by his mouth that day,[1] by this "wondrous sight,"[2] that the altar would be rent, and the ashes laden with the fat of the sacrifices poured out. Arrested by this uncompromising announcement from one whom he regarded as a daring fanatical intruder, the king turned quickly round, and stretching out his hand towards him, commanded : "Seize him!" But already a mightier Hand than King Jeroboam's was stretched out. Now, if ever, would Jehovah vindicate His authority, prove His Word, and show before all the people that He, Whose authority they had cast off, was the Living God. Then and there must it be shown, in the idol-temple, at the first consecration of that spurious altar, at the first false feast, and upon King Jeroboam, in the pomp of his splendour and the boastfulness of his supposed power (comp. here Acts xii. 22, 23). The king had put forth his hand, but he could not draw it back : the Hand of the LORD held it. Some mysterious stroke had fallen upon him ; and while he thus stood, himself a sign, the top of the altar suddenly parted, and the ashes, clogged and heavy with the fat of idol-sacrifices, poured out around him. No hand was stretched out to seize the "man of God." Nor was there need of it—the "man of God" had neither design nor desire to escape. Rather was it now the king's turn, not to command but to entreat. In the expressive language of the original : "And the king answered" (to the unspoken word of Jehovah in the stroke that had arrested his hand), "and said,

---

need to suppose that, contrary to the universal canon of prophecy, a prediction would give a name 300 years before the time. Of course, fully believing, as we do, in the reality of prophecy, we admit that this would be quite possible ; but on the grounds mentioned, and on others which will readily suggest themselves, it seems so unlikely, that we have adopted a view, supported, if not suggested, by the reference to Samaria in ver. 32. True and reverent faith in Divine revelation will make us only the more careful in our study of its exact meaning.

[1] 1 Kings xiii. 3 reads : "This is the portent (marvellous sign) that Jehovah hath spoken" (not "which Jehovah hath spoken," as in our Authorised Version).

[2] The Hebrew word means a *marvellous sign.*

Soften now the Face of Jehovah thy God, and make entreaty on my behalf, and " (or, that) " my hand shall return to me."

It was as he craved—for the prophecy and controversy were not with the king, but with the Altar. And all this had been only a sign, which had fulfilled its purpose, and would fulfil it still more, if the same Power that had appeared in the sudden stroke would again become manifest in its equally sudden removal. As for Jeroboam, Jehovah had no contro- versy with him then and there, nor indeed anywhere. The judgment of his sins would soon enough overtake him and his house. It might, indeed, seem passing strange that the king could now invite this "man of God" to his palace and table, and even promise him "a reward," if we did not bear in mind the circumstances of the times, and the heathen idea of miracles. To the heathen the miraculous, as direct Divine manifestation, was not something extraordinary and unexpected. Heathenism—may we not say, the ancient world ?—*expected* the miraculous ; and hence in those times God's manifestation by miracles might almost be designated not as an extraordinary, but, according to the then notions, as the ordinary mode of teaching. Moreover, heathenism regarded miracles as simply manifestations of *power*, and the worker of miracles as a magician, possessed of power—the question being, whether the power of the deity whom he represented was greater than that of other gods, or not. It was, no doubt, in this light that Jeroboam regarded this "man of *Elohim*"—the name Elohim itself expressing especially "*power*." [1] This, as well as know- ledge of the character of his own "prophets," and perhaps a secret hope that he might attach him to himself by a "reward," prompted the words of the king. He would do honour to the man of power, and, through him, to the deity whom he repre- sented—perhaps even gain the man of God. [2]

[1] In contradistinction to *Jehovah*, which added the idea of the *covenant* to that of power.

[2] I prefer this to the view that Jeroboam's conduct was merely prompted by the wish to nullify the effect upon the people. Such a motive seems, psychologically, unlikely in the circumstances.

It need scarcely be said, that the mere fact of the "man of God" entering the king's palace and sharing his feast—probably a sacrificial idol-feast—would not only have been contrary to the whole scope and spirit of his embassy, but have destroyed the moral effect of the scene enacted before the people. So, to mention a much lower parallelism, is the moral effect of all Christian testimony, whether by word or life, annulled by every act of conformity to, and fellowship with the world (comp. Rom. xii. 1, 2). But in the present instance any danger of this kind had by anticipation been averted. God had given His messenger express command, neither to eat bread nor to drink water in that place, nor even to return by the way that he had come. These directions had, of course, a much deeper and symbolical meaning. They indicated that Bethel lay under the ban; that no fellowship of any kind was to be held with it; and that even the way by which the messenger of God had come, was to be regarded as consecrated, and not to be retraced.[1] In the discharge of the commission entrusted to him, the "man of God," who had "come in the word of Jehovah," was to consider himself as an impersonal being—till he was beyond the place to which, and the road by which he had been sent. Whatever view, therefore, we may take of his after-conduct, it cannot at least surprise us, that at that moment no earthly temptation could have induced him to accept the king's offer (1 Kings xiii. 8, 9).

Yet, as we think of it, the answer of the "man of God" seems to us disappointing. It is like that of Balaam to the messengers of Balak (Numb. xxii. 13, 18), and yet we know that all along his heart was with them, and that he afterwards yielded to their solicitations, to his own destruction. We would have expected more from the "man of God" than a mere recital of his orders—some expression of feeling like that of Daniel under analogous circumstances (Dan. v. 17). But, in repeating

---

[1] The general explanation, that this was added, in order that it should not be known what route he took, so that he might be fetched back, needs no refutation.

before all the people the express command which God had given him, the "man of God," like Balaam of old, also pronounced his own necessary doom, if he swerved from the injunction laid upon him. He had borne testimony—and by the testimony of his own mouth he must be content to be judged; he was quite certain of the command which God had laid upon him, and by that certainty he must abide.

And at first it seemed as if he would have done so. His message delivered, he left Bethel by another way than that which he had come. Among his astonished audience that day had been the sons of an old resident in Bethel, whose real character it is not easy to read.[1] In the sacred narrative he is throughout designated as *Navi*, or Prophet (literally: one who "wells forth"), while the Divine messenger from Judah is always described as "man of Elohim"—a distinction which must have its meaning. On their return from the idol-temple, the eldest of his sons[2] described to the old prophet the scene which they had witnessed. Inquiring from them what road the "man of God" had taken—which they, and probably many others had watched[3]—he hastily rode after him, and overtook him. The "man of Elohim" was resting under "the terebinth"—apparently a well-known spot where travellers were wont to unlade their beasts of burden, and to halt for shelter and repose (a kind of "Travellers' Rest"). Repeating the invitation of Jeroboam, he received the same answer as the king. There could be even less hesitation now, since the "man of God" had actually left Bethel, nor could he possibly have

[1] See the remarks further on.

[2] In the second clause of ver. 11 the singular is used, "his son," not, as in our Authorised Version, "sons." The plural which follows shows, however, that several sons were present, though one was the spokesman. From the presence of the "old prophet" in Bethel, and that of Ahijah in Shiloh, we infer that, if there was a migration of pious laity into the territory of Rehoboam—which, however, is *not* expressly stated in 2 Chron. xi. 16—it must have been that of a minority.

[3] This disposes of the argument quoted in the previous page as to the reason why the "man of God" was to return by another road.

deemed it right to return thither. Upon this the old prophet addressed him as a colleague, and falsely pretended, not indeed that Jehovah, but that "*an angel* in the word of Jehovah," had directed him to fetch him back, when the other immediately complied. As the two sat at table in Bethel, suddenly "the word of Jehovah was upon the prophet [1] who had brought him back." Because he had "resisted (rebelled against) the mouth of Jehovah, and not kept the commandment which Jehovah had commanded him," [2] his dead body should not come into the sepulchre [3] of his fathers. Startling as such an announce. ment must have been, it would set two points vividly before him : his disobedience and his impending punishment—the latter very real, according to the views prevailing at the time (Gen. xlvii. 30; xlix. 29; l. 25; 2 Sam. xix. 37, etc.), although not implying either immediate or even violent death. It is very surprising to us—and indicative of the absence of the higher moral and spiritual elements — that this announce- ment was not followed by any expression of sorrow or repent- ance, but that the meal seems to have continued uninter- rupted to the end. Did the old prophet seem to the other only under an access of ecstatic frenzy? Did the fact that he announced not immediate death blunt the edge of his message? Had disobedience to the Divine command carried as its consequence immediate spiritual callousness? Or had the return of the "man of God" to Bethel after all been the result of a deeper estrangement from God, of which the first manifestation had already appeared in what we have described as his strangely insufficient answer to Jeroboam's invitation and offer? These are necessarily only suggestions—and yet it seems to us as if all these elements had been present and at work to bring about the final result.

[1] So literally.   [2] So literally.
[3] The sepulchres in Palestine were not like ours, but generally rock- hewn, and consisted of an ante-chamber and an inner cave in which the bodies were deposited in niches—the entrance to the sepulchre being guarded by a stone. For details, comp. *Sketches of Jewish Social Life in the Days of Christ*, p. 171.

The meal was past, and the "old prophet" saddled his ass to convey his guest to his destination. But the end of the journey was never reached. As some travellers were passing that way, they saw an unwonted spectacle which must have induced them to hasten on their journey. Close by the roadside lay a dead body, and beside it stood the ass [1] which the unhappy man had ridden—both guarded, as it were, by the lion, who had killed the man, evidently by the weight of his paw as he knocked him down,[2] without, however, rending him, or attempting to feed on his carcase. Who the dead man was, the travellers seem not to have known, nor would they, of course, pause by the road. On passing through Bethel—which from the narrative does not seem to have been their ultimate destination, but the first station which they reached—they naturally "talked in the town" about what they had just seen in its neighbourhood. When the rumour reached the "old prophet," he immediately understood the meaning of all. Riding to the spot, he reverently carried home with him the dead body of the "man of God," mourned over, and buried him in his own sepulchre, marking the place by a monumental pillar to distinguish this from other tombs, and to keep the event in perpetual remembrance. But to his sons he gave solemn direction to lay him in the same tomb—in the rock-niche by the side of that in which the "man of God" rested. This was to be a dying testimony to "the man of God:" that his embassy of God had been real, and that surely the "thing would be" (that it would happen) "which he had cried in the word of Jehovah against the altar which (was) at Bethel, and against all the *Bamoth*-houses which (are)[3] in the cities of Samaria." With this

[1] From 2 Kings ii. 24 we gather, that the forest around Bethel was the haunt of wild beasts. It will be easily understood, that it was almost necessary the lion should remain by the dead body, alike to show the Divine character of the judgment, and to induce the passers-by to make haste on their journey.

[2] This is clearly implied by the word "broken" in 1 Kings xiii. 26, marginal rendering.

[3] So literally. The reference to the other *Bamoth*-houses, besides those of Bethel and Dan, is, of course, prophetic.

profession of faith in the truth of Jehovah's message, and in the power of the LORD certainly to bring it to pass at some future time, would the old prophet henceforth live. With it would he die and be buried—laying his bones close to those of the "man of God," sharing his grave, and nestling, as it were, for shelter in the shadow of that great Reality which "the man of God" had cast over Bethel. So would he, in life and death, speak of, and cling to Jehovah—as the True and the Living God.

More than three hundred years later, and nearly a century had passed since the children of Israel had been carried away from their homes. *Then* it was that what, centuries before, the "man of God" had foretold, became literally true (2 Kings xxiii. 15-18). The idol-temple, in which Jeroboam had stood in his power and glory on that opening day, was burned by Josiah; the *Bamoth* were cast down; and on that altar, to defile it, they gathered from the neighbouring sepulchres the bones of its former worshippers, and burned them there. Yet in their terrible search of vengeance one monument arrested their attention. They asked of them at Bethel. It marked the spot where the bones of "the man of God" and of his host the "old prophet" of Samaria [1] lay. And they reverently left the bones in their resting-places, side by side—as in life, death, and burial, so still and for aye witnesses to Jehovah; and safe in their witness-bearing. But three centuries and more between the prediction and the final fulfilment: and in that time symbolic rending of the altar, changes, wars, final ruin, and desolation! And still the word seemed to slumber all those centuries of silence, before it was literally fulfilled. There is something absolutely overawing in this absence of all haste on the part of God, in this certainty of the final event, with apparent utter unconcern of what may

---

[1] The mention of Samaria here and in 1 Kings xiii. 32 must have been explanatory additions by the writer, since Samaria was only built by Omri (1 Kings xvi. 24). This, of course, confirms the view we have expressed about the mention of the name of Josiah. It need scarcely be stated, that this in no way invalidates the truthfulness of the narrative, but rather confirms it.

happen during the long centuries that intervene, which makes us tremble as we realise how much of buried seed of warning or of promise may sleep in the ground, and how unexpectedly, but how certainly, it will ripen as in one day into a harvest of judgment or of mercy.

But too many questions and lessons are involved in this history to pass it without further study. Who was this "old prophet?" was he a true prophet of Jehovah? and why did he thus "lie" to the destruction of the "man of God?" Again, why was such severe punishment meted out to the "man of God?" did he deserve any for what might have been only an error of judgment? and why did his tempter and seducer apparently escape all punishment? To begin with the old "prophet" of Bethel—we do not regard him as simply a false prophet, whose object it was to seduce "the man of God," either from jealousy or to destroy the effect of his mission.[1] On the other hand, it seems equally incorrect to speak of him as a true prophet of God, roused from sinful conformity with those around by the sudden appearance of the Judæan messenger of Jehovah, and anxious to recover himself by fellowship with "the man of God," even if that intercourse could only be secured by means of a falsehood.[2] Nor would we describe his conduct as intended to try the steadfast obedience of the "man of God." The truth seems to lie between these extreme opinions. Putting aside the general question of heathen divination, which we have not sufficient materials satisfactorily to answer, it is at least certain that not every *Navi* was a prophet of Jehovah. That God should have sent a message through one who was not His prophet, need not surprise us when we recall the history of Balaam. Moreover, it was peculiarly appropriate, that the announcement of guilt and punishment should come to the "man of God" through the person who had misled him by false pretence

---

[1] This, in one form or another, is the view of Josephus, the Targum, and of most of the Rabbinical and Christian commentators.

[2] So Ephr. Syr., Theodor., Witsius, Hengstenberg, Keil, and Bähr.

of an angelic command, and at the very meal to which the
" man of God" should never have sat down. Again, it is
evident that, from the moment he heard of the scene in
the idol-temple, the " old prophet" believed in the genuine-
ness and authority of the message brought to Bethel. Every
stage in the history deepened this conviction, till at last it
became, so to speak, the fundamental fact of his religious
life, which must have determined his whole after-conduct.
May it not have been that this " old *Navi*" was one of
the fruits of the " Schools of the Prophets "—the prophetic
order having apparently been widely revived during the later
part of Solomon's reign? Settling in Bethel (as Lot in
Sodom), he may have gradually lapsed into toleration of
evil—as the attendance of his children in the idol-temple
seems to imply—without, however, surrendering his character,
perhaps his office of " Prophet," the more so as the service
of Jehovah might be supposed to be only altered in form, not
abolished, by the adoption of the symbol of the Golden Calves.
In that case his immediate recognition of the " man of God,"
and his deepening conviction may be easily understood ; his
earnest desire to claim and have fellowship with a direct
messenger of God seems natural ; and even his unscrupulous
use of falsehood is accounted for.

These considerations will help to show that there was an
essential difference between him and "the man of God,"
and that the punishment which overtook the latter bears
no possible relation to the apparent impunity of the " old
prophet." That terrible judgment ought to be viewed from
two different points : as it were, absolutely—from heaven
downwards ; and relatively to the person whom it overtook
—from earth heavenwards. The most superficial consideration will convince, that, from the nature of the case, the
authority of God must have been vindicated, and that by a
patent and terrible judgment, if the object and meaning of
the message which He had sent were not to be nullified.
When " the man of God " publicly proclaimed in the temple

the terms which God had prescribed, he pronounced his own sentence in case of disobedience. Besides, the main idea underlying the Divine employment of such messengers was that of their absolute and unquestioning execution of the exact terms of their commission. This essential condition of the prophetic office it was the more necessary to vindicate in Bethel, as also at the commencement of a period marked by a succession of prophets in Israel, who, in the absence of the God-ordained services, were to keep alive the knowledge of Jehovah, and, by their warnings and teaching, to avert, if possible, the catastrophe of national judgment which would overtake apostate Israel.

As regards "the man of God" himself, we have already noticed the increasing spiritual callousness, consequent upon his first unfaithfulness. But putting this aside, surely there never could have been any serious question in his mind as to his duty. By his own testimony, he had received express and unmistakable command of God, which Scripture again and again repeats, for the sake of emphasis; and his conduct should have been guided on the plain principle, that an obvious and known duty can never be set aside by another seeming duty. Besides, what evidence had he that an angel had really spoken to the "old prophet;" or even that his tempter was a "prophet" at all, or, if a prophet, acted in the prophetic spirit? All these points are so obvious, that the conduct of the "man of God" would seem almost incredible, if we did not recall how often in every-day life we are tempted to turn aside from the plain demands of right and duty by a false call in contravention to it. In all moral and spiritual questions it is ever most dangerous to reason: simple obedience and not argument is the only safe path (comp. here Gal. i. 8). One duty can never contravene another—and the plainly known and clear command of God must silence all side-questions.

Viewing the conduct of the "man of God" as a fall and a sin, all becomes plain. He had publicly announced his duty, and he had publicly contravened it; and his punishment was, through the remarkable, though not miraculous, circumstances [1] under which it overtook him, equally publicly known. Throughout the whole history there is, so to speak, a remarkable equipoise in the circumstances of his sin and of his punishment, as also in the vindication of God's authority. And yet even so, the moral effect of God's message was apparently weakened through the sin of His messenger. So terribly fatal in their consequences are our sins, even when publicly punished. For it is scarcely possible to believe that, had it not been so, Jeroboam would "after this thing" have uninterruptedly continued his former course of defiance of the authority of God. But here the history also turns from Israel to its wretched king, and in a narrative of deepest pathos shows us at the same time the punishment of his sin, and the wonderful tenderness of God's dealings towards those who, in the midst of greatest temptations, have kept their hearts true to Him, and are preserved by His mercy from the evil to come. And most comforting is it to know that God has and keeps His own—even though it be in the family of a Jeroboam, and that true piety finds its respectful acknowledgment, even among a people so sunken as was Israel at that time.

If it were necessary to show how unhappiness and sin go hand in hand, the history about to be told would furnish ample evidence of it. The main reason of its insertion in the Biblical record is, of course, that it gave occasion to announce the Divine punishment upon the race of Jeroboam, as having traversed the fundamental condition on which the possibility of the new dynasty rested (1 Kings xi. 38). At the same time, it seems also to cast an important side-light on the transaction between Ahijah the prophet and Jeroboam, when the former first announced to him his future elevation to the kingdom (1 Kings xi. 29–39). Keil renders 1 Kings xiv. 7 : "Thus saith Jehovah, the God of Israel: Therefore, because thou hast

---

[1] It is well known that lions do not prey upon dead bodies, except through stress of hunger.

elevated thyself from amongst the people, and I have given thee ruler over My people Israel " If this rendering is correct, it would imply that his elevation, or leadership of Israel, was in the first place entirely Jeroboam's own act, and that, having so elevated himself and assumed the leadership, God afterwards bestowed on him the rule to which he aspired, leaving for future trial the fitness of his race for the kingdom.

But, besides the higher Divine meaning of this history, it possesses also a deep human interest. It gives us a glimpse into the inner family-life of the wretched king, as, divested of crown and purple, and having cast aside state-craft and religious falsehood, he staggers under a sore blow. For once we see the man, not the king, and, as each man appears truest, when stricken to the heart by a sorrow which no earthly power can turn aside. From Shechem the royal residence had been transferred to the ancient Canaanite city (Josh. xii. 24) Tirzah, the beautiful (Cant. vi. 4), two hours to the north of Samaria, amidst cultivated fruit-and-olive-clad hills, up on a swelling height, with glorious outlook over the hills and valleys of rich Samaria.[1] The royal palace seems to have stood at the entering in of the city (comp. 1 Kings xiv. 17 with ver. 12). But within its stately apartments reigned silence and sorrow. Abijah, Jeroboam's son, and apparently the intended successor to his throne, lay sick. He seems like the last link that bound Jeroboam to his former better self. The very name of the child—*Abijah,* " Jehovah is my Father," or else " my Desire "—indicates this, even if it were not for the touching notice, that in him was " found a good thing towards Jehovah, the God of Israel, in the house of Jeroboam " (ver. 13) We can conceive how this " good thing " may have sprung up; but to keep and to cause it to grow in such surroundings, surely needed the gracious tending of the Good Husbandman. It was the one green spot in Jeroboam's life and home; the

[1] The fullest description is that in Guérin's *Samarie,* tome i., pp. 365-368. It is the modern *Thallusah* : comp. Böttger, *Topogr. Histor. Lex. zu Flavius Josephus,* p. 243.

one germ of hope. And as his father loved him truly, so all Israel had set their hopes on him. Upon the inner life of this child—its struggles and its victories—lies the veil of Scripture-silence ; and best that it should be so. But now his pulses were beating quick and weak, and that life of love and hope seemed fast ebbing. None with the father in those hours of darkness—neither counsellor, courtier, prophet, nor priest—save the child's mother. As they two kept sad watch, helpless and hopeless, the past, to which this child bound him, must have come back to Jeroboam. One event in it chiefly stood out : it was his first meeting with Ahijah the Shilonite. That was a true prophet—bold, uncompromising withal. With that impulse of despair which comes upon men in their agony, when all the delusions of a misspent life are swept away, he turned to the opening of his life, so full of hope and happy possibility, ere ambition had urged him upon the path of reckless sacrifice of all that had been dearest and holiest ; ere unlimited possession had dazzled his sight and the sound of flattery deafened his ears. As to Saul of old on the eve of that fatal battle, when God and man had become equally silent to him, the figure of Samuel had stood out—that which to us might seem the most unlikely he could have wished to encounter—so now to Jeroboam that of Ahijah. Could he have wished to blot out, as it were, all that had intervened, and to stand before the prophet as on the day when first he met him, when great but not yet unholy thoughts rose within him ? Had he some unspoken hope of him who had first announced to him his reign ? Or did he only in sheer despair long to know what would come to the child, even though he were to learn the worst ? Be this as it may, he must have word from Ahijah, whatever it might be.

In that hour he has no friend nor helper save the mother of his child. She must go, in her love, to the old prophet in Shiloh. But how dare she, Jeroboam's wife, present herself there ? Nay, the people also must not know what or whither her errand was. And so she must disguise herself as a poor

woman, carrying with her, indeed, as customary, a gift to
the prophet, but one such as only the poorest in the land would
offer.   While alone and in humble disguise the wife of Jeroboam goes on her heavy embassy, across the hills of Samaria,
past royal Shechem, Another has already brought her message
to Shiloh.   No need for the queen to disguise herself, so far
as Ahijah was concerned, since age had blinded his eyes.
But Jehovah had spoken to His aged servant, and charged
him concerning this matter.   And as he heard the sound of
her feet within the door, he knew who his unseen visitor was,
and addressed her not as queen but as the wife of Jeroboam.
Stern, terrible things they were which he was commissioned
to tell her ; and with unswerving faithfulness and unbending
truth he spake them, though his heart must have bled within
him as he repeated what himself called "hard *tidings.*"[1]   All
the more deeply must the aged prophet have felt them, that
it was he who had announced to Jeroboam his future elevation.
They concerned Jeroboam ; but they also touched every heart-
string in the wife and the mother, and must well nigh have torn
each one of them as they swept across her.   First :[2] an uncompromising recital of the past, and a sternly true representation
of the present—all glare, dazzle, and self-delusion dispelled, till
it stood in naked reality before her.   Only two persons are in
this picture, Jehovah and Jeroboam—all else is in the far
background.   That is enough ; and now once in full sight of
those two persons, the wife, the mother, must hear it all, though
her ears tingle and her knees tremble.   Not this child only,
but every child, nay, every descendant, down to the meanest,
whether it be child or adult[3]—swept away : " And I will sweep

[1]   In the original it is simply "*hard.*"
[2]   Commentators have noted in the ten verses of Ahijah's message
(vers. 7-16) a rhythmic arrangement, viz., twice 5 verses—the first stanza
(vers. 7-11) consisting of 3 + 2, the last stanza (vers. 12-16) of 2 + 3
verses.
[3]   This seems to be the correct meaning of a proverbial expression which
scarcely occurs except during the period from the time of David to that
of Jehu.

out after the house of Jeroboam, as one sweepeth out dirt till it is quite gone" (1 Kings xiv. 10).[1] And not only this, but also horrible judgment; the carcases of her children lying like carrion in street and on field, their flesh torn and eaten by the wild, unclean dogs that prowl about, or picked from their limbs by birds of prey who swoop round them with hoarse croaking.[2] Thus far for Jeroboam. And now as for the child that lay sick in the palace of Tirzah—it shall be in God's keeping, removed from the evil to come. As her feet touched the threshold of her doomed home, it would die. As it were, such heavy tidings shall not be brought within where he sleeps; its terrors shall not darken his bed. Before they can reach him, he shall be beyond their shadow and in the light. But around that sole-honoured grave all Israel shall be the mourners, and God Himself wills to put this mark of honour upon His one child in that now cursed family. Lastly, as for apostate Israel, another king raised up to execute the judgment of God—nay, all this not merely in the dim future, but the scene seems to shift, and the prophet sees it already in the present.[3] Israel shaken as a reed in the water by wind and waves; Israel uprooted from their land,—cast away and scattered among the heathen beyond the river, and given up to be trampled under foot. Such is the end of the sins of Jeroboam and of his people; such, in the bold figure of Scripture, is the sequel of casting Jehovah "behind their back."[4]

Of the further course of this history we know no more.

[1] This is the literal, and, as will be perceived, much more forcible rendering.

[2] Comp. here Exod. xx. 4, 5; Deut. xxviii. 26. Even the alteration of this latter passage in 1 Kings xiv. 11 is in favour of the earlier age of the Book of Deuter.—since the addition about the "dogs" points to Eastern *town*-life, where the wild dogs act as scavengers of cities.

[3] The words of the original are somewhat difficult to render on account of the abruptness of the speech; but the above, which corresponds with our Authorised Version, gives the correct meaning.

[4] It is remarkable, that the same strong expression occurs only in Ezek. xxiii. 35, in reference to the same sin of apostate Judah as followed by the same punishment as that of Israel.

The queen and mother went back, stricken, to her home; and it was as the prophet had told her from Jehovah. And this literal fulfilment would be to her for ever afterwards the terrible pledge of what was yet to come.

Nor do we read any more of Jeroboam. It almost seems as if Holy Scripture had nothing further to say of him—not even concerning his later and disastrous war with the son of Rehoboam (2 Chron. xiii. 2-20). That is told in connection with the reign of the second king of Judah. Of Jeroboam we only read that he "reigned two and twenty years," that "he slept with his fathers," and that "Nadab his son reigned in his stead."[1]

---

[1] We subjoin the following as the most interesting of the Rabbinical notices about Jeroboam (comp. the *Nachalath Shimoni*, vol. i., p. 37, *b* and *c*) : The name of Jeroboam is explained as "making contest among the people," either in reference to their relationship to God, or as between Israel and Judah (*Sanh.* 101, *b*). His father Nebat is identified with Micah, and even with Sheba, the son of Bichri (*Sanh.* ib.). The Talmud records various legendary accounts of Jeroboam's quarrel with Solomon, in which the former appears more in the right (*Sanh.* ib.), although he is blamed alike for the public expression of his feelings and for his rebellion. That rebellion is regarded as the outward manifestation of long-existing disunion. The government of Jeroboam is looked upon as distinguished by firmness, and he is praised for his wisdom, which had given rise to great hope. Pride is stated to have been the reason of his apostasy from God (*Sanh.* 102 *a*). The promise to Jacob in Gen. xxxv. 11, "Kings shall come out of thee," is applied in *Bereshith R.* 82 (ed. Warsh. p. 146, *b*), to Jeroboam; but he is regarded as not having share in the world to come. Seven such are mentioned : three kings—Jeroboam, Ahab, and Manasseh, and four private persons—Balaam, Doeg, Ahithophel, and Gehazi (*Sanh.* 90, *a*). He is also mentioned among those who are condemned eternally to Gehenna in *Rosh ha-Shanah*, 17, *a*.

CHAPTER XII.

ABIJAH AND ASA (2*nd* & 3*rd*) KINGS OF JUDAH.

*Accession of Abijah—His Idolatry—War between Judah and Israel—Abijah's
Address to Israel and Victory—Deaths of Jeroboam and of Abijah—
Accession of Asa—Religious Reformation in Judah—Invasion by Zerah
the Ethiopian—Victory of Zephathah—Azariah's Message to the Army
of Asa—Great Sacrificial Feast at Jerusalem—Renewal of the Covenant
with Jehovah.*

(1 KINGS XV. 1–15; 2 CHRON. XIII.–XV.)

JEROBOAM did not only survive Rehoboam, but he witnessed
the accession of two other kings of Judah, Abijah
and Asa. The reign of Abijah [1] was very brief. Both in
1 Kings xv. 2 and in 2 Chron. xiii. 2 it is said to have lasted
three years—an expression which must be understood according
to this canon laid down by the Rabbis, that the commencement of a year in the reign of a king is to be reckoned as
a full year. Thus, as Abijah ascended the throne in the
eighteenth (1 Kings xv. 1), and Asa in the twentieth (ver. 9)
year of Jeroboam's reign, it follows that the former actually
reigned only somewhat over two years. Two things are
specially noticed concerning Abijah: his relation towards
Jehovah (in 1 Kings xv. 3–5), and his relation to the kingdom
of Jeroboam (2 Chron. xiii. 2–20).

To begin with the former. It is stated that "he walked in

---

[1] *Abijah*—"my father Jehovah!" Two other forms of the name occur.
In the Book of Kings he is always called *Abijam*, while in 2 Chron. xiii. 21
he is also designated (in the Hebrew) *Abijahu*. Probably *Abijam* (in
1 Kings) was the older form—and it is not impossible that it may have
been altered into *Abijah*, when that monarch made his loud profession of
Jehovahism (2 Chron. xiii. 4, etc.).

all the sins of his father," and that "his heart was not perfect with Jehovah his God." These two statements are not explanatory of, but supplementary to, each other. We know that Rehoboam had not abolished the service of Jehovah (see, for example, 1 Kings xiv. 28), but that, by its side, a spurious worship had been tolerated, if not encouraged, which, in the view of Holy Scripture, was equal to idolatry. In this matter Rehoboam had not only followed the example of his father Solomon, during his later years, but greatly increased the evil which had then begun. A similar remark applies to the reign of Abijah, as compared with that of Rehoboam. That the idolatry of the reign of Rehoboam had grown both worse in character and more general in practice under that of Abijah, appears from the notices of the reformation instituted by his successor, Asa. The former circumstance is implied in the terms by which the idolatry of that period is described (2 Chron. xiv. 3, 5), and by the circumstance that "the queen-mother" (Maachah, Abijah's mother and Asa's grandmother),[1] who under Abijah held the official rank of *Gevirah*, "Queen" (the modern *Sultana Valide*), had made and set up "a horror for Asherah"[2]—some horrible wooden representation, equally vile and idolatrous in its character. Again, that idolatry had become more widely spread, and that its hold was stronger, we infer from the fact that, despite Asa's example, admonitions, and exertions (2 Chron. xiv. 4, 5), "the high places did not cease" (1 Kings xv. 14). This progressive spiritual decline under the reigns of Solomon, Rehoboam, and Abijah was so marked as to have deserved the removal of the family of David from the throne, had it not been for God's faithfulness to His covenant-promises (1 Kings xv. 4, 5). But, although such

[1] As Maachah, the daughter (granddaughter) of Abishalom (Absalom) was the mother of Abijah, she must have been the grandmother of Asa. She is designated as "Queen," or rather (in the original) as *Gevirah*, which is an *official* title.

[2] It is needless to inquire into the nameless abominations connected with what the original designates as a "horror," rendered in the Authorised Version "idol."

was the state of religion, Abijah not only made loud profession of the worship of Jehovah, but even brought votive
offerings to the Temple, probably of part of the spoil taken
in war (1 Kings xv. 15 ; comp. 2 Chron. xiii. 16–19).

Concerning the relations of Judah to the neighbouring kingdom of Israel, it may be said that the chronic state of warfare
which had existed during the time of Rehoboam now changed
into one of open hostilities. Two reasons for this may be given.
Abijah was a much more vigorous ruler than his father, and
the power of Egypt, on which Jeroboam relied for support,
seems at that time to have decreased. This we gather, not
only from the non-interference of Egypt in the war between
Abijah and Jeroboam, but from the fact that, when Egypt at
length sought to recover its lost ascendancy, it was under
the rule of Zerah the Ethiopian (probably Osorkon ii.), who
was not the son, but the son-in-law, of the preceding monarch
(2 Chron. xiv. 9) ; and we know the fate that overtook the
huge, undisciplined army which Zerah led.

The language of the sacred narrative (2 Chron. xiii. 2, 3)
implies, that the war between Judah and Israel was begun
by Abijah. On both sides a levy of all capable of bearing arms
was raised, though, so far as the numerical strength of the
two armies was concerned, the response seems not to have
been so universal in Judah as in Israel.[1] But perhaps the

---

[1] The numbers : 400,000 for Judah, 800,000 for Israel, and 500,000
killed, have always seemed a difficulty. Bishop Kennicott and others
have regarded these numerals as a copyist's mistake. But it seems difficult
to imagine three consecutive errors in copying. Professor Rawlinson
(in the *Speaker's Commentary*, vol. iii., p. 306) thinks, that both the
combatants and the slain represent those engaged throughout the whole
war. But this scarcely removes the difficulty. Two points may help our
better understanding of the matter, though we would only suggest them
hypothetically. First, comparing these numbers with more exact numerical details, as in 2 Chron. v.–vii., and xii., they read rather like what
might be called "round numbers" than as precise numeration. Secondly,
comparing these numbers with the census under King David (2 Sam.
xxiv. 9), we find that the number of the Israelites is exactly the same in
both cases, while that of Judah is larger by 100,000 in the census of David

seeming discrepancy may be explained by the necessity of leaving strong garrisons in the south to watch the Egyptian frontier (comp. 2 Chron. xiv. 9). The two armies met at the boundary of the two kingdoms, though, as we judge, within the territory of Israel. They camped in close proximity, only separated by Mount Zemaraim,[1] a height to the east of Bethel and some distance north of Jericho, forming part of the ridge known as "Mount Ephraim," which stretched from the plain of Esdraelon southwards. From this height Abijah addressed the army of Israel just before the battle began, in the hope of securing their voluntary submission, or at least weakening their resistance. Ignoring all that told against himself,[2] Abijah tried to impress on his opponents that right was wholly on his side.[3] In language full of irony he set before them their weakness, as the necessary result of their apostasy from Jehovah, the God of their fathers, and of their adoption of a worship neither conformable to their ancient faith nor even respectable in the sight of men. Lastly, he loudly protested that, since Judah had gone to war under the leadership of Jehovah and in the manner appointed by Him, Israel was really fighting against Jehovah, the God of their fathers, and could not expect success. Whatever hollowness there may have been in this profession on the part of Abijah, it was at least the true war-cry of Israel which he raised. It found an echo in the hearts

---

than in the army of Abijah, though it included Benjamin. If we assume that Abijah invaded Israel with a regular army — "began the war with an army of war-heroes," and that in defence Jeroboam raised a levy of all capable of bearing arms, we can understand the use of these "round numbers," derived from a previous census. In that case the number of the slain would represent rather the proportion of those who fell during the war than a numerically exact statement.

[1] The *Semaron* of Josephus (*Ant.* viii. 11, 2), probably the modern *Kharbet-es-Somera* (Guerin, *La Samarie*, vol. i. pp. 226, 227; vol. ii. p. 175). But this localisation is by no means certain.

[2] Such as the conditions of David's royalty (Ps. cxxxii. 12), the sin of Solomon, the folly and sin of Rehoboam, and his own unfaithfulness to the LORD.

[3] "A covenant of salt"—comp. Lev. ii. 13; Numb. xviii. 19.

of his followers. In vain Jeroboam, by a cleverly executed movement, attacked Judah both in front and rear. The terror excited by finding themselves surrounded only led the people to cry unto Jehovah (2 Chron. xiii. 14), and He was faithful to His promise (Numb. x. 9). The shout of the combatants mingled with the blast of the priests' trumpets, as Judah rushed to the attack. Israel fled in wild disorder, and a terrible carnage ensued. The fugitives were followed by the army of Judah, and Abijah recovered from Israel the border-cities,[1] with the districts around them. In consequence of this victory the power of Jeroboam was henceforth on the wane, and that of Abijah in the ascendancy Not long afterwards Jehovah struck Jeroboam, either suddenly or with lingering disease, of which he died. He had, however, survived his rival, Abijah,[2] for more than two years.

Abijah was succeeded on the throne of Judah by his son, Asa, probably at the time a boy of only ten or eleven years.[3] This may in part account for his pious up-bringing, as, during his minority he would be chiefly under the official guardianship of the High-priest (comp. 2 Chron. xxii. 12). It also explains how a bold, resolute woman, such as Maachah, could still retain her official position as *Gevirah*, or "queen-mother," till, on attaining majority, the young king commenced his religious reformation. During the first ten years of Asa's reign the land had rest (2 Chron. xiv. 1). While devoutly acknowledging the goodness of God in this, it is easy to understand the outward circumstances by which it was brought about. The

---

[1] The localisation of "Jeshanah" and "Ephrain" has not been satisfactorily made out. But in all probability these towns were not at a great distance from Bethel.

[2] The expression (2 Chron. xiii. 21): "Abijah waxed mighty," or rather "strengthened himself," may also refer to his league with Syria (2 Chron. xvi. 3). The notice of his wives and children includes, of course, an earlier period of his life.

[3] If Rehoboam was twenty-one years old at his accession, and reigned eighteen years, and then after two or three years was followed by his grandson, the latter could scarcely have been more than ten or eleven years old.

temporary weakness of Egypt, the defeat of Jeroboam, and an alliance which Abijah seems to have contracted with Syria (2 Chron. xvi. 3), as well as afterwards the rapid succession of rival dynasties in Israel, sufficiently explain it.   For, during his long reign of forty-one years, Asa saw no fewer than seven kings ascend the throne of Israel.[1]   The first work which Asa took in hand was a thorough religious reformation ; his next, the strengthening of the defences of the country.   For this the temporary state of security prevailing offered a happy opportunity—" the land " being " still before them "—open and free from every enemy, though it was not difficult to foresee that such would not long be the case.   And, as king and people owned that this time of rest had been granted them by Jehovah, so their preparations [2] against future attacks were carried on in dependence upon Him.   The period of trial came only too soon.

An almost countless [3] Egyptian host, under the leadership of Zerah,[4] the Ethiopian, swarmed into Judah.   Advancing by the south-west, through the border of the Philistines, who, no doubt, made common cause with the Egyptians (2 Chron. xiv. 14), they appeared before Mareshah (comp. Josh. xv. 44). This was one of the border fortresses which Jeroboam had built (2 Chron. xi. 8).   The natural capabilities of the place and its situation, so near the south-western angle of the country, and almost midway between Hebron and Ashdod, must have marked it as one of the most important strategical points in the Jewish line of defensive works against Philistia, or rather,

[1] At his accession Jeroboam reigned in Israel.   The other seven were : Nadab, Baasha, Elah, Zimri, Tibni, Omri, and Ahab.   These seven kings represented four rival dynasties.

[2] Evidently all the males capable of bearing weapons were trained to arms.   The proportion of Benjamin relatively to Judah, though great, is not excessive (comp. Gen. xlix. 27).

[3] We regard these numerals also as round numbers.

[4] Brügsch regards Zerah not as Osorkon, but as an independent Ethiopian monarch.   But there is no evidence in support of this hypothesis.

against Egypt.[1] About two miles north of Mareshah **a**
beautiful valley debouches from between the hills.[2] This
is the valley of Zephathah, where the relieving army of Asa,
coming from the north-east, now took up its position. Here a
decisive battle took place, which ended in the complete rout of
the Egyptians. It has been well noted,[3] that this is the only
occasion on which the armies of Judah ventured to meet, and
with success, either Egypt or Babylon *in the open field* (not
behind fortifications). On the only other occasion when a battle
in the open was fought (2 Chron. xxv. 20–24), it ended in the
signal defeat of Judah. But this is only one of the circumstances which made the victory of Asa so remarkable. Although
the battle-field (a valley) must have been unfavourable for
handling so unwieldy a mass of soldiers and for deploying their
war-chariots, yet the host of Egypt was nearly double that of
Asa, and must have included well-disciplined and long-trained
battalions. But, on the other hand, never before had a battle
been fought in the same manner ; never had there been more
distinct negation of things seen and affirmation of things unseen—which constitutes the essence of faith—nor yet more
trustful application of it than in Asa's prayer before the battle :
" Is it not with Thee to help between the much (the mighty)
relatively to no strength (in regard to the weak) ?[4] Help us,
Jehovah our God, for upon Thee do we put our trust ; and in
Thy name have we come (do we come) upon this multitude.
O Jehovah, Thou art our God (the God of power, *Elohim*) : let
not man retain *strength* by the side of Thee (have power before

---

[1] The *Marissa* of Josephus, the modern *Marâsh*. Comp. Robinson's
Bibl. Researches, vol. ii. pp. 67, 68. Its importance as a fortress is shewn
by the part it sustained in later Jewish history, having been taken and
retaken several times at different periods.

[2] Not where Robinson finds it (*u.s.* p. 31).

[3] Professor Rawlinson in the *Speaker's Commentary*.

[4] The words are not easy of exact rendering, though their meaning is
plain. Different translations have been proposed. We have ventured to
put it interrogatively. If this view be not adopted, that which would most
commend itself to us would be : "It is nothing with Thee, Jehovah, to
help between the mighty in regard to the weak."

Thee) !" Such an appeal could not be in vain. In the significant language of Holy Scripture, it was "Jehovah" Who
"smote" the Ethiopians, and "Asa and the people that were
with him" only "pursued them."[1]   Far away to Gerar, three
hours south-east from the border-city, Gaza, continued the chase
amidst unnumbered slain, and still the destroying sword of
Jehovah was before His host (2 Chron. xiv. 13), and His fear
fell upon all the cities round about. To wrest the hostile cities
of the Philistines and to carry away much spoil was only one
sequence.   Henceforth Egypt ceased to be a source of terror
or of danger, and full 330 years passed before its army was
again arrayed against Judah.[2]

The occasion was too favourable not to have been improved.
Asa had entered on a course of right-doing, and the LORD,
upon Whom he and his people had called, had proved a faithful and prayer-hearing God.   If the religious reformation so
happily begun, and the religious revival which had appeared,
only issued in a thorough return to the LORD, the evil which
had been in the far and near past and which threatened in the
future, might yet be averted. The morrow of the great God-
given victory seemed the most suitable time for urging this upon
Judah.   Accordingly, Azariah, the son of Oded,[3] was Divinely
commissioned to meet the returning victorious army of Asa,
and to urge such considerations upon the people. "The Spirit
of Elohim" was upon him, and what he spake bore reference not
only to the past and the present, but also to the future. Hence
his message is rightly described as both "words" and "a prophecy" (2 Chron. xv. 8). Carefully examined, it contains alike
an address and a prophecy. For it were a mistake to suppose,

[1] In 2 Chron. xiv. 13 the Hebrew expression is : "they were broken before
Jehovah"—as it were by the weight of His Hand.

[2] In the reign of Josiah (2 Chron. xxxv. 20–24).

[3] There is no reason for supposing that Oded was Iddo the prophet. In
2 Chron. xv. 8 the words : "Of Oded the prophet," are either defective, or
more probably a gloss. This is evident, not only from the ascription of the
prophecy to Oded, but from the fact that the grammatical structure requires
either the omission of these words or the addition to them of others.

that the picture which Azariah drew of Israel's sin and its consequence in vers. 3, 5, 6 was only that of the far past in the
time of the Judges, of the religious decline under Jeroboam
and Abijah, or even of their future apostasy and its punishment. *All these* were included in what the prophet set before
the people.[1] And not only so, but his words extended
beyond Judah, and applied to all Israel, as if the whole
people were viewed as still united, and ideally one in their
relation to the Lord.[2] Accordingly, it deserves special notice,
that neither in ver. 3 nor in ver. 5 any verb is used, as if
to indicate the general application of the "prophecy." But
its present bearing, alike as regarded Judah's sin and repentance, and God's judgment and mercy, was an earnest call
to carry on and complete the good work which had already
been begun (ver. 7).

/ And king and people hearkened to the voice of God through
His prophet. Again and more energetically than before, the
religious reformation was taken in hand. The idol-"abominations" were removed, not only from Judah and Benjamin,
but from the conquered cities of the north, and the great altar
of burnt-offering in the Temple was repaired. The earnestness of this movement attracted the pious laity from the neighbouring tribes, and even led those of Simeon (in the far south)
who, apparently, had hitherto sympathised with the northern
kingdom, as they shared their idolatry (comp. Amos iv. 4; v. 5;
viii. 14), to join the ranks of Judah. At a great sacrificial feast,
which the king held in Jerusalem, the solemn covenant into which
Israel had originally entered with Jehovah (Ex. xxiv. 3–8) was
renewed, in repentant acknowledgment that it had been broken,
and in believing choice of Jehovah as henceforth their God—
just as it was afterwards renewed on two analogous occasions:

---

[1] As regards the past compare Judges ii. 10; iii. 14; v. 6; vi. 2; xii. 4;
xx. As regards the future compare here, Deut. iv. 27–30; xxviii. 20;
Is. ix. 17–20; lv. 6; Jer. xxxi. 1; Ezek. xxxvi. 24; Amos iii. 9; Zechar.
xiv. 13.

[2] In regard to Israel comp. here Hos. iii. 5; v. 13–15.

in the time of Josiah (2 Kings xxiii. 3; 2 Chron. xxxiv. 31), and in that of Nehemiah (Nehem. x. 28–39). The movement was the outcome of heart-conviction and earnest purpose, and consisted, on the one hand, in an undertaking that any intro- duction of idolatry should be punished by death[1] (according to Deut. xiii. 9), and, on the other, in an act of solemn national consecration to Jehovah.

To Asa at least all this was a reality, although, as regarded his subjects, the religious revival does not seem to have been equally deep or permanent (2 Chron. xv. 17). But the king kept his part of the solemn engagement. However difficult it might be, he removed "the Queen-mother" from her exalted position, and thus showed an example of sincerity and earnest- ness in his own household. And, in token of his consecra- tion to Jehovah, he brought into His House alike those war- spoils which his father had, after the victory over Jeroboam, set apart as the portion for God, and what he himself now consecrated from the spoil taken in the war with Egypt. These measures were followed by a period of happy rest for the land —even to the twenty-fifth[2] year of King Asa's reign.

[1] The Authorised Version conveys the impression, that in every case want of personal piety would be punished by death. Such, however, is not the meaning of the original. It only implies, that the introduction of idolatry by any person should be punishable by death (comp. Deut. xvii. 2-7).

[2] As the dates in 2 Chron. xv. 19; xvi. 1 are incompatible with that of Baasha's death (1 Kings xvi. 8), and consequently, of course, with that of Baasha's war against Asa, commentators have tried to obviate the diffi- culty, either by supposing that the numeral 35 refers, not to the date of Asa's accession, but to that of the separation of the kingdoms of Judah and Israel, or else by emendating the numeral in the Book of Chronicles. The latter is, evidently, the only satisfactory solution. There is manifestly here a copyist's mistake, and the numeral which we would substitute for 35 is not 15 (as by most German commentators) but 25—and this for reasons too long to explain (כה instead of לה).

CHAPTER XIII.

ASA (*3rd*) KING OF JUDAH — NADAB, BAASHA, ELAH, ZIMRI, TIBNI, AND OMRI (*2nd, 3rd, 4th, 5th, 6th, 7th*) KINGS OF ISRAEL.

Reign of Nadab—His Murder by Baasha—War between Judah and Israel—Baasha's Alliance with Syria—Asa gains over Ben-hadad—Prophetic Message to Asa—Resentment of the King—Asa's Religious Decline—Death of Asa—Death of Baasha—Reign of Elah—His Murder by Zimri—Omri dethrones Zimri—War between Omri and Tibni—Rebuilding of Samaria.

(1 KINGS XV. 16-XVI. 28; 2 CHRON. XVI.)

WHILE these things were going on in Judah, the judgment, which the LORD had, through Ahijah, pronounced upon Jeroboam and his house, was rapidly preparing. After an apparently uneventful reign of only two years, Nadab, the son and successor of Jeroboam, was murdered while engaged in the siege of Gibbethon (the *Gabatha* and *Gabothane* of Josephus). This border-city, on the edge of the plain of Esdraelon (not many miles south-west of Nazareth, and originally in the possession of Dan, Josh. xix. 44), must have been of great importance as a defence against incursions from the west—to judge from the circumstance that not only Nadab but his successors sought, although in vain, to wrest it from the Philistines (comp. 1 Kings xvi. 15). No other event in the reign of Nadab is recorded. " He walked in the way of his father, and in his sin," and sudden destruction overtook him. Baasha—probably the leader of a military revolution—murdered him, and usurped his throne. The first measure of the new king was, in true Oriental fashion, to kill the whole family of his predecessor.   Although the judgment of God upon Jeroboam and his house, as announced by the prophet, was thus fulfilled, it must not for a moment be thought that the foul deed of Baasha was thereby lessened in guilt.   *On the contrary, Holy Scripture expressly marks this crime as one of the grounds of Baasha's later judgment* (1 Kings xvi. 7).   It is perhaps not easy, and yet it is of supreme importance for the understanding of the Old Testament, to distinguish in these events the action of man from the overruling direction of God. Thus when, after his accession, the prophet Jehu, the son of Hanani,[1] was commissioned to denounce the sin, and to announce the judgment of Baasha, these two points were clearly put forward in his message : The sin of Baasha in the murder of Jeroboam's house, and the fact that his exaltation was due to the LORD (1 Kings xvi. 7 ; comp. ver. 2).[2]

Baasha had sprung from a tribe wholly undistinguished by warlike achievements,[3] and from a family apparently ignoble and unknown (1 Kings xvi. 2).   His only claim to the crown lay in his military prowess, which the neighbouring kingdom of Judah was soon to experience.   Under his reign the state of chronic warfare between the two countries once more changed into one of active hostility.   From the concordant accounts in the Books of Kings and Chronicles (1 Kings xv. 16–22 ; 2 Chr. xvi. 1–6), we gather what was Baasha's object in this war, and what his preparations for it had been.   It seems, that Asa's father, Abijah, had formed an alliance with the rising power of Syria under Tabrimon (" good is Rimmon "),[4] with the view

[1] As to Jehu comp. 2 Chron. xix. 2, 3 ; his death xx. 34. As to Hanani, comp. 2 Chron. xvi. 7–10.

[2] In fact the last clause in 1 Kings xvi. 7 seems added to explain the statement in ver. 2.

[3] The tribe of Issachar ; comp. Gen. xlix. 14, 15.   That tribe furnished the Judge Jola (Judg. x. 1).

[4] The god Rimmon—or more probably Hadad-Rimmon, the Sun-god of the Syrians, 2 Kings v. 18.   Hadad, " the sun," seems from ancient history to have been a royal title both in Syria and Edom.   As stated

of holding Israel in check by placing it between two enemies—
Syria in the north and Judah in the south. This "league"
was, as we infer, discontinued by Asa during the earlier part
of his reign, when his confidence was more entirely placed
in Jehovah his God. In these circumstances Baasha eagerly
sought and entered upon an alliance with Syria. His primary
object was to arrest the migration of Israelites into the kingdom
of Judah, and the growing influence of Asa upon his own
subjects, consequent, as we know, upon his great religious
reformation (1 Kings xv. 17). His secondary object was so
to overawe Jerusalem, as virtually to paralyse the power of
Judah. The invasion was at first successful, and Baasha
penetrated as far as Ramah, about midway between Bethel
and Jerusalem, thus obtaining command of the two roads
which led from the north and the east to the Jewish capital.
This, of course, implied not only the re-conquest of the towns
which Abijah had taken from Israel (2 Chron. xiii. 19 ; comp.
also xv. 8), but the complete isolation and domination of
Jerusalem. Ramah was to be immediately converted into a
strong fortress.

In these straits Asa seems to have forgotten the manner in
which his former brilliant victory over Zerah had been obtained.
Instead of relying wholly on Jehovah his God, he appears to
have imagined that his former policy in regard to Syria had
been a mistake. Like many who, on losing the first freshness
of their faith, seek to combine trust in the Lord with what they
regard as most likely means of worldly success, Asa entered
into a new alliance [1] with Ben-Hadad, purchasing it with the
silver and gold treasured up in the Temple and in the royal

---

in a previous note, there seem to have been four kings of Syria who
bore that name: Hadad-ezer, in time of David ; Hezion (Hadad II.) in
that of Rehoboam ; Tab-Rimmon (Hadad III.) in the time of Abijah ; and
Ben-Hadad (Hadad IV.) in the time of Asa. It is doubtful, whether the
Rezon in the time of Solomon (1 Kings xi. 23–25) was identical with Hezion,
or whether the former was a usurper.

[1] The meaning of 1 Kings xv. 19 is : Let there be a league.

palace. He may have argued, that this did not imply a renunciation of his former allegiance to Jehovah; that he had no personal intercourse with Syria, which, indeed, was far separated from his dominions; that his was only a countermove to Baasha's schemes; and that a similar league had, during the reign of his father, proved eminently successful. But the result of an alliance so incongruous, and purchased in so dubious a manner, proved the beginning of spiritual declension and of little honour or real benefit to his country.

Ben-Hadad was only too ready to entertain Asa's proposals. It could never have been his real policy to strengthen the neighbour-state of Israel, and to weaken that of Judah. On receiving the rich bribe, which made Judah virtually tributary to him, he broke his league with Baasha, and immediately invaded Israel, overrunning the northern territory, penetrating as far as the district of Chinneroth (Josh. xi. 2; xii. 3; xix. 35),—which gave its name to the Lake of Gennesaret,—and occupying the land of Naphtali. This threatening danger in the north of his dominions obliged Baasha hastily to quit Ramah. Asa now summoned all Judah. The materials accumulated for the fortress of Ramah were removed, and used for building two new forts: Geba ("the height") and Mizpah ("the outlook") (comp. Josh. xviii. 24, 26; also Jer. xli. 5–9). Both these cities lay within the territory of Benjamin, about three miles to the north of Ramah, in very strong positions, and commanded the two roads to Jerusalem.

But with the retreat of Baasha from Ramah, the troubles of Asa did not end; rather did they only then begin. When, alone and unaided, he had, in the might of Jehovah, encountered the hosts of Egypt, signal success had been his; peace and prosperity had followed; and God's prophet had been specially sent to meet the returning army with good and encouraging tidings. It was all otherwise now. Hanani the prophet was directed to meet Asa with a message of reproof and judgment; instead of, as formerly, peace, there would henceforth be continual warfare (2 Chron. xvi. 9); and the alliance with Syria would prove neither to honour nor profit. On the other hand, even had his fears been realised, and the combined armies of Israel and Syria invaded Judah, yet if, instead of buying the alliance of Ben-Hadad, he had gone forward in the name of the LORD, victory such as that over the Ethiopians would again have been his (2 Chron. xvi. 7). As it was, Asa had chosen a worldly policy, and by its issue he must abide. Henceforth it was no more Jehovah Who was arrayed against the might of man, but the contest would be simply one of cunning and strength, as between man and man (2 Chron. xvi. 9).

Hanani had spoken, as all the prophets of Jehovah, fearlessly, faithfully, and only too truly. It was probably conviction of this which, in the unhumbled state of the king, kindled his anger against "the seer." Once more it might seem to Asa as not implying rebellion against God, only a necessary precaution against disunion and dissatisfaction among his own subjects, threatening to upset his political calculations and combinations, to use measures of severity against the prophet from which he would have shrunk at a former period of his reign. All the more requisite might these appear, since his unwelcome monitor evidently commanded the sympathies of an influential part of the community. But it was an unheard-of proceeding, which happily found imitation only in the worst times of Israel (1 Kings xxii. 26–29; Jer. xx. 2; xxix. 26; Acts xvi. 24), to put the prophet of the LORD "in the house of stocks"[1] on account of his faithfulness, and by a series of persecutions to oppress, and, if possible, crush[2] those who sympathised with him.

Nor was this all. The fatal tendency which had showed itself in the Syrian alliance, and still more in the measures

---

[1] Two terms are used in Hebrew for "the stocks." That here employed combined the pillory for the body with the stocks for the legs. It was, in fact, an instrument of torture, the neck and arms being confined, and the body in a bent position.

[2] The verb really means "to crush." It is generally used in connection with cruel oppression, as in Deut. xxviii. 33; 1 Sam. xii. 3, etc.

against Hanani and his sympathisers, continued and increased
with the lapse of years. Two years before his death, Asa was
attacked by some disease[1] in his feet. In this "also"[2] "he
sought not Jehovah but in (by) the physicians."[3] It is not
necessary to explain the blame which Holy Scripture evidently
attaches to this, on the ground that these physicians were
so called "medicine-men" (as among the heathen), nor to
suppose that they used idolatrous or even superstitious means.
The example of Hezekiah (2 Kings xx.; 2 Chron. xxxii. 24)
sufficiently shows, how one who fully trusted in the LORD
would have felt and acted in these circumstances. On the
other hand, Asa displayed in this instance the same want of
practical religion as in his alliance with Syria—a state of mind
which Bengel rightly characterises as theoretical orthodoxy
combined with practical atheism. And—as formerly the prophet had summed up what Asa had no doubt regarded as the
height of political wisdom in the curt, if somewhat harsh,
criticism : "Thou hast acted stupidly over this" (2 Chron. xvi.
9)—so might it have been said of him in this matter also.
He had not sought Jehovah, but had sought in the physicians
—and by the help which he had sought he must abide. He
had not trusted in the supernatural, but applied to the natural :
and in the natural course of events his disease ended in death.
It was not wrong to employ means, indeed such were used in
the miraculous cure of Hezekiah (2 Kings xx. 7), just as in
the miraculous rescue of St. Paul's companions from shipwreck
(Acts xxvii. 23, 24, 43, 44). And, if one lesson more than
another has been impressed on our minds in the course of this
history, it is that of the use of natural means, in the ordinary

[1] According to the Talmud (*Sotah* 10 *a*) it was the gout.
[2] So 2 Chron. xvi. 12 literally.
[3] It deserves to be noticed that, when the true seeking of Jehovah is referred
to, the original uses simply the accusative, as if to indicate the directness of
the address ; while in all spurious enquiries or requests the preposition *in*
or *by* is employed, as if, while marking the means by which the object is
sought, at the same time to indicate that any result still comes only from God.
For, the Hebrew may be designated as the only theologically true language.

and rational succession of events, for the accomplishment of supernatural and Divinely-announced purposes. But the error and sin of Asa consisted in seeking an object, however lawful and even desirable, in, by, and through secondary means, without first seeking Jehovah. Such conduct carried with it its natural result. For, what a man soweth, that—the very kind of grain—shall he also reap; just as, none the less, that we work for it (or perhaps have it supplied to our hands), but on the contrary, all the more because of it, we first pray: "Give us this day our daily bread," and then receive as directly from His hand the consecrated fruit of our labour.

There was the same sad consistency about Asa's death as in his life. He seems to have built him a special mausoleum in the city of David; and there they laid him in almost Egyptian pomp on a bed of spices, and burnt at his burying, whether for the first time in royal funerals, or according to a more ancient practice,[1] a large quantity of costly spices and perfumes.

But in following the narrative of Holy Scripture, we have been really anticipating the course of this history. For, as previously stated, Asa not only outlived Baasha, but altogether saw eight kings on the throne of Israel. Baasha seems to have survived his defeat little more than a year. He was succeeded by his son Elah, in the twenty-sixth year of King Asa's reign. The rule of Elah lasted only two years, or, more exactly, part of two years. Baasha had set the example of military revolutions, in which the favourite of the soldiery ascended the throne by the murder of his predecessor, and the extirpation of all who might have rival claims to the crown. The precedent was a dangerous one; and henceforth the throne of Israel was occupied by a series of military adventurers, whose

---

[1] The former seems to me the most probable. It need scarcely be said that the heathen practice of *cremation* was unknown. On this subject, and on the burning of spices at such funerals, comp. Geier, *De Ebræorum Luctu*, pp. 104–119. According to Rabbinical writings, Asa was one of the model-kings.

line did not extend beyond their immediate successors. The son of Baasha was a cowardly debauchee, who, forgetful even of the decorum of Eastern princes, indulged in orgies in the houses of his favourites, while his army was fighting before Gibbethon. He fell a victim to a court conspiracy. We know only two of the actors in it: Arza, the steward of the king's palace (or rather, his *major-domo*), in whose house Elah was drinking himself drunk, and the king's murderer and successor Zimri, who filled the post of chief over half his "chariots," or perhaps his cavalry. The reign of Zimri lasted only seven days, but they were stained by even more than the bloodshed usual on such occasions. For Zimri destroyed not only the family of his predecessor, but killed all the "blood-avengers" (relatives, kinsfolk), and even "the friends" of the late king.

Whether, as Josephus explains (*Ant.* viii. 12, 4), Zimri had chosen for his rebellion the moment when all the leading officers were in camp, or Omri himself was originally in the conspiracy, certain it is that the army was not disposed to acknowledge the new usurper. It immediately proclaimed their general Omri, and under his leadership marched back upon Tirzah. Zimri held out till the city was taken, when he retired into "the citadel of the king's palace," [1] which he set on fire, perishing in its flames. But Omri had not at first undisputed possession of the throne. For four years the people were divided between him and another pretender to the crown, Tibni, the son of Genath. At length Omri prevailed, and "Tibni died"—either in battle or, as Josephus seems to imply (*Ant.* viii. 12, 5), by command of his rival.

Omri occupied the throne altogether twelve (or part of twelve) years. The first four of these passed in contests with Tibni. During the next two years he resided in Tirzah. After that he bought from Shemer for two talents of silver (about £780) the hill of Samaria. On this commanding position he built the new capital of Israel, which, according to the sacred text, he named

---

[1] This is the correct rendering of the original.

Shomeron,[1] after the former owner of the site. But on other grounds it deserved to be called "watch-mountain," as the name may be rendered. Situated about the centre of the land, six miles north-west of Shechem, it occupied a commanding hill, rising from a broad valley, and surrounded on all sides by mountains, through which there was only a narrow entrance from the west. The approach to the plateau on which Samaria stood is steep on all sides. Thus the site of the new capital, which was also distinguished by great beauty, was singularly adapted both for observation and defence. The country around was very rich, and the place well supplied with water. A more suitable spot could not have been chosen by monarch or general. This accounts for the continued importance of Samaria through all the varying fortunes of the country and its people. The modern miserable village of *Sebustiyeh* (the ancient *Sebaste*), inhabited by less than one thousand people, which occupies the site of the once splendid city, where Omri, Ahab, and their successors held high court, contains but few remains of its ancient grandeur. But these are sufficiently remarkable.[2] The ancient Acropolis, or temple, palace, and citadel, seems to have stood on the western brow of the hill, and its site is still marked by the ruins of a most magnificent colonnade composed of graceful monoliths. The approach to the castle must have been by ascending terraces, which, no doubt, were covered with houses and palaces. Of these not a trace is left. Only on the topmost height—from which, west-wards, the Mediterranean, and eastwards, across swelling mountains, a landscape of unrivalled beauty and fertility were full in view—a few broken and upturned pillars mark the site of the royal castle. The dynasties that reigned

[1] It is remarkable that in the older Assyrian monuments the city is still denominated as that of Omri, its later name appearing only in the time of Tiglath-pileser, nearly two hundred years after its building by Omri. This is a noteworthy confirmation of the Scriptural narrative. According to tradition, John the Baptist was buried in Samaria.

[2] See the very full description by M. Guérin (*La Samarie,* vol. ii. pages 188-210).

there have long been swept away; the people over whom they ruled carried into a captivity over which the veil of impenetrable mystery lies. Only the word of the LORD has stood firm and immovable. Of Nadab, of Baasha, of Elah, of Zimri, and of Omri, Scripture has only one and the same thing to say: that they walked in the way and in the sin of Jeroboam, the son of Nebat, "wherewith he made Israel to sin, to provoke Jehovah, the God of Israel, to anger." And over each and all did the same judgment sweep. And yet there were more grievous sins to follow, and more terrible judgments to come.[1]

CHAPTER XIV.

ASA AND JEHOSHAPHAT (3rd and 4th) KINGS OF JUDAH—AHAB (8th) KING OF ISRAEL.

Accession of Ahab—Further Religious Decline in Israel—Political Relations between Israel and Judah—Accession of Jehoshaphat—Ahab's marriage with Jezebel—The Worship of Baal and Astarte established in Israel—Character of Ahab—Religious Reforms in Judah—Jehoshaphat joins affinity with Ahab—Marriage of Jehoram with Athaliah, and its consequences.

(1 KINGS XVI. 29-33; XXII. 41-44; 2 CHRON. XVII.; XVIII. 1, 2.)

OMRI was succeeded on the throne of Israel by his son Ahab, in the thirty-eighth year of the reign of Asa, king of Judah. With the accession of Ahab a new period may be said to commence in the history of Israel, and this alike religiously and politically. In regard to the former, Omri had already prepared the way for further terrible progression in Israel's

---

[1] The Talmud (*Sank.* 102 *b*) asks whether Omri was worthy of the kingdom—the answer being, that he added a city to the land of Israel.

apostasy. In the language of Holy Scripture (1 Kings xvi. 25), he "did worse than all that were before him." Whatever the special "statutes" or ordinances in this respect which he introduced, they marked an era in the history of Israel's religious decline (Micah vi. 16). But Ahab far out-distanced even his father's wickedness, first by entering into a matrimonial alliance with the vile dynasty of Ethbaal, and then by formally making the worship of Baal the established religion of Israel, with all of vileness and of persecution which this implied. In these circumstances, surely, we may look for extraordinary interposition on the part of Jehovah. For, with such a king and queen, and with a people, not only deprived of the Temple services and the Levitical priesthood, but among whom the infamous rites of Baal and Astarte had become the established worship, ordinary means would manifestly have been in vain. Again and again had messengers sent from God spoken His Word and announced His judgments, without producing even a passing effect. It needed more than this, if the worship of Baal was to be effectually checked. Accordingly, this period of Israel's history is also marked by a great extension of the Prophetic order and mission. It was theirs to keep alive the knowledge of Jehovah in the land; theirs also to meet the gross and daring idolatry of king and people by a display of *power* which could neither be resisted nor gainsaid. Hence the unparalleled frequency of miracles, mostly intended to prove the vainness of idols as against the power of the Living God, the reality of the prophets' mission, and of the authority which the LORD had delegated to His messengers. Only thus could any effect be produced. It was an extraordinary period—and God raised up in it an extraordinary agency. We have already indicated that, in general, considering the notions and expectations of the times, miracles might almost be said to have been God's ordinary mode of teaching the men of that age. This holds specially true of the period now under consideration. Hence the unusual accumulation of the miraculous—and that chiefly in its aspect of power—as

N

displayed by an Elijah and an Elisha, so far from seeming strange or unaccountable, appears eminently called for.

Politically speaking also, this was a period of great change. For, whereas hitherto the two kingdoms of Israel and Judah had been in a state of constant warfare, an alliance between them was now formed. At first, indeed, it seemed otherwise. As Ahab ascended the throne of Israel during the lifetime of Asa, the relations between the two kingdoms continued as before. And when, in the fourth year of King Ahab's reign, Jehoshaphat succeeded his father Asa (1 Kings xxii. 41), it appeared as if the prospect of an alliance between the sister-countries were more remote than ever. Jehoshaphat began his reign by strengthening the defences of his country against Israel (2 Chron. xvii. 1, 2). His religious measures were in the opposite direction from those of Ahab. Himself earnestly and decidedly pious, it is expressly stated that he walked "not after the doings of Israel." On the other hand, Ahab entered, probably at the beginning of his reign, into an alliance with the most wicked dynasty then in power, by marrying Jezebel,[1] the daughter of Ethbaal (or Ithobalus, "Baal is with him"). Josephus has preserved to us the history of this royal family (*Against Ap.* i. 18). It appears that Ethbaal was originally the High-priest of the great temple of Astarte in Tyre; that he murdered his king, and usurped the throne, which he occupied for thirty-two years; and that his dynasty continued for at least sixty-two years after his death. These notices will sufficiently explain the upbringing of Jezebel. A clever, strong, bold, and unscrupulous woman, she was by conviction a devotee to the most base and revolting idolatry which the world has ever known, combining with this the reckless contempt of the rights and consciences of others, and the utter indifference as to the means employed, which characterise the worst aspect of Eastern despotism. That she would hate the religion of Jehovah, and

---

[1] The classical student will be interested to know that Jezebel was the grand-aunt of Dido, the founder of Carthage. The notices in Josephus are taken from Mezander.

seek utterly to destroy it—and, indeed, whatever would not bend to her imperious will; that she would prove the implacable foe of all that was pious or even free in Israel; and that she would not shrink from the wholesale murder of those who resisted or opposed her, follows almost as a matter of course. Yet, strange as it may sound, there is something grand about this strong, determined, bold woman, which appears all the more strikingly from its contrast with her husband. Jezebel was every inch a Queen—though of the type of the Phœnician Priest-King who had usurped the throne by murder.

The immediate consequence of this ill-fated union was, that the religion of Jezebel became the worship of the land of Israel. Ahab built in Samaria a temple to "the Baal"[1]—the Sun-god (the producing principle in Nature)—in which he erected not only an altar, but, as we gather from 2 Kings iii. 2; x. 27, also one of those pillars which were distinctive of its vile services. As usual, where these rites were fully carried out, he also "made the Asherah"[2]—Astarte, the Moon-goddess (the receptive principle in Nature)—so that the Phœnician worship was now established in its entirety. As we infer from later notices, there was a "vestry" attached to these temples, where special festive garments, worn on great occasions, were kept (2 Kings x. 22). Ahab—or perhaps rather Jezebel—appointed not less than 450 priests of Baal and 400 of Asherah, who were supported by the bounty of the queen (1 Kings xviii. 19; xxii. 6). The forced introduction of this new worship led to a systematic persecution of the prophets, and even of the openly professed worshippers of Jehovah, which had their complete extermination for its object (1 Kings xviii. 13; xix. 10; 2 Kings ix. 7).

[1] With the article — the supreme Phœnician and Assyrian deity, worshipped under different designations throughout that part of Asia. The critical study of the mythology of these countries has yielded many interesting results, and shown, with striking similarities in designation of the deity, the most absolute contrast to the religion of Jehovah as regards doctrine and life, so as to bring the heavenly origin of the latter into marked prominence.

[2] *Not* as in the Authorised Version (1 Kings xvi. 33): "And Ahab made a grove."

These measures were wholly due to the absolute power which
Jezebel exercised over her husband. Left to himself, Ahab
might have yielded to better influences (comp. 1 Kings xviii.
39–46; xx. 13, etc.; xxi. 27–29). Altogether Ahab presents a
strange, though by no means uncommon mixture of the good
and the evil, the noble and the mean, issuing finally not in
decision for God and what was right and true, but in the triumph
of evil, to his own destruction and that of his race. For
he possessed qualities which, if directed by the fear of God,
might have made him even a great king. He was at times
brave, even chivalrous (comp. for example 1 Kings xx. 11, and
even verse 32); royal in his tastes and undertakings (1 Kings
xxii. 39; 2 Chron. xviii. 2); and ready, under temporary
emotion, to yield to the voice of conscience. But all this was
marred by fatal weakness, selfishness, uncontrolled self-indulgence, an utter want of religion, and especially the influence of
his wife, so that in the language of Holy Scripture he "sold
himself to work wickedness in the sight of Jehovah," incited
thereto by his wife Jezebel (1 Kings xxi. 25).

While these influences were at work in Israel, Jehoshaphat,
encouraged by the blessing which rested on his kingdom, once
more vigorously resumed the work of religious reformation in
Judah (2 Chron. xvii. 6–9). Not only did he take away the
"high places and groves," but, in the third year of his reign,[1]
he sent five of his princes, accompanied by nine of the principal
Levites and two priests, throughout the towns of Judah to teach
the people the Law—no doubt the Pentateuch,[2] of which they
took with them an authorised copy. The actual instruction
would unquestionably be committed to the priestly members of
this commission (comp. Lev. x. 11; Deut. xvii. 8, 9), whilst
the presence of the princes would not only secure the authority
of the teachers and the efficiency of their work, but also be

---

[1] It has been ingeniously suggested (by Hitzig), that this was a Year of
Jubilee, viz. 912 B.C.

[2] Thus the Pentateuch in its present form circulated ten centuries before
the time of our LORD.

requisite for civil purposes, since the Law of Moses affected many of the social relations of life, and accordingly required for its enforcement the authority of the magistrates. Once more signal marks of the Divine approbation followed. Some of the Philistine chiefs rendered voluntary homage to Jehoshaphat; the Arab tribes, whom Asa had subdued during his pursuit of Zerah, the Ethiopian, again paid their tribute; new castles for the defence of the country were built, "store-cities" provided, and the various towns provisioned;[1] while a large army was ready prepared,[2] of which the five chiefs resided in Jerusalem, to be under the personal orders of the king.[3]

It was in circumstances of such marked prosperity that Jehoshaphat "joined affinity with Ahab." The sacred text specially notes this (2 Chron. xviii. 1), partly to show that Jehoshaphat had not even an excuse for such a step, and partly, as we think, to indicate that this alliance must, in the first place, have been sought by Ahab. The motives which would influence the King of Israel are not difficult to understand. The power of the country had been greatly weakened by Syria during the reign of Omri. Not only had Ben-Hadad possessed himself of a number of cities, both east (Ramoth-Gilead, for example) and west of the Jordan, but the country had become virtually subject to him, since he claimed even in the capital, Samaria, the right of having "streets," or rather "squares," that is, Syrian quarters of the town, which owned his dominion (comp. 1 Kings xx. 34). And now Ben-Hadad had been succeeded by a son of the same name, equally warlike

---

[1] This seems the real meaning of the Hebrew, and not "much business," as in the Authorised Version of 2 Chron. xvii. 13.

[2] A very ingenious defence of the accuracy of the numbers of this army has been lately attempted. But to us these numerals seem corrupt, though it is impossible in this place to furnish proof for the assertion. Probably they were illegible or blotted out, and the copyist seems to have supplied the two first from chap. xiv. 8, while the other three were formed by deducting 100,000 from each of them. The sum total is *double* that of chapter xiv. 8.

[3] This seems to be the true meaning of the Hebrew text.

and ambitious. In these circumstances it was of the utmost importance to Ahab to secure permanent peace on his southern or Judæan frontier, and, if possible, to engage as an active ally so powerful and wealthy a monarch as Jehoshaphat. On the other hand, it is not so easy to perceive the reasons which influenced the King of Judah. Of course he could not have wished to see the power of Syria paramount so close to his borders. Did he, besides, desire to have the long-standing (seventy years') breach between Judah and Israel healed? Had he a dim hope that, by the marriage of his son with the daughter of Ahab, the two realms might again be joined, and an undivided kingdom once more established in the house of David? Or did he only allow himself to be carried along by events, too weak to resist, and too confident to dread evil? We can only make these suggestions, since the sacred text affords no clue to this political riddle.

It was, as we reckon, about the eighth year of Jehoshaphat's reign, and consequently about the twelfth of that of Ahab, that Jehoram, the son of Jehoshaphat—then a lad of about fifteen or sixteen years—was married to Athaliah, the daughter of Ahab and Jezebel (2 Chron. xxi. 6).[1] Jehoshaphat lived to see some

---

[1] We arrive at this conclusion as follows : When eight or nine years later — that is, in the seventeenth year of Jehoshaphat, the latter paid his memorable visit to Ahab (1 Kings xxii. 2), Ahaziah, the son of Jehoram, must have been already about eight or nine years old, since he ascended the throne about thirteen years later, after the death of his grandfather and his father, at the age of twenty-two (2 Kings viii. 26). But it must be admitted that the chronology of these reigns is involved and somewhat difficult. Indeed, a perfect agreement is impossible. For the dates are given not according to any *fixed* standard (such as the Creation, or the Birth of Christ), but according to the reigns of the various kings. But, according to Jewish practice, a year of a king's reign is counted from *Nisan* (April) to *Nisan*, so that any time before or after Nisan would be counted as an integral year. Thus a prince who ascended the throne in *Adar* (March) of one year and died in *Ijar* (May) of the next, although only reigning fourteen months, would be said to have reigned *three years*. This difference, when applied to the reigns of the various kings, or to a comparison between the dates of the kings of Israel and Judah, constitutes one of the main practical difficulties in establishing a perfect agreement.

of the bitter fruits of the rash and unholy alliance which he had sanctioned. Eight or nine years later, he went on that visit to Ahab which led to the disastrous war with Syria, in which Ahab himself perished (2 Chron. xviii.). Then followed the joint maritime expedition of Jehoshaphat and the son of Ahab, which ended in loss. But the worst was to come after the death of Jehoshaphat. / His son and successor, the husband of Athaliah, introduced in Judah the idolatry of his wife, and brought shame and loss upon his people./ The next occupant of the throne—the son of Athaliah—followed the example of his father, and perished by command of Jehu. Lastly came the terrible tragedy of the wholesale murder of the royal princes by Athaliah, then her reign, and finally her tragic death.

It was not by means such as those which Jehoshaphat employed that good could come to Judah, the breach be healed between the severed tribes, the kingdom of David restored, or even peace and righteousness return to Israel. But already God had been preparing a new instrumentality to accomplish His own purposes. A Voice would be raised loud enough to make itself heard to the ends of the land; a Hand, strong enough not only to resist the power of Ahab and Jezebel, but to break that of Baal in the land. And all this not by worldly might or craftiness, but by the manifestation of the power of Jehovah as the Living God.[1]

---

[1] A few Talmudic notices about Ahab may here find a place. They are chiefly derived from the Tractate *Sanhedrin* (102 *b*—103 *b*). His outward prosperity, and enjoyment of the pleasures of this world in contrast with those of the next, are emphatically dwelt upon. He is characterised as naturally cold and weak—his sinfulness being chiefly ascribed to his wife ; hence this proverb : He who walks in the counsel of his wife will fall into Gehenna (*Baba Mez.* 59). The heaviest sins of Jeroboam had only been like the lightest of Ahab ; in fact, he was guilty of all kinds of idolatry, and even inscribed on the gates of Samaria : Ahab denies the God of Israel ! Nevertheless he was allowed to reign twenty-two years because he had shown respect to the Law (as in the embassy of Ben-Hadad to him, in his temporary repentance, etc.), the Law being written with twenty-two letters (which constitute the Hebrew alphabet). Ahab was one of those who were supposed to have no part in the world to come. To dream of King Ahab was an evil omen (*Ber.* 57 *b*).

CHAPTER XV.

AHAB, (8*th*) KING OF ISRAEL.

*Rebuilding of Jericho—The Mission of Elijah—His Character and Life—
Elijah's First Appearance—Parallelism with Noah, Moses, and John
the Baptist—Elijah's Message to King Ahab—Sojourn by the Brook
Cherith—Elijah with the Widow of Sarepta—The Barrel of Meal wastes
not, nor does the Cruse of Oil fail—Lessons of his Sojourn—Sickness
and Death of the Widow's Son—He is miraculously restored to life.*

(1 KINGS XVI. 34–XVII.)

WITH the enthronement of Ahab and Jezebel, the establishment of the worship of Baal as the state-religion, and
the attempted extermination of the prophets and followers of
the LORD, the apostasy of Israel had reached its high point.
As if to mark alike the general disregard in Israel of the
threatened judgments of God, and the coming vindication
of Jehovah's Kingship, Holy Scripture here inserts a notice
of the daring rebuilding of the walls of Jericho, and of the
literal fulfilment of Joshua's curse upon its builder [1] (1 Kings
xvi. 34; comp. Josh. vi. 26). Indeed, the land was now ripe
for the sickle of judgment. Yet as the long-suffering of God
had waited in the days of Noah, so in those of Ahab; and as
then the preacher of righteousness had raised the voice of
warning, while giving evidence of the coming destruction, so
was Elijah now commissioned to present to the men of his
age in symbolic deed the alternative of serving Jehovah or Baal,
with all that the choice implied. The difference between Noah

---

[1] Jericho seems to have belonged to Ahab. On its rebuilding see Vol.
III. of this History, p. 66. The remarks of the Talmud on the subject
(*Sanh.* 113 *a*) are, to say the least, very far-fetched.

and Elijah was only that of times and circumstances: the one was before, the other after the giving of the Law; the one was sent into an apostate world, the other to an apostatising covenant-people. But there is also another aspect of the matter. On the one side were arrayed Ahab, Jezebel, Baal, and Israel—on the other stood Jehovah. It was a question of reality and of power: and Elijah was to be, so to speak, the embodiment of the Divine Power, the Minister of the Living and True God. The contest between them could not be decided by words, but by deeds. The Divine would become manifest in its reality and irresistible greatness, and whoever or whatever came in contact with it would, for good or for evil, experience its Presence. We might almost say, that in his prophetic capacity Elijah was an impersonal being—the mere medium of the Divine. Throughout his history other prophets also were employed on various occasions: he only to do what none other had ever done or could do. His path was alone, such as none other had trodden nor could tread. He was the impersonation of the Old Testament in one of its aspects: that of grandeur and judgment—the living realisation of the topmost height of the mount, which burned with fire, around which lightnings played and thunder rolled, and from out of whose terrible glory spake the Voice of Jehovah, the God of Israel. We have the highest authority for saying that he was the type of John the Baptist. But chiefly in this respect, that he lifted the axe to the root of the tree, yet, ere it fell, called for fruits meet for repentance. He was not the forerunner of the LORD, save in judgment; he was the forerunner of the King, not of the Kingdom; and the destruction of the state and people of Israel, not the salvation of the world, followed upon his announcement.

A grander figure never stood out even against the Old Testament sky than that of Elijah. As Israel's apostasy had reached its highest point in the time of Ahab, so the Old Testament antagonism to it in the person and mission of Elijah. The analogy and parallelism between his history and that of Moses, even to minute details, is obvious on comparison of the two ;[1] and accordingly we find him, significantly, along with Moses on the Mount of Transfiguration. Yet much as Scripture tells of him, we feel that we have only dim outlines of his prophetic greatness before us. By his side other men, even an Elisha, seem small. As we view him as Jehovah's representative, almost plenipotentiary, we recall his unswerving faithfulness to, and absolutely fearless discharge of his trust. And yet this strong man had his hours of felt weakness and loneliness, as when he fled before Ahab and Jezebel, and would fain have laid him down to die in the wilderness. As we recall his almost unlimited power, we remember that its spring was in constant prayer. As we think of his unbending sternness, of his sharp irony on Mount Carmel, of his impassioned zeal, and of his unfaltering severity, we also remember that deep in his heart soft and warm feelings glowed, as when he made himself the guest of the poor widow, and by agonising prayer brought back her son to life. Such as this must have been intended by God, in His mercy, as an outlet and precious relief to his feelings, showing him that all his work and mission were not of sorrow and judgment, but that the joy of Divine comfort was his also. And truly human, full of intense pathos, are those days of wilderness-journey, and those hours on Mount Horeb, when in deepest sadness of soul the strong man, who but yesterday had defiantly met Ahab and achieved on Mount Carmel such triumph as none other, bent and was shaken, like the reed in the storm. A life this full of contrasts—of fierce light and deep shadows—not a happy, joyous, prosperous life ; not one even streaked with peace or gladness, but wholly devoted to God : a bush on the wilderness-mount, burning yet not consumed. A life full of the miraculous it is

[1] Jewish tradition extols him almost to blasphemy, to show how absolutely God had delegated to Elijah His power—or, as the Rabbis express it : His three keys—those of rain, of children, and of raising to life. With special application of Hos. xii. 13 to Moses and Elijah, Jewish tradition traces a very minute and instructive parallelism between the various incidents in the lives of Moses and Elijah (*Yalkut* vol. ii. p. 32. *d*).

and must be, from the character of his mission—and yet himself one of the greatest wonders in it, and the success of his mission the best attestation of, because the greatest of the miracles of his history. For, alone and unaided, save of God, he *did* conquer in the contest, and he *did* break the power of Baal in Israel.

His first appearance—alike in the manner and suddenness of it—was emblematic of all that was to follow. Of his birth and early circumstances, we know next to nothing. Josephus assumes (*Ant.* viii. 13, 2) that the Tishbah which gave him his name (1 Kings xvii. 1) lay on the eastern side of Jordan, in the land of Gilead; and some modern writers have found the name in the village of *Tisieh*, to the south of Busrah. But this view has been shown (by Keil) to be untenable. Even more fanciful is the suggestion, that. the Hebrew expression means that he was "a stranger among the strangers of Gilead" —possibly a Gentile by birth. Most likelihood attaches to the generally received view, that his birthplace was the Tishbi in Upper Galilee (within the territory of Naphtali), known to us from apocryphal story (Tobit i, 2, LXX) — and that, for some unascertained reason, he had migrated into Gilead, without, however, becoming one of its citizens. This the sacred text conveys by the expression, "Elijah the Tishbite from among the dwellers (strangers dwelling) in Gilead." Another inference as to his character may be drawn from his name *Elijah:* My God Jehovah! though it is scarcely necessary to say that he did not assume it himself.[1]

With the same, or perhaps with even more startling unexpectedness and strangeness than that which characterised the appearance of John the Baptist—and with precisely the same object in it—Elijah suddenly presented himself in Samaria and

---

[1] Later Jewish tradition has represented him as of priestly descent, presumably on account of his sacrifice on Mount Carmel. But even so the illegality of a sacrifice outside Jerusalem would require special vindication. Even Jewish legalism, however, admits the plea of exceptional necessity in this instance. Tradition represents Elijah as a disciple of Ahijah, the Shilonite.

before Ahab. It was, and intended to be—to adapt the figure of the Son of Sirach (Ecclus. xlviii. 1)—like a fire that kindled suddenly, like a torch that blazed up in the still darkness of the night. There was, indeed, sufficient here to rouse the dullest mind. We can imagine the stern figure of the Tishbite, arrayed in an upper garment of black camel's hair[1]—which henceforth seems to have become the distinctive garb of the prophets (Zechar. xiii. 4)—girt about his loins with a leathern girdle. The dress betokened poverty, renunciation of the world, mourning, almost stern judgment, while the girdle, which, as the badge of office, was always the richest part of the dress, was such as only the poorest of the land wore. It was an unwonted sight, and, as he made his way up through the terraced streets of rich luxurious Samaria, its inhabitants would whisper with awe that this was a new prophet come from the wilds of Gilead, and follow him. What a contrast between those Baal-debauched Samaritans and this man; what a greater contrast still between the effeminate decrepit priests of Baal, in their white linen garments and high-pointed bonnets,[2] and this stern prophet of Jehovah! And now he had reached the height where palace and castle stand, and met Ahab himself, perhaps at the magnificent entrance to that splendid colonnade which overlooked such a scene of beauty and fertility. His message to the king was abrupt and curt, as became the circumstances[3]—after all, only a repetition of Jehovah's denunciation of judgment upon an apostate people (Lev. xxvi. 19,

---

[1] The rendering, 2 Kings i. 8, "a hairy man" is incorrect. The expression means a man arrayed in a hairy garment—as we gather, of black camel's hair.

[2] This was the official dress of the priests of Baal.

[3] The Talmud (*Sanh.* 113. *a*) mars the whole subject by a discussion, at the close of which Elijah's words are introduced. Both he and King Ahab are supposed to have come on a visit of condolence to Hiel, after the death of his children (1 Kings xvi. 34). Elijah explains that this terrible calamity was the consequence of the neglect of Joshua's warning, to which Ahab objects that it was incredible the disciple's word should become true, if the master's were not. But since the threatening of Moses in regard to idolatry had not been fulfilled, he could not believe in the warning of Joshua. Upon this Elijah bursts into the words mentioned in the text.

etc.; Deut. xi. 16, etc.; xxviii. 23, etc.; comp. 1 Kings viii. 35; Amos iv. 7); but with this addition, that the cessation of dew and rain should last these years—whether many or few —"except" by his word. This latter perhaps was intended to emphasize the impotence of Ahab's prophets and priests as against Jehovah.

It was all most startling: the sudden, strange, wild apparition; the bold confronting of king and people there in Samaria; the announcement apparently so incredible in itself, and in such contrast to the scene of wealth and fruitfulness all around; the unexpected pronunciation of the name Jehovah in such a place; the authority which he pleaded and the power which he claimed—in general, even the terms of his message: "Lives Jehovah, the God of Israel, which I stand before His Face! If there be these years dew or rain, except by the mouth (the spoken means) of my word!"[1] What answer Ahab made, what impression it produced on him or his people, Holy Scripture, in its Divine self-consciousness and sublime indifference to what may be called "effect," does not condescend even to notice. Nay, here also silence is best— and the prophet himself must withdraw as suddenly as he had come, hide himself from human ken, not be within reach of question or answer, and let God work, alone and unseen. An absolute pause with that thunder-cloud overhead—unremoved and apparently unremovable—in presence of which man and Baal shall be absolutely powerless: such was the fitting sequence to Elijah's announcement.

Elijah's first direction was to the Wady Cherith—probably east of the Jordan[2]—one of those many wide water-courses which drain into the river of Palestine. In this wild solitude, like Moses, nay, like our LORD Himself, he was to be alone with God—to plead for Israel, and to prepare for his further

[1] So in strict literality.
[2] This appears probable from the Hebrew expression rendered in the Authorised Version "before Jordan," but meaning literally, "in face of Jordan."

work. So long as water was left in the brook—for there is nothing needlessly miraculous, even in the story of Elijah— and so long as Jehovah had such strange provisioners as " the ravens"[1] to act as His messengers — for there is nothing that is merely natural in this history, and the miraculous always appears by the side of the natural,—the prophet would not want needed support. In this also there were lessons of deepest significance to Elijah (compare as to God's strange messengers, Job xxxvii. 10; Psa. lxxviii. 23; Isa. v. 6; Amos ix. 3). When in the course of time the waters of Cherith failed, owing to the long drought, Elijah was directed to go to Zarephath (*Sarepta*, Luke iv. 26[2]), where God had "com- manded" for him even a more strange provisioner than the ravens : a poor, almost famishing widow, and she a Gentile![3]

Here again everything is significant. Sarepta was not only a heathen city, outside the bounds of Israel, midway between Sidon and Tyre, but actually within the domains of Jezebel's father. The prophet, who was not safe from Jezebel in Israel would be safe within Jezebel's own country; he for whom Ahab had so earnestly but vainly searched, not only throughout his own land, but in all neighbouring countries (1 Kings xviii.

---

[1] Surely, it is one of the strangest freaks of criticism (Jewish and Christian) to make of these " ravens " either " Arabs," or " merchants," or " Orebites," from a supposed town of Oreb. We can understand the difficulty of the Rabbis, arising from the circumstance that Elijah should be fed by ravens, which were unclean animals. Those of them who take the literal translation comfort themselves with the fact, that the ravens at least brought him levitically clean food, either from one of the 7000 in Israel who had not bent the knee to Baal, or from the table of Ahab, or from that of Jehoshaphat. But these Rabbinical comments are so far evi- dential of the truth of this narrative, that we see how differently a later writer would have constructed this history, had he invented a Jewish legend. Hess adduces parallel instances of the support of people by wild beasts ; but they are of little interest, since the provision for Elijah was manifestly miraculous.

[2] Corresponding to the modern village of *Surafend*, though the latter seems farther from the sea than the ancient Sarepta.

[3] The Rabbis represent her as a Jewess, and make her the mother of Jonah.

10), would be securely concealed in the land most hostile to Elijah's mission, and most friendly to Ahab's purposes. But there are even deeper lessons. It is only one of these, that, cast out of his own country and by his own people, God can find a safe refuge for His servant in most unlikely circumstances; and that, when faith seems to fail, where most we might have expected it, God will show that He has His own where least we would look for them. Again, the reference of our LORD to this history (Luke iv. 25), shows these three things: that the entertainment of Elijah was a distinguishing honour conferred on the widow of Sarepta; that it proved of real spiritual benefit to her (as will be shown in the course of this history); and that it implied, that God had purposes of grace beyond the narrow bounds of Israel, unbelieving as it was—in the language of St. Paul, that He was not the God of the Jews only, but also of the Gentiles (Rom. iii. 29). May we not go a step farther, and see in this mission of Elijah to, and entertainment by a heathen widow, an anticipation at least of the announcement of that "Kingdom of God" in its world-wide bearing, which formed part of the message of his antitype, John the Baptist?

Once more the support of Elijah, though miraculous, was to be secured in the course of natural and easily intelligible events. Yet withal, as it had been Jehovah Who "commanded"[1] the ravens, so it was He also Who "commanded" the widow of Sarepta, all unconscious as she was of it, to sustain Elijah. But how should the prophet recognise her? He must go, trusting to God's direction, and, watching such natural indications as would appear, be guided to whither he was supernaturally sent. Arrived at the gate of Sarepta, he saw a widow, whose poverty was evidenced by her searching for a little brushwood. Was she the woman who would sustain him? There was a preliminary test ready to hand. She must have recognised the stranger by his dress as a

[1] The Rabbis note, that, when God is said to have "commanded" the ravens, He put it in their heart—a gloss this of manifold application.

prophet of Jehovah. Would she, the heathen, be willing to hold friendly communication with him? So he handed her the drinking-vessel which he had brought, with the request to interrupt her weary work in order to fetch him some water. Even this first test proved that God had, as of old (Gen. xxiv. 12–21), and as afterwards (Luke xix. 30–34; xxii. 9–12), by anticipation provided for His servant. And, assuredly, as ever, " the cup of cold water " given in the name of the LORD was soon to receive rich reward.

But there was yet another and a sharper test by which to ascertain whether she were the widow to whom Elijah was Divinely sent. If she would hold communion with a servant of Jehovah—did she truly believe in Jehovah Himself; and if so, was her faith such that she would venture her last means of support upon her trust in Him and in His word? To put it in another manner: heathen as she was, though thus far pre-pared, was there, if not activeness, yet receptiveness of faith in her, of sufficient capacity for such spiritual provision as that which was afterwards miraculously supplied for her temporal wants? This would be the last and decisive test. As she was going to fetch the water, without hesitating or murmuring at the interruption of the old, or at the imposition of the new task, Elijah arrested her with a request yet stranger and far harder than the first. She was evidently a poor widow, and we know from profane history [1] that the famine, consequent on the want of rain in Israel, had also extended to Tyre. But when Elijah addressed to her what, even in these circumstances, would have seemed the modest request for " a morsel of the bread " in her hand—that is, in her possession [2]—he could

---

[1] Menander in Josephus' *Ant.* viii. 13, 2. According to Menander the actual famine in Tyre lasted one whole year. We may here remark, that if any one wishes to be impressed with the sublimeness of the Scriptural account of this event he can do no better than compare it with the wretched rationalistic prose of Josephus' version of it.

[2] The words "in thine hand" do not refer to the verb "bring," but to "bread," and mean that Elijah spoke as if she had some bread at home. So the LXX render it.

not have been aware of the terrible straits to which his future hostess was reduced. It was not unwillingness to give even to a complete stranger part of her scanty provision, but that she had absolutely none left. Despair breaks down the barriers of reserve—at least to fellow-sufferers, and, as in this case, to fellow-believers. With the adjuration: "Lives Jehovah, thy God," which attested alike her knowledge of Elijah's profession and her own faith, she told how nothing but a handful of meal was left in the small *Cad*[1] that held her provisions, and a little oil in her cruse. She had now come to gather by the highway a few sticks, with which to cook a last meal for herself and her child. After that they must lie down and die.

It is difficult to know which most to wonder at: Elijah's calmness, consistency, and readiness of faith, or the widow's almost incredible simplicity of trustfulness. Elijah was not taken aback; he did not hesitate to go on with the trial of his hostess to the end; least of all, was he afraid of the possible consequences. As in every real trial of our trust, there was first a general promise, and, on the ground of it, a specific demand, followed by an assurance to conquering faith ("the cad of meal shall not come to an end, nor the cruse of oil fail"). But, if it was as he told her, why this demand in its sharply trying severity: *first*, to use for Elijah part of the very little she had, and to bring it to him, and only after that to go back[2] and prepare for herself and her son? Needless, indeed, the trial would seem, except as a test of her faith; yet not a mere test, since if she stood it and inherited the promise, it would be such confirmation of it, such help and blessing to her—alike spiritually and temporally—as to constitute the beginning of a new life. And so it ever is; and therefore

[1] The *Cad* was a small—probably the smallest—barrel. The word has passed into the Latin, the Greek, and the Sanscrit. Curiously enough, our English representative of it is the word "Caddy."

[2] This is clearly implied in the original, and must have been a much greater trial of her faith than if Elijah had at once returned with her, and the miracle begun then and there.

O

does every specific demand upon our faith stand between a general promise and a special assurance, that, resting upon the one, we may climb the other; and thus every specific trial— and every trial is also one of our faith—may become a fresh starting-point in the spiritual life.

And the widow of Sarepta obeyed. It requires no exercise of imagination to realise what her difficulties in so doing must have been. Did Elijah go back with her after she had brought him the cake, almost the last provision for herself and her child,—to watch as, with wonderment and awe, she prepared the first meal from her new store; or did he allow her to return home alone, perhaps wondering as she went whether it would be as the prophet had said, or whether perhaps she would never again see the Israelite stranger? One thing at least is clear: that this heathen woman, whose knowledge of Jehovah could only have been rudimentary and incipient, and who yet, at the word of a stranger, could give up her own and her son's last meal, because a prophet had bidden it, and promised her miraculous supply for the future, must have had the most simple childlike trustfulness in the God of Israel. What a lesson this, and how full of comfort, to Elijah! There *was* faith not only in Israel, but wherever He had planted its seed. Elijah had spread the wings of the God of Israel's promise (1 Kings xvii. 14), and this poor heathen had sought shelter under them. There, almost hourly these many " days," [1] the promise proved true, and, day by day, as when Israel gathered the manna in the wilderness, did an unseen Hand provide—and that not only for herself and her son, but for all " her household." It was a constant miracle; but then we need, and we have a God Who doeth wonders — not one of the idols of the heathen, nor yet a mere abstraction, but the Living and the True God. And we need in our Bible such a history as this,

---

[1] The word "many" in 1 Kings xvii. 15 is not in the original (as indicated by the italics). The expression marks an indefinite period of time— yet, as it seems to me, with the peculiar Old Testament idea of time, as "day by day."

to give us the pledge of personal assurance, when our hearts well-nigh sink within us in the bitter trials of life—something which to all time may serve as evidence that Jehovah reigneth, and that we can venture our all upon it. And yet as great as this miracle of daily providing seems that other of the faith of the widow of Sarepta !

It was soon to be put to even greater trial—and, as before, not only she, but Elijah also, would learn precious lessons by it. "Days" (time) had passed in happy quiet since God had daily spread the table in the widow's home, when her son became ill. The sickness increased, till, in the language of the sacred text, "there was not left in him breath."[1] There is something in the immediate contact with the Divine, which, from its contrast, brings sin to our remembrance, and in consequence makes us feel as if it were impossible to stand unpunished before Him—until our thoughts of the Divine Holiness, which in this view seems as consuming fire, pass into the higher realisation of the infinite love of God, which seeks and saves that which is lost (comp. Luke v. 8 ; also Isa. vi. 5). It was certainly not the wish that the prophet should be gone from her home, nor yet regret that he had ever come to it, which wrung from the agonised woman, as she carried to him her dead child in her bosom, these wild words, in which despair mingled with the consciousness of sin and the searching after the higher and better : "What have I to do with thee (what to [between] me and thee [2]), man of the Elohim ? Come art thou to me to bring to remembrance my sin, and (thus) to cause the death of my son !" The Divine, as represented by Elijah, having no commonality with her; its fierce light

---

[1] Since the same or at least a very similar expression in Dan. x. 17 does not imply actual death, it would be rash to assert that the child was really dead. This is well pointed out by Kimchi. Similarly, Josephus has it that the child only seemed dead (was "as one dead," in New Testament language). The circumstance that his mother still carried him in her bosom seems to imply the same.

[2] Comp. Judg. xi. 12 ; 2 Sam. xvi. 10 ; 2 Kings iii. 13 ; Matt. viii. 29 ; John ii. 4.

bringing out her sin, and her sin bringing down condign punishment—such were the only clearly conscious thoughts of this incipient believer—though with much of the higher and better, as yet unconsciously, in the background.

Elijah made no other answer than to ask for her son. He took him from her bosom, carried him to the *Alijah* (upper chamber) where he dwelt, and there laid him on his own bed. In truth, it was not a time for teaching by words, but by deeds. And Elijah himself was deeply moved. These "many days" had been a happy, quiet, resting time to him—perhaps the only quiet happy season in all his life. And as day by day he had been the dispenser of God's goodness to the widow and her household, and had watched the unfolding of her faith, it must have been a time of strengthening and of joy to his heart. As St. Chrysostom has it : Elijah had to learn compassion in the house of the widow of Sarepta, before he was sent to preach to his own people. He learned more than this in that heathen home. Already he had learned that experience of faith, which, as St. Paul tells us, worketh a hope that maketh not ashamed (Rom. v. 4, 5). But now it seemed as if it were all otherwise ; as if he were only a messenger of judgment ; as if his appearance had not only boded misery to his own people Israel, but brought it even upon the poor widow who had given him shelter. But it could not be so—and in the agony of prayer he cast this burden upon his God. Three times—as when the Name of Jehovah is laid in blessing on His people (Numb. vi. 24, etc.), and as when the Seraphim raise their voice of praise (Isa. vi. 3)— he stretched himself in symbolic action upon the child, calling upon Jehovah as his God : laying the living upon the dead, pouring his life, as it were, into the child, with the agony of believing prayer. But it was *Jehovah* Who restored the child to life, hearkening to the voice of His servant.

They are truly human traits, full of intense pathos, which follow—though also fraught with deep spiritual lessons. We can almost see Elijah as he takes down the child to his mother in that darkened room, and says to her only these words of deep emotion, not unmingled with loving reproof: "See, thy son liveth!" Words these, which our blessed LORD has said to many a weeping mother when holding her child, whether in life or in death. And thus we can understand the words of the mother of Sarepta, and those of many a mother in like circumstances: "Now—thus—I know that a Man of Elohim thou, and that the Word of Jehovah in thy mouth *is* truth!" She had learned it when first she received him; she had seen it day by day at her table; she had known it when God had answered her unspoken thought, her unuttered prayer, by showing that mercy and not judgment, love and forgiveness, not punishment and vengeance, were the highest meaning of His dealings.

The Rabbis see in this story an anticipation of the resurrection of the dead. We perceive this and more in it—an emblem also of the resurrection from spiritual death: a manifestation to Elijah and to us all, that "He quickeneth the dead, and calleth those things which be not as though they were" (Rom. iv. 17).

END OF VOLUME V.

CHRONOLOGICAL TABLE

OF THE KINGS OF JUDAH AND ISRAEL, AND OF CONTEMPORARY EVENTS,

According to Keil, Winer, Ewald, Clinton, and the Margin of our Authorised Version (Ussher[1]).

Year from the Separation of the Two Kingdoms.	KINGS OF JUDAH. Reigned:	Year from the Accession of the Kings of Judah.	KINGS OF ISRAEL. Reigned:	Year from the Accession of the Kings of Israel.	CONTEMPORARY EVENTS.	DATE BEFORE CHRIST.				
						Keil.	Winer.	Ewald.	Clinton.	Authorised Version.
1	REHOBOAM, 17 years	1st	JEROBOAM, 22 years	1st	Shishak King of Egypt	975	975	985	976	975
18	ABIJAM, 3 years	2nd		18th	Shishak enters Jerusalem	971	970	968	959	958
20	ASA, 41 years	3rd		20th		957	957	965	956	955
22			NADAB, 2 years			965	955	963	955	954
23			BAASHA, 24 years			953	954	961	954	953
					Zerah the Ethiopian	952	953			
					Ben-Hadad I. of Syria	940				
45			ELAH, 2 years	26th		930	930	937	930	930
46			ZIMRI, 7 days	27th		929	928	935	930	929
46			OMRI and TIBNI, 4 years	27th		929	928	935	930	929
50			OMRI, sole king 8 years	31st	Building of Samaria	925	924			
					Ethbaal, King of Tyre and Sidon	924	923			
57	JEHOSHAPHAT, 25 years	38th	AHAB, 22 years	4th	Ben-Hadad II. of Syria	918	918	919	919	918
61					Battle of Ramoth-gilead	914	914	917	915	914
78	JEHORAM, co-regent for 2 years?	17th	AHAZIAH, 2 years	5th	War of Israel and Judah against Moab (Moabite Stone)	897	897	897	896	898
						897	897			
79	JEHORAM, sole ruler 6 yrs	18th	JEHORAM, 12 years	12th		896	896	895	895	896
86					Hazael, King of Syria	891	889	893	891	892
						889				
91	AHAZIAH, 1 year				Second Battle of Ramoth-gilead	884	885	885	884	885

No.	King of Judah		King of Israel		Events					
92	ATHALIAH, 6 years	7th	JEHU, 28 years		Murder of Ahaziah and Jehoram by Jehu / Lycurgus in Sparta, 884. His sister Athaliah slain	883	884	883	883	884
98	JOASH, 40 years				Pygmalion, King of Tyre. Dido founds Carthage, 143 years after the building of the Temple	877	878	877	877	878
119		22nd?	JEHOAHAZ, 17 years			856	856	855	855	856
135		37th	JOASH, 16 years		Judah invaded and Jerusalem threatened by the Syrians	840	840	839	839	841
137	AMAZIAH, 29 years	2nd			Ben-Hadad III., King of Syria / Joash, King of Judah, murdered / War of Amaziah against Edom / Attack of Moab upon Israel / War between Judah and Israel / Jerusalem occupied by the Israelites	838	838	837	837	839
151	UZZIAH, 52 years	15th	JEROBOAM II., 41 years		Successful War of Israel against Syria	824	825	823	823	825
165		15th?			Ammon becomes tributary to Judah / The Philistines humbled	810	809	808	808	810
192			Death of JEROBOAM II., Interregnum for 11 yrs.		First year of the Olympiads, 776	783	784			
203			ZACHARIAH, 6 months	38th		772	772	771	770	773
204			SHALLUM, 1 month	39th		771	771	770	770	772
204			MENAHEM, 10 years	39th	Pul, King of Assyria / Israel becomes tributary to Assyria	771	771	769	769	772
215	JOTHAM, 16 years		PEKAHIAH, 2 years	50th	Murder of Pekahiah	760	760	759	759	761
216		2nd	PEKAH, 20 years	52nd	Building of Rome, 753 / Nabonassar, King of Babylon, 747 / Rezin, King of Syria	759	758	757	757	759
217						758	758	756	756	758
233	AHAZ, 16 years	17th			Ahaz invokes the help of Assyria against Syria and Israel / Tiglath-pileser, King of Assyria / The Assyrians occupy the land east of the Jordan, and the north of Palestine, and lead the people captive	742	741	740	741	742

1 For Events from the Exodus to the building of the Temple by Solomon, see the Chronological Table at the beginning of Vol. III. of this History.

Year from the Separation of the Two Kingdoms.	Kings of Judah. Reigned:	Year from the Accession of the Kings of Judah.	Kings of Israel. Reigned;	Year from the Accession of the Kings of Israel.	Contemporary Events.	Keil.	Winer.	Ewald.	Clinton.	Authorised Version.
236		4th	PEKAH murdered. Interregnum 8½ years?		The Philistines conquer the western part of Judah	739	738			
245		12th	HOSHEA, 9 years, tributary to Assyria		So, King of Egypt	730	729	728	730	730
248	HEZEKIAH, 29 years			3rd	Shalmaneser, King of Assyria (Media and Babylonia). Growth of the Assyrian Empire in Asia	727	725 722	724	726	726
253		6th	DESTRUCTION OF THE COMMONWEALTH OF ISRAEL		Attempt of Hoshea to rebel against Assyria. Invasion of the Assyrians. Siege of Samaria. Deportation of the Ten Tribes	722	721	719	721	721
261					Sargon, King of Assyria. Siege of Ashdod (Isa. xx. 1) Alliance between Judah and Egypt. Siege of Jerusalem by Sennacherib. War between Sennacherib and Tirhakah. Destruction of the Assyrians by "the Angel of the Lord." Embassy from Merodach-baladan	714	712			
277	MANASSEH, 55 years				Esarhaddon, King of Assyria, sends fresh Colonists to Samaria. Scythian hordes pass through Palestine (Herod. I, 104, etc.)	698	696	695	697	698
332	AMON, 2 years				Murder of Amon	643	641	640	642	643
334	JOSIAH, 31 years				Nabopolassar, founder of the Babylonian Temple, father of Nebuchadnezzar. Draco in Athens	641 626	639 625	638	640	641

						610	609
365	**JEHOAHAZ, 3 months** / **JEHOIAKIM, 11 years**	Invasion of Assyria by Egypt. Alliance of Assyria and Judah. Victory of Megiddo by Pharaoh-nechoh, Josiah slain	610	610	609	608	610	610
365		Jehoiakim put on the throne by the King of Egypt. Judah subject to Egypt	609	609	608	607	600	609
369	Commencement of the Exile	The Egyptians beaten by the Chaldees in the Battle of Carchemish. Taking of Jerusalem by Nebuchadnezzar	609	609	607	600	610	610
						607		
376	**JEHOIACHIN, 3 months**	Second Conquest of Jerusalem and Deportation.	599	598	597	598	599	599
376	**ZEDEKIAH, 11 years**	Jerusalem and the Temple plundered by the Chaldees	599	598	596	598	599	599
		Zedekiah made king by the Chaldees. Zedekiah rebels against Nebuchadnezzar, and turns towards Pharaoh-hophra, King of Egypt (Jer. xliv. 30; Ezek. xvii. 15). Jerusalem besieged. Attempted relief of Jerusalem by the Egyptians (Jer. xxxvii. 5, etc.; Ezek. xvii. 17, etc.)	599	590				
387	**DESTRUCTION OF JERUSALEM** / Gedaliah Babylonian Governor in Judah, 2 mths.	Death of Zedekiah. Majority of the Jews carried to Babylon (3rd deportation)	588	588	587	588	588	588
387		Gedaliah murdered. Many of the Jews retire into Egypt	588	588			588	588
391	Last Deportation of the Jews to Babylon (Jos. *Ant.* x. 97; comp. Jer. lii. 30?)		584	584			584	584

Judah lies desolate (2 Chron. xxxvi. 21; Zech. vii. 14). Occupation of part of the country by the Philistines and Edomites. The latter take the southern territory (Ezek. xxxv. 10). Hebron part of Idumea (Jos. *Jew. Wars*, iv. 9, 7).

The Chronology of the two Kingdoms after their separation is in many respects involved, and, from the want of sufficient data to guide us, sometimes so difficult as to baffle all efforts at certain solution. But the final result shows that these divergences are rather nice than important, the total difference being at most only that of a few years. Special difficulties are considered in the text as they arise. Two points ought to be here kept in view, as on the one hand accounting for, and on the other helping us to solve most of the minor difficulties. They are: *first*, the dates are not reckoned according to a fixed standard, such as the Creation of the World, or the Exodus, but according to the accession of the various kings of Judah and Israel; while *secondly*, the duration of the reign of these kings is computed from the month Nisan to the month Nisan of each year, so that even a single day before or after the 1st of Nisan is reckoned equivalent to a whole year. This mode of computation, which is distinctly asserted in the Talmud (*Rosh-ha-Shâ, 2a–3a passim*), was that according to which Josephus reckoned. Compare the detailed proof in Wieseler's *Synopse*, pp. 53, etc.